MEETING COMMUNITY NEEDS WITH JOB & CAREER SERVICES

A How-To-Do-It Manual
For Librarians

JOAN C. DURRANCE

HOW-TO-DO-IT MANUALS FOR LIBRARIANS

Number 42

NEAL-SCHUMAN PUBLISHERS, INC.
New York, London

Published by Neal-Schuman Publishers, Inc.
100 Varick Street
New York, NY 10013

Printed and bound in the United States of America

Library of Congress Cataloging-in-Publication Data

Durrance, Joan C.
Meeting community needs with job & career services : a how-to-do-it manual / Joan Durrance.
p. cm. -- (How-to-do-it manuals for libraries : 42)
ISBN 1-55570-177-9
1. Vocational guidance--United States--Information services. 2. Labor supply--United States--Information services. 3. Public libraries--United States--Services to the unemployed. 4. Libraries and community--United States. 5. Libraries and labor--United States I. Title. II. Series: How-to-do-it manuals for libraries : no. 42.
HFB382.5.U5D87 1994
025.06'331702--dc20 94-16462
CIP

CONTENTS

CREDITS

These individuals contributed to the following sections of this book:

Chapter 2: Catherine Allen and Paula Gibbons

Chapter 4: Cheryl Burley

Chapter 5: Cheryl Burley

Layout: Cheryl Burley and Susan Schweitzer

Illustrations: Cheryl Burley

Index: Meegan Niemira

ACKNOWLEDGMENTS

The W. K. Kellogg Foundation played a large part in the development in many libraries of education, and job and career information centers. Its project officers Arlon Elser, Joel Orosz, and Gail McClure had the vision to help librarians stretch their professional practice in order to provide need-based services that are described in this book. The Kellogg Foundation's commitment to encouraging the development of services which anticipate the needs of adults for education and career information and assistance resulted in the generous support of the creation of these services in a number of states. I am grateful that the Foundation provided me with the support which permitted me to visit over 40 job and career information centers in five states. These visits formed the basis for this book.

Each chapter of this book is richer due to the experience and contributions of the staff of scores of job and career center staff. Everywhere I traveled, librarians and other job center staff told me how working at the job center had changed the way they thought about what they did. Time and again, these staff told me how much what they do means to the people who use the job centers. They know that what they do makes a difference. This book is filled with illustrations sent to me by directors of job and career information centers from all over the country. These illustrations can be used as models for public relations materials and service development. The testimonials and anecdotal material have also been provided by the staff of these centers. I appreciate the generosity of the staff who shared them with me.

I would also like to acknowledge the time, effort, and expertise provided by some of the profession's most skilled practitioners—Jackie Thresher, Mary Jo Ryan, Steve Oserman, Stephen Mallinger, Vera Green, Dorothy Puryear, Ruth Schwab, and Jeanne Patterson. The book is better because of their work.

I appreciate the efforts made by my research assistants at the University of Michigan for the fine work they contributed at various stages in the Kellogg Project. These included Jan Hartley, Cathy Allen, Cheryl Burley, Paula Gibbons, Heidi Wiese, Susan Schweitzer, and Meegan Niemira.

Cheryl Burley worked with me to identify and select the illustrations. She also worked with me to develop the chapter on raising awareness. Cathy Allen and I collected and wrote the library profiles. Cheryl and Cathy made very strong contributions to the book.

1 SERVICES THAT START WITH THE NEED

Since before the turn of the century, librarians have responded to the needs of the citizens in their communities. They have done this primarily by providing needed resources. Public librarians had horse-drawn book carriages which carried books to people in remote locations even before the advent of the automobile. From the turn of the century on, librarians have worked with immigrant populations. Then and now they helped make Americans out of the people who used public libraries to learn English and find out how to function in a democracy. During the depression, libraries served as the people's university for those who were out of work. For many decades people have learned to read at the public library. It is clear from the diverse groups of people who have been served throughout the decades of the 20th century by librarians, that the public library has long attempted to serve the need of the citizens in their communities.

From the 1970s, public libraries have rediscovered their community roots and have strengthened their services to the citizens of their communities. The first community information services were those that identified and organized a wide range of social service information that was desperately needed by the people. These services were called Information and Referral Services (I & R) when they developed in major cities across the nation. They responded to real needs in the community. (Durrance 1984). The emphasis of these services was both on identifying and organizing information and on providing librarians with the interviewing skills necessary to refer citizens to appropriate social services and other agencies in the community. Likewise, adult outreach services that flourished particularly in the 1920s and 1930s, experienced a resurgence in the 1970s and 1980s due to funds from the Library Services and Constructions Act (LSCA) earmarked for reaching out to the disadvantaged.

Community information services in the 1970s and 1980s paved the way for the development of this book. These services have helped librarians more effectively serve as a wide constituent base. Community information services have shown librarians that they can best serve the needs of multiple constituencies by learning more about these groups and their information needs. Because work is a part of nearly every individual's life, developing viable services that meet the real needs of job seekers and career changers should be a high priority for most public libraries. The experience of many community information librarians has shown that providing books and other resources is not enough. Librarians who seek to respond effectively to community information needs must know more about those needs. This book distills the experience of a number of librarians who have developed job and career centers in libraries across the nation.

THE NEED

Under normal circumstances, most adults will make a major employment change or need additional education at least several times during their adult work lives. During recessionary times even more people need job or education information. In the last decade millions of people found themselves out of work. They had been white collar and blue collar workers, sales people, professionals, and managers. They had worked in banks, insurance companies, newspapers, the automobile industry, local governments. Many of these people had never been laid off before, and some had worked in their jobs for most of their lives.

A recent Gallup survey showed that "almost two-thirds of adult Americans would try to get more information about their career options if they could chart their careers again."[1] The survey found that 79% of black Americans and 74% of people under age 25 felt even more strongly about the need for more information about job options.

Nearly one in four adults indicated that when they were making a decision about jobs, information was not available. Minorities, people with less than a high school education, and older adults, were more likely to have problems than college graduates. The survey found that "an estimated 12.5 million U.S. adults (7 percent of the adult population) a year needed help in selecting, changing, or getting a job."[2] People need help, the Gallup survey notes, "to use the information to make decisions about their participation in the labor force."[3]

The Executive Director of the National Occupational Information Coordinating Committee which sponsored the survey indicated the following:

> "The findings of this survey point to a critical need by all Americans for information about jobs and careers. It is vital that we do all we can to see to it that people are aware of the available information."[4]

PUBLIC LIBRARIES AND THE NEED

Across the country, librarians are helping people make use of job, career, and education information. Many librarians provide a wide range of services designed to help job seekers and career changers. In some communities people come to their local library seeking more than information. They seek and get help in assessing their own interests and abilities, putting together a resume, preparing for a job interview, finding training and education programs, learning about jobs and employers, and starting a small business. They may also learn how to improve their job prospects, find out about educational alternatives, or college financial aid opportunities.

This guide is built on the experience of scores of librarians who work in public library services called variously Career Center, Economic Development Center, Procurement Center, or by acronyms or names which are reflective of the service, EIC (Education Information Center), EJIC (Education and Job Information Center), WORKPLACE, InfoPLACE, and JOBLINC. When librarians name their local job and career center, they tend to choose a name which describes the types of services provided, and which is easily understandable by their potential clientele.

As this guide will demonstrate, job centers vary from one library to another. What they all have in common is a dedicated staff who works closely with others in the community to develop services which are needed by the people who live in their community. Job and career centers have been well received by those who need and use them.

JOB AND CAREER CENTER CLIENTELE

A four state study of users of job and career information centers in libraries found that a wide variety of people reported that they had received help from the staff of job and career information centers. They include the following:

- Women who are returning to work because their households can no longer subsist without a second income.
- Displaced workers from the automobile, steel, and lumber industries and from the agricultural sector.

- Single mothers who are heads of households.
- Workers in the lumber mills or automobile factories who did not finish high school, are functionally illiterate and now have to pass tests in order to continue their employment.
- Career changers, who may be employed but are exploring other careers and/or job possibilities.
- Underemployed workers including people who are overqualified for their jobs and part-time workers.
- Injured workers who must change jobs for health reasons.
- High-school students who are in the process of planning for their futures.
- People who are new in town and seeking employment.[5]

The range of needs for people who come to the public library job and career information centers is quite varied. People come to the Job and Career Information Centers to do the following:

Make a decision;

Find needed information about different types of jobs;

Learn how to write resumes, complete job applications, and/or conduct job interviews;

Assess their skills, interests and what additional training or education they needed to compete for the careers they wanted to pursue;

Increase their awareness of options, and

Gain confidence in themselves.[6]

Job and career center clientele are often not previous library users. Statistics from the Pennsylvania State Library show that the people who come to library job and career centers called in Pennsylvania, WORKPLACE centers, have the following characteristics:

About 70% of WORKPLACE patrons are not library users and need library cards;

The sex ratio is about 55% women;

The average age is 35;

Most have been out of work for about a year, and

> The average client has about one year of post high school education (often a JTPA vocational retraining program).

No statistics were kept on the number who found jobs, but the vast majority of WORKPLACE patrons report that they increased the number of interviews they received and learned how to be more effective in their job search skills. Similar use patterns have been seen in job and career centers in other states.

Scattered throughout this guide are anecdotes and testimonial letters from agencies and people that show how these services have helped real people. They provide excellent examples to give decision makers. These vignettes show that librarians in job and career centers have developed a number of different strategies aimed at helping people use information and resources in their lives.

The vignettes, testimonials, and letters in this manual show that people believe that they can get help for real problems at the library. Grateful users frequently sing the praises of services that have helped them turn their lives around or get past a temporary setback. Staff at these centers report that they regularly receive letters, phone calls, and notes from ecstatic users of these services.

WHY PUBLIC LIBRARIANS ATTEMPT TO MEET THESE NEEDS

Should the library take on yet another service? Most library staff have more than enough to do. The following section describes some of the benefits these services bring to the community and the library, and reflect what several administrators have to say about them.

Gloria Coles, Director of the Flint Public Library, has dealt with tight budgets during the entire time she has been director. The city of Flint has severe economic problems, high unemployment, a decline in the automobile industry, deteriorating housing, and limited revenues. The library has suffered budget cuts. Yet, Ms. Coles considers Flint Public Library's Career Opportunities and Planning for Employmentthe COPE Centerto be an essential part of the services which the Flint Public Library brings to its community. The COPE Center was started with Kellogg Funds. However, when these funds ran out, Ms. Coles had no problem in deciding that this service should continue. She notes:

> "This service meets the needs both of our traditional clientele and people who just haven't seen the need to use our library in the past. This service makes a difference in the lives of the people who use it. It is essential."

David Remington, Deputy Director of the State Library of Washington, developed the job and career service at Pend Oreille County Library in eastern Washington. He says, "People have changed the way they think about the library here. They now see that we can help them with solutions to their everyday problems."

Dorothy Puryear, Director of Special Services, Nassau Library System in New York, former president of PLA's Community Information Section, and Information and Referral and job and career center pioneer, sees a bright future for these services in public libraries. The hardest part of assuming the role, she finds, is initially selling librarians on the idea—a problem faced by all innovators. Puryear remarks:

> "Librarians who have accepted the idea of job and career information services are amazed at the satisfaction that comes in helping clients solve educational and job problems, plan for the future, and get their lives on track. It is very rewarding. These services may be the most critical and needed services a local public library can offer its community."

Directors are increasingly concerned that their library meets the needs of the community. This service brings in a diverse clientele. Paul Savedow of the Free Library of Philadelphia says:

> "We get a lot of underemployed peoplethose with liberal arts degrees who have been working in bars or bookstores for the last 10 years but have never established a career. And we also serve people in job readiness programs, those who may be homeless or on welfare. The number of white-collar workers using our services has definitely grown in the past year. These people are college grads, aged 25-50, who may be laid off or looking for a career change." (SIGI Plus Newsletter, Win 1992)

Directors of public libraries with these services regularly receive testimonials from members of the community which eagerly extol the virtues of these services. Many proudly point to the accomplishments of these services which have provided proof that the library is serving a vital function in the community.

> "I get more letters from satisfied users about this program than any other service."
>
> "People have told us they were surprised to find the library such a helpful place."

The letter below, written on agency letterhead was addressed to the director of a library with a career center. It eloquently speaks of the trauma which the unemployed experience, even well-educated, capable individuals who are only briefly out of work.

> Dear Mike,
>
> As a recent member of that diverse group known as the "temporarily unemployed," I wish to extend my warmest thanks to the people who planned and executed the "Job Information Center." My wife's position [resulted in a move to this city]. Unfortunately, our move here dropped me into a "brave new world" which lacked bearings and contacts.
>
> My first stop (after contacting the utilities and unpacking the broken china) was the public library. Discovering the "Job Information Center" was like finding a desert oasis. It contains an extensive selection of reference works, personal presentation texts, and employment listings (not to mention the self-evaluation books and computer programs). Having searched for employment in a wide variety of locations across America, I have not seen another library space so adequately designed to aid an individual in one of the most challenging and life-changing tasks he will face.
>
> Though the space and the collection would be adequate by themselves, your choice of supervisory personnel is truly brilliant. [Your JIC director] provides a marvelous blend of experience, familiarity and therapy. The latter component may not often be associated with a public library, but let's pursue this further. What one "does" is an integral part of "who" one is. When a person is unemployed, that critical portion of identity is missing. This can be a threatening, stressful and often traumatic period. Besides the helpful information and contacts, she brings an under-

> standing, concern and a positive attitude which leaves people feeling that there is light at the end of the tunnel.
>
> The collection, arrangement, and management of this "crucial corner" in the Library should be considered a feather in [the community's] cap. You, your administrative board, and your staff should be proud of the product and services you provide!
>
> Sincerely,

These services change the way that the public library relates to the community. These services have opened the eyes of the community to the role of the library as a vital part of the community. Job and career librarians across the nation point to the new relationships they have developed with human service agencies and other organizations in the community.

These new relationships bring new clients to the library because agency staff who have come to understand the role of the library, now refer their clients to the library. As a result they often bring benefits to the library.

> "The staff and I are increasingly being asked to serve on the boards of community agencies."
>
> "The job center has helped our image."

Many directors have found these services to be an invigorating force for the staff.

> "Starting this new type of service has generated much excitement and energized the staff."

Librarians who work with job seekers and career changers report becoming more reflective practitioners. They have accomplished the following:

- Become more skilled at listening and communicating—keys to excellence in librarianship;
- Learned to work more effectively with people;
- Grown professionally on the job;
- Developed a greater knowledge of their community;

- Increased their public speaking skills through workshops and public presentations; and/or
- Become skilled at writing grant proposals.

Testimonials from librarians about the impact of developing need-based services include the following:

> "My experience with this program has made me a better professional."
>
> "By gaining insight into other people I've learned more about myself."

These services have changed the way that many libraries operate. Robert Trautwein of Columbus, Nebraska commented, "We have incorporated longer patron interactions and more empathy into our reference staff philosophy."

Ruth Schwab of Ossining, New York says, "This service utilizes the potential skills of librarians. As a result people who use our library have a new image of librarians as real people capable of helping them better understand the world of work."

The need for providing services to job seekers, career changers, entrepreneurs, and those who need more education is clear. Most people devote most of their adult lives to working, preparing to work, or changing jobs or careers. Public libraries have a long history of providing materials and resources that these people need. New knowledge about how to identify and respond to information needs has made it possible to create this planning approach which will make it easier for librarians to develop services which are based on actual needs. This manual should be both an inspiration and a guide.

RESOURCES

Adrift in a Sea of Change: California's Public Libraries Struggle to Meet the Information Needs of Multicultural Communities. California Center for Policy Development, 1990.

Formative Evaluation Research Associates (FERA). Final Report to the W.K. Kellogg Foundation. [Unpublished], 1990.

National Career Development Association (NCDA). *Work in America.* [Findings of a Gallup Poll], Washington, D.C., National Occupational Information Coordinating Committee, 1990.

NOTES

1. National Career Development Association (NCDA). *Work in America.* [Findings of a Gallup Poll], Washington, D.C.: National Occupational Information Coordinating Committee, 1990.
2. National Career Development Association (NCDA). *Work in America.* [Findings of a Gallup Poll], Washington, D.C.: National Occupational Information Coordinating Committee, 1990.
3. National Career Development Association (NCDA). *Work in America.* [Findings of a Gallup Poll], Washington, D.C.: National Occupational Information Coordinating Committee, 1990.
4. National Career Development Association (NCDA). *Work in America.* [Findings of a Gallup Poll], Washington, D.C.: National Occupational Information Coordinating Committee, 1990.
5. FERA. Final Report to the W.K. Kellogg Foundation.
6. FERA. Final Report to the W.K. Kellogg Foundation.

2 PROFILES OF NEED-BASED SERVICES

Although job and career centers do not fit easily into a single, cohesive model, these services do bear the indelible imprint of an approach to practice that starts with need. It recognizes the value of working with other agencies in the community and focuses squarely on the person who needs assistance.

The model that emerges consists of a range of strategies designed to respond to the needs of adults who need education, job, and career information and assistance. Although not all of the strategies are used in all libraries, generally staff at these centers are likely to do the following:

- Focus on and learn about the employment and education environment.
- Purchase and make available a wide range of resources, including career advising software, and other relative computer software.
- Develop approaches which result in the users exhibiting more effective listening and communication skills.
- Attempt to understand the specific problems and concerns of the people who come for assistance.
- Use a variety of techniques to respond to these problems including advising, help with resume writing, and developing workshops on a variety of needs.
- Work closely with other agencies and professionals in the community (linking and referring clients).
- Raise awareness among agencies and people who need these services, and about their nature (including a range of outreach activities).

This chapter provides profiles of job and career centers and economic development services in 25 public libraries in communities of all sizes. Many of these services were started as the result of a grant written by an interested staff member. Some of the libraries described in this manual got their start with money from the W. K. Kellogg Foundation or the federal government as long ago as the 1970s. Long after their outside funding disappeared, these job and career centers have continued. Their growth and longevity attest to the staying power of these services and their importance to their communities.

The profiles reflect the ingenuity of library staff in responding to the needs of a particular community. There is a considerable variation in services from one community to the next. In public libraries in rural Nebraska, they are just part of the regular service with no specially assigned staff. Everyone in the library works with people who need help with education, job, and career decision making. On the other hand, the Cuyahoga County (OH) Public Library's InfoPLACE is an example of a service that grew over the years and now employs several full-time librarians and counselors.

To show how librarians have described their services to the citizens of their community, actual brochures and flyers from some of these libraries are used as illustrations. The profiles in this chapter show a wide range of service possibilities in many different places. They are arranged by size, from Pend Oreille County Library District in Newport, WA (population, 1665) to the Free Library of Philadelphia, PA (population, 1,688,212). The profile of each job and career center or economic development program was written from responses to a survey of job and career center services or from information obtained directly from the program. We often include how the service started. The text reflects the wording used in responding to the survey. I appreciate all of the input from these librarians.

PROFILES OF JOB AND CAREER CENTERS IN PUBLIC LIBRARIES

LIBRARIES IN COMMUNITIES OF LESS THAN 15,000

PEND OREILLE COUNTY LIBRARY DISTRICT-NEWPORT (WA)

Profile of the Library

Size of Community: 1,691

Population Served: 8,883

Staff: 10

Profile of the Education and Job Information Center

This center was started with Kellogg funds in 1987; the Education and Job Information Center (EJIC) was originally an outreach center of the Spokane Public Library. The library is seen in the community as an action agency with the ability to provide practical solutions to problems at the local level. Its aim is to "empower individuals." Like Nebraska libraries, the job center is considered an integral part of service of the small town library. Services vary but have included individual assessments, computerized career software, group instruction and mock interviews. An "information station" provides computer software programs to assist clients in their career analysis and testing, and training in the use of major computer software applications. Weekly seminars are given in the use of the computer and a wide range of software. The Pend Oreille library pioneered in the use of a toll-free telephone hotline to the state employment office in Olympia, the State Capitol.

BELLEVUE (IA) PUBLIC LIBRARY

Profile of the Library

Size of Community: 2,239

Population Served: 2,475

Staff: not available

Economic Development Activities

Bellevue Public Library staff has been active in enhancing the economic situation in their community for several years. With help from Iowa state government's Community Economic Preparedness Program (CEPP), the library has prepared an information packet for businesses considering locating in Bellevue. The packet includes a cost-of-living index for the area, a 30-page community fact file, a detailed survey of residents, and a video about Bellevue. This package is especially important because Bellevue's main asset is the quality of its work force. The efforts of the librarian and his/her staff have attracted many businesses to Bellevue. and have lead to the librarian's new role in the community as head of Bellevue's economic development agency.

BROKEN BOW (NE) PUBLIC LIBRARY

Profile of the Library

Size of Community: 3,778

Population Served: 3,979

Staff: 7

Profile of the Education Information Center

Broken Bow is approximately 70 miles from a university branch campus. This library, located in a rural area in western Nebraska, has addressed economic and rural development issues and worked with other agencies. The Education Information Center (EIC) was started in 1987 with a grant from the W. F. Kellogg Foundation; it is now supported by local funds. The program is incorporated into the regular library service and considered part of the basic work load. Services include DISCOVER and other computer software, advising, developing materials, and group workshopsa joint effort of the job career center.

Various groups visit the job and career center. Outreach efforts include taking job and career center resources to other libraries for a month at a time. Cooperating agencies include County Extension, Broken Bow Literacy Project (encourages the use of computer services), the Department of Social Services, the local Chamber of Commerce, and the Broken Bow School Systemjuniors and seniors use the job and career center for career decision-making; adult education classes also make use of the job and career center. Residents of the Broken Bow area who are studying at the university provide, on an occasional basis, assistance in utilizing the job and career center to their Broken Bow neighbors. The library is a service site for Nebraska Online, a statewide electronic communications and job listing service.

BUTLER AREA (PA) PUBLIC LIBRARY WORKPLACE

Profile of the Library

Size of Community: 15,714

Staff: 13

Profile of WORKPLACE

This WORKPLACE site is one of approximately 65 SITES which have spun off from the original six Kellogg funded WORKPLACE sites in Pennsylvania. WORKPLACE in Butler got its start through a basic grant with a computer, VCR, Karli tapes, resume writing, and other software and training from the state library. In addition to receiving state training, the coordinator spent a day observing Vera Green at the WORKPLACE Center at the Carnegie Oakland in Pittsburgh. The two and a half day state library training program, which included experienced librarians, software developers, and other trainers, was an invaluable aid to getting started. It gave the Butler WORKPLACE coordinator ideas, approaches, and the personal contacts she needed to get started. She believes that, although the computers and software are helpful, the most important thing is the one-on-one interactions she has with people who come to her for assistance. The training showed her how to identify needs and how to respond to them, and how to work effectively with people "Human beings need someone to help." This small library has spun off another generation of WORKPLACE by funding small satellite collections ("The Basic Job Search Shelf") in six other libraries in Butler county through a small grant from the County Economic Development program.

ALPENA (MI) COUNTY LIBRARY

Profile of the Library

Size of Community: 11,354

Population Served: 30,000

Staff: not available

Profile of Job Launch and M-LINK

Alpena is a small community with 12,000 residents on Lake Huron. The Alpena County Library serves over 30,000 people in the county. Job Launch (Employment Information Center) was established in January 1990 with funds from an LSCA grant. The unemployment rate is high and it is the only section of Michigan with no four year college within easy driving distance. Job Launch is located in a separate area in the Reference Department designated to focus on the vocational and small business needs of the community. One-to-one assistance is provided in accessing information from SIGI Plus and Michigan Occupational Information System (MOIS) computer guidance systems, as well as from books, journals, pamphlets, and audio-visual aids. Weekly clinics offer help in resume preparation and job search strategies. A network of local cooperation and support has aided in the growth and popularity of the service. An important adjunct to the Job Launch program has been M-LINK, a program funded by the W. K. Kellogg Foundation and administered by the University of Michigan Library. M-LINK seeks to foster economic development in the community. The Alpena County Library has also developed an adult literacy program called READ. Job Launch is an obvious next step for people whose newly developed skills have prepared them for the job market. These three programs make economic information more accessible for Alpena County residents.

CAMDEN COUNTY (NJ) FREE LIBRARY [VOORHEES, NJ]

Profile of the Library

Size of Community: 12,919

Population Served: 250,000

Staff: 63

Profile of the Job & Career Information Center

Camden County (NJ) Library's Job & Career Information Center began in 1981 as part of a W. K. Kellogg Foundation program and is now funded internally. The coordinator is a career counselor. The services include the following:

1. providing information on the current job market and other topics,
2. books, magazines, and directories related to jobs and careers,
3. individual assistance with the job search,
4. workshops on resumes, interviews and other aspects of the job search process, and
5. DISCOVER, a computer career guidance system.

A simple two-sided flyer (see Figure 2-1) reminds people that the library is not an unemployment agency, but it can provide valuable assistance in the job search or education planning process.

ALLIANCE (NE) PUBLIC LIBRARY

Profile of the Library

Size of Community: 9,765

Population Served: 9,869

Staff: not available

Profile of the Education Information Center

Alliance, Nebraska is "miles from everywhere," according to one of the staff members there, meaning it takes several hours to drive to most cities of any size in Nebraska. It is a little closer to Denver, but that is still a couple of hundred miles. Alliance is a town of 5,000 people, a large town for this area. The nearest college, a community college, is in another town 60 miles away. That community

FIGURE 2-1: On The Job For You—Camden County (NJ) Library

JOB & CAREER INFORMATION CENTER

at the Camden County Library

ON THE JOB FOR YOU

- INDIVIDUAL ASSISTANCE with your job search
- WORKSHOPS on resumes, interviews & more
- "DISCOVER" career planning by computer
- BOOKS, MAGAZINES, DIRECTORIES related to jobs & careers
- INFORMATION on current labor market

ALL SERVICES ARE FREE

WHEN YOU ARE . . .

- Looking for a job
- Changing careers
- Re-entering the work force
- Choosing a career
- Seeking part-time or temporary work
- Planning your education

MAKE YOUR FIRST STOP . . .

JOB & CAREER INFORMATION CENTER
CAMDEN COUNTY LIBRARY
LAUREL ROAD
VOORHEES, N.J. 08043
(609) 772-1636

JACIC is not an employment agency, but a special library service designed to help you organize a job search or choose a career.

college offers some courses in the library meeting room in the basement. The library is understaffed, but the director of the library has undertaken a number of projects. Alliance staff welcomed becoming a job and career center site. All staff at the public library answer education, and job and career questions. The library purchased DISCOVER with Kellogg funds and made it available to area adults and high school students. The presence of this computer program changed the way one high school teacher presented the senior theme. It became an exploration of a career, starting with the use of DISCOVER. One staff member, commenting on the addition of this resource commented: "DISCOVER is so helpful. It helps people think about their own needs and it asks them about themselves."

LIBRARIES IN COMMUNITIES OF 15,000 - 50,000

OSSINING (NY) PUBLIC LIBRARY

Profile of the Library

Size of Community: 22,582

Population Served: 27,486

Staff: 17

Profile of the Education/Job Information Center

The Education/Job Information Center at Ossining Public Library, a library serving a population of 34,000, was started in 1978 as part of the Westchester Educational Brokerage System (WEBS) program, funded by the W. K. Kellogg Foundation. Funding is now primarily internal. All reference librarians answer E/JIC questions as part of their regular duties; Ruth Schwab coordinates the service. Services include contract counseling, individual librarian assistance, career development workshops, small business information, video and software programs, and referrals. The program contributes to the image of the library as a helping institution and a vital part of the community.

CLINTON-ESSEX-FRANKLIN LIBRARY SYSTEM [PLATTSBURGH, NY]

Profile of the Library

Size of Community: 21,255

Population Served: 169,661

Staff: 24

Profile of the Job & Education Information Center

This JEIC's three-fold flyer (see Figure 2-2) shouts "YOU CAN FIND A JOB!". Its three inside panels introduce ways that people can get help at the library. Clinton-Essex-Franklin (NY) Library System services for job seekers have included: Skills assessment questionnaires, a variety of ways to explore careers and vocations such as SIGI Plus, tips on how to start and finance a business. For the individual who needs educational information the library provides college catalogs, directories of educational and training opportunities, and educational testing assistance. This library has acquired specialized job-related materials, including newspapers, employment journals, and job-related videos and films. The staff have developed workshops to help people gain skills in resume writing and interviewing. This center was one of the early Kellogg-funded programs.

PETER WHITE PUBLIC LIBRARY—MARQUETTE (MI)

Profile of the Library

Size of Community: 21,977

Population Served: 37,882

Staff: 28

Profile of the Education Information Center and Small Business Training Center

The Education Information Center (EIC) at the Peter White Public Library in Marquette, MI, was one of six job and career centers in Michigan started in 1986 with W. K. Kellogg Foundation funding. It now is supported by internal funds. The job and career center, located in a separate room in the basement of the library, answers over 300 user inquiries monthly and is coordinated by an educator. Computer software is available to patrons for career exploration. Advising services include help with resumes, interviewing, and the job search process. A related service, the Small Business Training Center, jointly sponsored by the Library and Northern Michigan University, provides one-on-one assistance to people starting a small business. The job and career center maintains a collection of print and audiotape materials, and publishes a series of bibliographies on job and education related topics. Staff have joined several community networks. The library acquired a WATS line for area libraries as part of their outreach program. Additionally they are helping three area libraries develop collections.

FIGURE 2-2: You Can Find A Job!—Clinton-Essex-Franklin (NY) Library System

You Can Find A Job!

Job & Education Information Center
Clinton-Essex-Franklin Library System

The Job & Education Information Center

We are part of the Clinton-Essex-Franklin Library System.

Located within the Saranac Lake Free Library (Main Street, Saranac Lake, N.Y.)

Materials are available for your use during regular library hours:

Mon.-Sat. - 10:00am - 5:30pm

The Job & Education Information Center is funded by the Clinton-Essex-Franklin Library System, the State of New York and a federal Library Services and Construction Act Title I grant.

For more information call:

(518) 563-8370

Job & Education Information Center
Clinton-Essex-Franklin Library System

Career Information

SKILLS ASSESSMENT QUESTIONNAIRES
Self-testing, matching personal aptitudes and interests with career choices.

CAREER EXPLORATION/ VOCATIONAL GUIDANCE
Job descriptions, including average salaries, employment growth outlook, and training requirements. Format varies from brief articles to in-depth books. Resources include such materials as: **high paying blue collar jobs, top careers for the 90's, non-traditional careers for women, and a variety of other topics.**

SMALL BUSINESS INFORMATION
Tips on how to start and finance a business, keep records, advertise effectively, etc.

Educational Information

COLLEGE CATALOGS
From the U.S. and Canada. Listings of college course offerings, with admission requirements, tuition, etc.

GUIDES TO COLLEGES AND TRADE SCHOOLS
Directories indicating where training is offered for different occupations and fields of study.

ALTERNATIVE EDUCATION
Programs designed to remove the barriers which have traditionally prevented working adults from completing their college education.

Apprenticeship Information - Formal agreements between workers and employers in which employee learns a skilled trade on-the-job.

Home Study & Correspondence Schools - Lists of available schools where you can study independently "by mail" and that are fully accredited.

Regents & Empire State College Degrees - Flexibility in arranging means of obtaining credit is the major focus, and degrees can be earned partially or entirely outside the normal classroom situation.

Educational Testing - Study Guides for examinations that can be used to obtain credit by studying independently such as High School Equivalency and CLEP exams.

Employment Information

SUNDAY NEWSPAPERS
Included in these are "help wanted" ads, and valuable real estate listings which can aid in relocation decisions.

STATE/COUNTY/FEDERAL CIVIL SERVICE INFORMATION
Postings of current openings, with sample examinations for study purposes.

STATE EMPLOYMENT TRENDS
Statistics on employment outlook by state in various career fields.

JOB SEEKING TECHNIQUES
Materials on resume writing, identifying employers, conducting an effective job search, and interviewing skills. Resume writing workshops, and free resume critiques are also provided.

NATIONAL EMPLOYMENT JOURNALS
Current job listings in fields such as nursing, social services, education, and business, as well as journals specializing in general career topics.

STATE INDUSTRIAL DIRECTORIES
Books from various states identifying large companies, and furnishing addresses, phone numbers, and key "contact" people.

FILMS & VIDEO
A variety of videos, films and filmstrips are available to community organizations on career & employment topics.

LONGVIEW (WA) PUBLIC LIBRARY

Profile of the Library

Size of Community: 31,499

Population Served: 32,030

Staff: 16

Profile of the Education/Job Information Center

Longview's Education/Job Information Center, started by the W. K. Kellogg Foundation in 1987 was created by, and is still managed, by a career counselor who seeks to help people with their job search and educational information needs—who also coordinates the literacy program. Now locally funded services include: Providing information, self-assessment, job and career advising and consulting, workshops and programs, and referrals. Computer career/education programs are used for assessment and career information. Informal networks with community agencies have been important in gaining support for the E/JIC and facilitating referrals. By keeping others in the community informed and working cooperatively, library services complement rather than duplicate community services.

HEMPSTEAD (NY) PUBLIC LIBRARY (NASSAU LIBRARY SYSTEM)

Profile of the Library

Size of Community: 49,453

Population Served: 41,389

Staff: 37

Profile of the Job and Education Information Center

The village of Hempstead has suffered economically for over a decade. The public library's Job and Education Information Center (JEIC) was started in the early 1980s as part of the original Kellogg-funded project to respond to a relatively high unemployment rate. Professional librarians and contract career counselors staff the JEIC. This center has been operating for more than a decade on local library tax-based funding, state aid, and LSCA funds. The flyer that describes the job and career center at the Hempstead (NY) Public Library, like most brochures which describe job and career centers, opens with questions that touch the lives of many people and follows with how they can get help at the library. The services at Hempstead Public Library start with special materials, including videos which help prepare people for job interviews. SIGI Plus is used for career advising, and for counselors who provide advising and workshops. Assessment is important and individualized, extended-time help is common. Staff can provide assistance to Spanish speakers (and others). Involvement in several networks extends the service into the community. Hempstead is a member of the Nassau County Library System.

LIBRARIES IN COMMUNITIES OF 50,000 - 250,000

SCHENECTADY COUNTY (NY) PUBLIC LIBRARY

Profile of the Library

Size of Community: 65,566

Population Served: 149,285

Staff· 79

Profile of the Education and Job Information Center

The Education and Job Information Center at Schenectady County Public Library is designed to serve people who are choosing or changing careers, writing a resume, looking for work, preparing for interviews or tests, starting a business, going back to school, looking for financial aid, working toward a GED, or who are involved in other education or job-related activities. The flyer states that the service is free and that specially trained staff members "can help you define your job and learning goals," find resources, and make contact with appropriate people and agencies in the community. The flyer describes the available educational and job resources, including directories and databases developed by the library.

FLINT (MI) PUBLIC LIBRARY

Profile of the Library

Size of Community: 140,761

Population Served: 159,611

Staff: 92

Profile of the Cope Center

The COPE Center(C)areer (O)pportunities and (P)lanning for (E)mployment began in 1986 with funding from the W. F. Kellogg Foundation and is now supported with internal funds as part of the

FIGURE 2-3: Job And Education Information Center—Hempstead (NY) Public Library

JEIC JOB AND EDUCATION INFORMATION CENTER

HEMPSTEAD PUBLIC LIBRARY 481-6990

- **Thinking about going back to school?**
- **Considering a career change?**
- **Looking for a different job?**

If you said 'yes' to any of the above, the place to go for free information and assistance is the JOB AND EDUCATION INFORMATION CENTER (JEIC) located in the Hempstead Public Library and available to all Nassau County residents.

You'll find all kinds of special materials — like the most current books for job seekers, directories, trade journals, out-of-town newspapers — and even videos on how to succeed on job interviews.

The friendly staff of career counselors and librarians can give you appropriate, individual assistance. You can schedule an appointment with a career counselor for a confidential meeting, or your own session with the computer for guidance in your career planning.

Throughout the year, workshops, lectures, seminars and film programs are offered upon request either at community facilities or at the Center. Some of the available subjects presented may be just the ones that interest you.

If you are non-English speaking or have other special concerns, you can be assured of staff interest and support.

Hundreds of people use JEIC every month. Come in and see why...for yourself!

The Job and Education Information Center provides free educational information and assistance which can help you to

- Get your high school diploma
- Select a college
- Locate a trade/technical school or training program
- Prepare for academic or employment tests
- Gain admission to school of your choice
- Find a source of financial aid/scholarship
- Study independently
- Find out about internship opportunities
- Pursue continuing education courses
- Use our computerized guidance system to help determine career direction
- Consult with our career counselor

The Job and Education Information Center may help you get the job you want by offering free career and employment information such as

- Resume writing assistance
- Videos on interviewing and job search skills
- Books and pamphlets on careers and job hunting
- Employment related magazines
- Help wanted ads from local/out-of-town listings
- Information on interstate listings including airlines, military, other fields
- Business directories describing companies
- Announcements of Civil Service jobs
- Job openings listed with the N.Y. State Employment Service
- Resources on how to start your own business

Flint Public Library. Declining population and high unemployment are two indicators of a community in economic distress. The COPE Center uses a number of approaches designed to respond to the needs of the Flint community. COPE's director is a Licensed Professional Counselor who works closely with library staff to provide service to patrons. A brochure emphasizes the kind of services patrons can expect to receive from the COPE Center. Career counseling, resume clinics, videotaping of mock interviews, college directories, and financial aid information, and Passport and MOIS computerized career search programs are available in the Center. Special programs and workshops focusing on careers and employability skills are also offered. COPE's director works closely with local agencies and organizations to address the career and job needs of the community. Users of the COPE Center indicate that the program is meeting crucial needs while bringing many traditional nonlibrary users into the library.

ONONDAGA COUNTY PUBLIC LIBRARY SYSTEM [SYRACUSE, NY]

Profile of the Library

Size of Community: 163,860

Population Served: 463,920

Staff: 212

Profile of the Regional Learning Service

The Regional Learning Service ("RLS"), coordinated by an adult educator, is a community-based education and career information and counseling organization. RLS was the nation's first education information center, opening in the mid 1970s, with funds from the W. K. Kellogg Foundation. It has served as a model for a number of programs. Because of special state-funding, RLS was able to reach out to special target audiences including people who are incarcerated, geographically isolated, educationally or economically deprived, minorities, and workers in transition. A telephone hotline, created and staffed by the Regional Learning Service and the public library, gives information on educational and training opportunities in seven counties in the Syracuse area (Onondaga, Oswego, Madison, Oneida, Cayuga, Tompins, and Cortland). RLS is built on a computerized Information and Referral Database of 500 subject areas. It represents the educational and training offerings of over

150 institutions, from basic literacy providers to degree granting institutions.

RLS employees include educational and career counselors who are available on a sliding scale basis. Counseling is enhanced by the use of SIGI Plus, computerized financial aid information, and resume writing software. Networking is critical in promoting cooperation and enhancing services. Promotion methods include radio public service announcements, and a weekly question and answer column called "Learn to Work," appears in the Sunday paper near the classified ads.

SPOKANE (WA) PUBLIC LIBRARY

Profile of the Library

Size of Community: 177,196

Population Served: 178,500

Staff: 118

Profile of the Education and Job Information Center

Spokane, often called "the hub of the inland empire" is the largest city between Seattle and Minneapolis. The economic base of the community includes "agriculture, mining, light manufacturing, and a diverse financial community made up of banking, insurance, and real estate concerns." Some of these industries have experienced major job losses and many workers have used the Spokane Public Library's Education and Job Information Center. Its flyer starts out with the following questions:

"Searching for a way to finance a college education?"

"Seeking employment?"

"Need to know how to write a resume?"

"Thinking about a career change?"

Karen Davis, a career counselor, coordinates the job center which includes: Information resourcesincluding print and video materials, software and databases; referral servicesto colleges, adult education programs, and other agencies; and personal assistance services including job search assistance and SIGI Plus. Staff help people write resumes and provide individual consultation on careers, job search strategies, and test preparation. A financial aid database provides financial aid opportunities in eastern Washington.

CORPUS CHRISTI (TX) PUBLIC LIBRARIES

Profile of the Library

Size of Community: 257,453

Population Served: 275,000

Staff: 67

Profile of the Career Center

The Career Center at Corpus Christi Public Library is the first center for job seekers in a public library in Texas. It began in 1987 with several grants from LSCA. There is a wide range of resources to help with the job search: Books and periodicals, videotapes, computer programs for exploring career options and interests and resumes, job listings, company information, and an electronic bulletin board with up-to-date job information. The Career Information Specialist, who has a Master's degree in counseling, is available for individual consultation and assistance with many aspects of the job search. Workshops, often brown bag lunchtime seminars or evening sessions, are offered on job search strategy, resume writing, interviewing skills, and many business and employment issues. The staff person is part of a network group to share business marketing ideas and assist each other in their own businesses. This active program receives regular media coverage. Local television stations and newspapers have started regular features on employment news and have frequent articles. The Career Center has a full-service image in the community: "We are the one-stop job search center of south Texas!"

LIBRARIES IN COMMUNITIES GREATER THAN 250,000

TOLEDO-LUCAS COUNTY (OH) PUBLIC LIBRARY

Profile of the Library

Size of Community: 332,943

Population Served: 462,361

Staff: 268

Profile of the Government Procurement Center

The Government Procurement Center (GPC) of the Toledo-Lucas County Public Library helps area businesses gain contracts from the federal government, worth over $100 million to date. Started in

FIGURE 2-4: Education/Job Information Center—Spokane (WA) Public Library

EDUCATION/JOB INFORMATION CENTERS

INLAND NORTHWEST

EJIC

Main Library
(509) 838-4728
Valley Library
(509) 926-6283
Pend Oreille County Library District
(509) 447-2111

Education/Job Information Centers, located at area public libraries, offer up-to-date information on:

- **Careers, vocations and occupations**
- **Career decision-making**
- **Techniques for successful job search and interviews**
- **Resume preparation**
- **Trade and vocational schools**
- **Colleges and universities**
- **Scholarships and individual grants**
- **Alternative routes to training — apprenticeship, military, correspondence**
- **Do-it-yourself lifelong and continuing education**
- **Test preparation for GED, college, civil service, and military**

EDUCATION/JOB INFORMATION CENTERS

INLAND NORTHWEST

EJIC

Spokane Public Library
West 906 Main Avenue
Spokane, Washington
99201

Searching for a way to finance a college education? Seeking employment? Need to know how to write a resume? Thinking about a career change? Get the facts you need from your library's Education/Job Information Center (EJIC).

Education/Job Information Centers offer up-to-date information on:

- **Careers, vocations, and occupations**
- **Career decision-making**
- **Resume preparation**
- **Techniques for successful job search and interviews**
- **Colleges and universities**
- **Trade and vocational schools**
- **Scholarships and individual grants**
- **Alternative routes to training — apprenticeship, military, correspondence**
- **Do-it-yourself lifelong and continuing education**
- **Test preparation for GED, college, civil service, and military**

Library staff members are available in the Centers to provide free assistance. Talks and orientations are available for individuals and groups. To make an appointment for specialized assistance contact the EJIC at your library.

Funds for EJIC were provided by a grant from the Kellogg Foundation. EJIC is a member of the Washington Occupation Information Service Network (WOIS).

1983 and housed at the Main Library in downtown Toledo, the GPC provides counseling and information to local businesses that are interested in participating in the federal purchasing process. The Library is especially pleased that the GPC is mainly used by small businesses, giving them access to the federal procurement network that they haven't had before. Very few public libraries support such a service, but Toledo markets its wealth of information strongly. The Center serves its clients with a variety of information/document retrievals, market development advice, and counseling on the federal procurement process. It also offers seminars on relevant topics. GPC staff reviews solicitations, bids, and correspondence relating to government contracting and serves as a client advocate, accompanying prospective contractors to meetings with government officials. The Government Procurement Center is totally staffed and primarily funded by Toledo-Lucas County Public Library with some financial assistance from the Ohio Department of Development.

TULSA (OK) CITY COUNTY LIBRARY

Profile of the Library

Size of Community: 367,302

Population Served: 503,341

Staff: 201

Profile of the Economic Development Information Center

The Economic Development Information Center, a cooperative project of the Tulsa City-County Library, the City and the Chamber of Commerce, has completed its fifth year of operation. The Center is located in the Business and Technology Department of the Central Library and is staffed by a full-time professional librarian. The Center gathers all existing economic development resources into a centralized location accessible to the entire community. Important activities include the creation and continual up-dating of a database with Tulsa's economic and demographic information and the publication of the Tulsa Data Book.

CARNEGIE LIBRARY OF PITTSBURGH (PA)

Profile of the Library

Size of Community: 369,879

Population Served: 1,336,449

Staff: 356

Profile of WORKPLACE

The aim of Carnegie Library of Pittsburgh's WORKPLACE initiated in the early 1980s with LSCA and Kellogg grants is to assist in career planning and researching the job market. This service, found in the main library and in several branches, is coordinated by librarians. A brochure widely distributed in Pittsburgh, explains WORKPLACE's goals and services.

WORKPLACE exists to help adults make job, career, and education decisions. Through computerized decision-making systems, WORKPLACE helps job seekers clarify their needs, assess their skills, explore today's world of work, and make career and job decisions. WORKPLACE offers workshops on all phases of the job search, provides information on specific jobs, and gathers information in one location on area agencies, programs, and educational opportunities that benefit the job seeker.

Advising is an important part of the program. DISCOVER and GIS interactive career assessment software packages, are used. A wide range of materials are available. Workshops are offered at the library and in the community in an adjoining meeting room. The program includes a job club. Staff, with other providers, have developed a local network of organizations which work with the unemployed. A WORKPLACE job developer works closely with area employers to help find jobs for WORKPLACE hard-to-place clients. Staff are developing more outreach and expanded services (in 1992, for example, they expanded services to Russian immigrants). JPTA and Pennsylvania Department of Commerce funds supplement library support.

CUYAHOGA COUNTY PUBLIC LIBRARY [PARMA, OH]

Profile of the Library

Size of Community: 87,876

Population Served: 614,474

Staff: 523

Profile of InfoPLACE

InfoPLACE(Info)rmation, (P)ublic (L)ibrary (A)dult (C)areer & (E)ducational service of the Cuyahoga County (OH) Public Library, is one of the nation's most comprehensive job and career information services. InfoPLACE is headquartered at the Maple Heights Regional Library but has services in a number of Cuyahoga County branches and regionals provided by a "circuit riding staff." The staff includes career counselors and librarians. The program began with LSCA funds, and it is now completely locally funded. InfoPLACE has two main components: 1) professional career guidance, job search assistance, and educational information; and 2) community information and referral service which focuses on providing current information to help solve educational, consumer, family, credit, and legal problems. This well-developed service has a wide range of counseling and advising services, DISCOVER and other computer software, many group workshops, and referrals. InfoPLACE staff provides consultation on career/life planning, educational decision-making, job-hunting strategies, resume writing, and interviewing skills. An individualized, labor-intensive counseling focus is especially strong, and often extended time is spent with each patron. There are strong links with other agencies and frequent collaboration.

Many excellent original materials, including *The Community Services Directory*, *The Educational Directory of Northeast Ohio*, *The Resume Guide*, *The Sourcebook For Career Planning and Job Search*, and *The Survival Guide* have been developed for use by patrons and in workshops. InfoPLACE staff present many extensive workshops for career changers and job seekers a year. The CAREER DECISION WORKSHOP includes: Self assessment, goal setting, researching occupations, library resources, and career planning tips. The JOB SEARCH PROCESS WORKSHOP includes: The hidden job market, interviewing skills, researching potential employers, resume writing, and library resources. The program is considered part of the "regular" library services, and is very popular and necessary in the community.

MEMPHIS-SHELBY COUNTY (TN) PUBLIC LIBRARY & INFORMATION CENTER

Profile of the Library

Size of Community: 610,337

Population Served: 828,082

Staff: 367

Profile of JOBLINC

The Memphis/Shelby County Public Library takes its job and career information service to the people on a 35-foot Bluebird bus called JOBLINCJOB (L)ibrary (IN)formation (C)enter. JOBLINC began in 1990 with funding from an LSCA grant, United Way, county gov-

FIGURE 2-5: WORKPLACE: Jobs, Careers, Education, Retraining At The Carnegie Library Of Pittsburgh

Workplace

JOBS
CAREERS
EDUCATION
RETRAINING

THE CARNEGIE
LIBRARY OF
PITTSBURGH

What is it?

The WORKPLACE is a special area of the library set apart to provide educational and career information. Although the center is not a job placement service, it offers the necessary tools--books, pamphlets, directories, government publications, and a computerized retrieval service--to assist in career planning and researching the job market.

Where is it?

The Carnegie Library of Pittsburgh operates WORKPLACE at the Main Library in Oakland as well as at the Hazelwood and West End Branches.

What are its goals?

WORKPLACE exists to help adults make job, career and education decisions. Through computerized decision-making systems, WORKPLACE helps job seekers clarify their needs, assess their skills, explore today's world of work and make career and job decisions. WORKPLACE offers workshops on all phases of the job search, provides information on specific jobs and gathers in one location information on area agencies, programs and educational opportunities that benefit the job seeker.

The WORKPLACE is operated through a grant from the State Library of Pennsylvania funded by the W. K. Kellogg Foundation.

Understanding yourself

Understanding the world of work

Making career decisions

The job search: taking action

The Carnegie Library of Pittsburgh and WORKPLACE have books on:

Resume preparation
Interviewing techniques
Company information
Careers
Job-hunting strategies

The Library also has:

Test manuals

Civil Service announcements

Audiovisual materials--
audiocassettes
microfiche
videocassettes
computer software

Computerized Pennsylvania databases
PAIS (Pennsylvania Financial Aid)
KEYS (Pennsylvania Schools)
Pennsylvania Careers

SERVICES

At WORKPLACE you will find information to help you...

- assess your abilities
- make a career decision
- write a resume and prepare for a job interview
- find training programs

Through the WORKPLACE, you will be able to...

- use career exploration software
- use Pennsylvania Careers, a state software package, to locate specific career opportunities
- find company information
- attend workshops
- identify community and state educational programs
- use books, films and software to help you in your career search
- use civil service listings

THE CARNEGIE LIBRARY OF PITTSBURGH WORKPLACE CENTERS

Main Library
4400 Forbes Avenue
First floor
622-3133
Library hours:

Mon., Tues., Wed., Fri. 9-9
Thurs., Sat. 9-5:30
Sun. 1-5
Closed Sundays in summer

WORKPLACE will be staffed Monday through Saturday, 10-5. CALL FOR AN APPOINTMENT.

Hazelwood Branch
4748 Monongahela Street
421-2517

Library hours:
Mon. 1-8
Tues., Wed., Fri. 1-6
Sat. 9-12

WORKPLACE will be staffed
1-8, Monday
3-6, 1st and 3rd Tuesday,
9-12, 2nd and 4th Saturday.
CALL FOR AN APPOINTMENT.

West End Branch
Wabash and Neptune Streets
921-1717

Library hours:
Mon.-Thurs. 1-8
Sat. 9-5

WORKPLACE will be staffed
1-8, 2nd and 4th Tuesday,
3-8, Wednesday, and
9-5, 1st and 3rd Saturday.
CALL FOR AN APPOINTMENT.

ernment, and special funds. The staff includes a library assistant, a social worker, a minister/counselor, and volunteers. The bus regularly goes to community centers, shopping malls, churches, social agencies and career fairs in the area. This fully-equipped job and career center has a host of resources on board. The array of job listings is widely used, and very important to many people. There are two computers with software for career and interest assessment, and resume writing. A video recording area is used to help assess interviewing skills and allow people to watch career videos. The collection contains books and materials on careers, education and training programs, continuing education and job skills, job search strategies, and other resources to help people with their needs for information and assistance. The library's information and referral files are available for social service assistance. The bus is connected by telephone and electronic mail to libraries in the area if further resources are needed. JOBLINC serves from 1,100-1,200 people per month and is responsive to public demand in a unique way. Taking the service to the people reaches a wider audience. This library service connects a public-service-oriented library to a definite community need and has become highly valued in the Memphis community.

FREE LIBRARY OF PHILADELPHIA (PA)

Profile of the Library

Size of Community: 1,585,577

Population Served: 1,688,210

Staff: 782

Profile of WORKPLACE

WORKPLACE at the Free Library of Philadelphia began in 1988 with funding by the Kellogg Foundation. Three librarians staff WORKPLACE and do workshops on such subjects as resume writing and career changing. A large number of computer programs support the need for career information, assessment and resume writing. Advising and informal information assessment are also available. There is some contact with agencies in the community especially for referral. WORKPLACE has Vocational Information Computer Systems (VICS), which is an occupational database. It includes information similar to that found in the Dictionary of Occupational Titles in a computerized form. Users are able to get information on where to get training to be qualified in a particular career, or what is the job outlook and salary for a particular occupation, all of which information is specific to the Philadelphia area. The service is available in most branch libraries, but WORKPLACE coordinates the printouts for the main branch of the Free Library of Philadelphia. WORKPLACE staff offers support and advice, examination of options, and provides workshops on job seeking and career decision making, among other topics. Workshops are staffed by librarians, and provide the camaraderie of people in similar situations. Paul Savedow, the director of WORKPLACE, thinks of WORKPLACE as a clearinghouse to use the library. Staff develop pathfinders and guides to help patrons use the resources of a large urban library.

BROOKLYN (NY) PUBLIC LIBRARY

Profile of the Library

Size of Community: (?)

Population Served: 2,230,936

Staff: 969

Profile of Education and Job Information Center

Brooklyn Public Library is one of the nation's largest public libraries. It serves 2.3 million people through its 58 branches and main library. Inspite of a series of severe budget cuts, for example a 12 percent cut from 1991-92 alone, resulting in major staff layoffs and branch closings, BPL has maintained its Education/Job Information Center, located at the Central Library at Grand Army Plaza. This job center, with a staff of five full-time librarians and one clerk, is the largest in the NYC Metropolitan area. The center provides a wide range of resources at various literacy levels for training, education, jobs and career choice, bibliographies, college catalogs, financial aid information, study guides for civil service and educational exams, how-to books for entrpreneurship and starting a small business, SIGI Plus career advising software, computerized job listings, and typewriters for writing resumes and cover letters.

The Center also provides directories of business firms and social agencies. The center works with adults and teens. Recently, by using LSCA funds, job and career center stafff worked with at-risk minority youth in a variety of ways. These at-risk young people were identified through community groups and school visits. Approaches taken included providing career guidance through SIGI Plus, class visits, provision of career videos, and a well-staffed job and career center reference desk. The experience of working with at-risk youth resulted in a greater number of referrals to English-as-a-second-language classes and literacy programs.

ADDITIONAL PROFILES

Women's Correctional Facility at Waynesburg Workplace

This WORKPLACE site is equipped with a computer loaded with a variety of career assessment software, including: DISCOVER and interactive programs developed by the Pennsylvania Higher Education Authority (PHEAA)Keys, an interactive guide to Pennsylvania Schools and programs, financial aid, and Pennsylvania Careers Outlook, shows job opportunities and the job outlook in Pennsylvania. In addition, there is resume writing softwareincluding Resume One and Perfect Resume. The software is supplemented by the employment outlook loose-leaf notebooks and other resources. Several job seeking videotapes, notably the Karli tapes designed for people with poor job skills are available for viewing on a portable monitor which can be used individually with a headset.

Funding for this site is provided by the Pennsylvania Corrections Department. Usually all of the tables are full. The library serves the legal (mandated) informational, and recreational needs of the population. Much of the work at this WORKPLACE site is done by inmates. Each inmate at the Correctional Facility has a job (farm workers, janitorial, food service, etc.). The position of Library Inmate Clerical is one of the more prestigious assignments in the prison. At the time of my site visit, three inmates were assigned to WORKPLACE.

An inmate must have a job plan or a school plan before she can be released from the prison. WORKPLACE fits into the other job oriented programs which have been developed at the prison. WORKPLACE is a voluntary option for release preparation, but there is some pressure to show a plan and WORKPLACE produces positive results.

Inmates work with inmates because of necessity there is not enough money to provide staff counseling. Peer counselors were used initially on an experimental basis, but the librarian has continued the program because it proved to be successful. Pragmatically, it makes possible a program unavailable otherwise. The librarian notes that there is probably more honesty on an inmate to inmate basis because the inmates like to impress the staff. For example, an inmate counselor might be told by an inmate, "I'm just here because my counselor sent me." This wouldn't be revealed to a staff member. Attitude does affect the session.

The inmates make heavy use of interactive software which helps users select occupations based on their own interests and abilities. Some of the WORKPLACE software packages generate letters to selected colleges and training schools that request enrollment information, college catalogs, financial aid, etc. These letters generate responses that fit in with the Parole Board requirements. They are also appreciated by the inmates because they yield results.

Peer counselors use computer software to help other inmates generate resumes. The only rule is that they may not be a party to falsifying information for a resume. The librarian looks for peer counselors who will respect confidentiality. She informs them about confidentiality in libraries. The librarian indicated that peer counselors are sensitive to inmates who have poor readings skills. They will say, "That screen looks a little blurry, it says . . . " and they read the information off the screen.

RESOURCES

American Library Directory, 1990-91 ed. New Providence, NJ: R.R. Bowker, 1990.

Materials developed by a number of Library Job and Career Information Centers.

SIGI Plus Newsletter, Winter 1992.

Telephone interviews by the staff of the University of Michigan Kellogg EJIC Project. Primary interviewers Paula Gibbons and Catherine Allen.

3 THE NEED BEHIND THE QUESTION

Each year millions of people face major changes in their lives, many involving their livelihood. Under normal circumstances most people are likely to change careers several times in their lives. Large numbers are forced by circumstances beyond their control into the job market often unprepared and even disheartened. Life changes can influence an individual and affect his or her ability to use information. Librarians can better help people who come to them for job information if they understand the kinds of situations or problems that interfere with using information.

Career counselors and others often refer to people who are undergoing major changes in their worklife as "adults in transition." Work-related transitions include: Leaving a job to relocate, being forced to leave a job for health reasons, retiring, being laid off or fired, starting a business, going bankrupt, being promoted or transferred, or going back to work after a long absence.

Mary Jo Ryan, Director of Public Relations at the Nebraska State Library says that all of the people described below—all adults in transition—found their way into Nebraska public libraries as part of their decision-making process.

- A laid-off railroader in Western Nebraska.
- A woman who hoped to start a mail-order country crafts business to keep the farm afloat.
- A bankrupt farm-implement dealer who lost everything including the family home.
- A young woman who wanted to start earning better money but "ain't going to spend the time at a four-year school."
- A man who just inherited a house full of old books, china, silver, and glassware and wondered if he should turn a casual interest into an occupation.

Whether or not they knew that information is a key ingredient in decision making, each of them found that the library in his or her community was the "information place" and a good first step. Coming to the library is one action. Getting the help that is needed involves a complicated communication process. Librarians have long known that people often don't ask the question they actually need a response to. Questions that people bring to librarians are often fairly far removed from the problems that they are trying to solve. By focusing on the problem, librarians can help questioners get the information they need more efficiently.

Information needs that result from the change process associated with seeking employment or career choice vary widely and depend on a number of factors associated with the person and with the problem. They can arise from the following:

The need for knowledge as well as the need to understand oneself;

The need to make decisions and solve problems, and

The need to prepare to take action.

This chapter focuses on the needs identified by career counselors and librarians as being associated with adults in job or career transitions. It provides a framework for anticipating needs in a community.

Job seekers who approach library staff may come asking questions that sound a lot like reference questions, such as " Where are your books on jobs?" Librarians who take a needs-based approach seek to find out more about the question in order to more effectively respond to the need. Librarians who develop job and career centers learn that when people come to the library for information about jobs, they often have other concerns which affect their ability to obtain and use information. During the course of working with an individual, a librarian may learn of these problems, some of which can be met by other professionals or agencies. Knowledge of an individual's situation, as well as knowledge of the resources in the community, gives librarians the ability to make appropriate referrals for such needs as counseling and emergency assistance.

THREE SUCCESS STORIES

The stories of how three people, Laurie, William, and Raoul—who were experiencing major changes in their work-life—received assistance at their local public library job center will serve to introduce a group of needs from the perspective of the people who experienced them. Laurie, William, and Raoul each had sustained interactions with their local library staff (librarians and/or career counselors) and were referred to resources in the community in the process of working with job and career information center staff. Each person came to the center with more than one set of needs. Notice what happened to these people when they worked with job and career center staff. The next several chapters discuss a wide range of strategies that can be used to help people. Some of them are mentioned in these stories.

LAURIE

When the glass factory in Washington County, Pennsylvania closed, the librarian at the Kellogg-funded job and career center, WORKPLACE, went to the factory and gave a seminar on job seeking skills. She told her audience that if they came to the library they could use the career advising software, check out materials on careers, or talk with her about choices and options. Laurie, a 32 year old single parent with a high school education, decided to investigate what the library had to offer. She had been laid off and felt that she had few options because she had worked all of her adult life at the glass factory. She was confused and thought at first that she should immediately try to get another job.

Over time, the WORKPLACE librarian worked with her by using career advising software, discussed her options with her, and provided her with encouragement. During that time Laurie decided that she wanted to go to college. Although she was excited about her decision to go to college, she was also apprehensive about this major life decision. College had not entered her mind before working with the WORKPLACE librarian. She was afraid that at 37 she was too old to start college.

The WORKPLACE librarian gave her encouragement on her decision, guidance on how to approach the admissions interview, and valuable information about financial aid. To let her know that she really cared about what happened to Laurie, the librarian suggested that she come back and let her know how things were progressing. Laurie is now preparing for a new career as a technician.

WILLIAM

William was referred to InfoPLACE by a relative who had been helped successfully in her own job search. All of his working life he had been with a company that manufactured steel tubing, first as a machinist and then as a foreman. In the year and a half after the company went out of business he had tried to find another job, first as a foreman, and then a machinist, and, finally, "just anything". His benefits had run out and he was taking any temporary job that he could find. He was worried about losing his home. Even though skilled machinists continue to be in short supply and high demand in the Cleveland area, William discovered that he lacked some essential current skills and knowledge—for example, computerized numerical control. William attended a library developed career decision workshop and learned steps in the process. He also worked with a counselor and explained his situation to her. Among other assistance, she linked him to a local trade school which she found had a JTPA contract to provide free training. When he was in her office she called the school, put William on the line, and he made an appointment for admissions testing. He called several days later to say that he had been accepted in a program that placed all of its graduates in good jobs.

RAOUL

Raoul is a young Hispanic man with a wife and a child to support. Not too long before coming to the United States from Mexico, Raoul graduated from college with an engineering degree. Unable to find a job that utilized his skills, Raoul had worked in a series of low-paying, menial jobs. His English-language skills were poor, he had very little confidence, and limited knowledge about how to find a job.

His local library had a contract program to bring in career counselors for appointments. A counselor helped him learn how to relate his background to finding a job. At the same time he worked with a librarian to identify appropriate information and materials designed to help him prepare his resume and to interview more effectively. Job and career center staff helped Raoul structure a job strategy and referred him to a local agency that helped minorities find employment. In just two weeks, Raoul found a job in an engineering company that had other Spanish-speaking employees. Shortly after that, he let the job and career center staff know that he was very pleased with his new job and that he had begun, on his own, to plan for continuing his education.

RESPONDING TO NEEDS

When librarians know more about people in job and career transition experience, they can better anticipate the kinds of needs that an individual mayhave. Typically, a career changer may need to learn more about some aspect of the world of work, to make a decision, or take some action such as making a job change. Many people, in

FIGURE 3-1: Spanish Version, Job-Seeker Survival Kit—Hempstead (NY) Public Library

BUSCAR EMPLEO:

CÓMO CONSEGUIR EL TRABAJO QUE USTED DESEA (Y MERECE)

Centro de Información sobre Empleos

HEMPSTEAD PUBLIC LIBRARY
115 NICHOLS CT., HEMPSTEAD, N.Y. 11550
(516) 481-6990

CONTENIDO

Este proyecto está apoyado por fondos federales, Titulo I. Federal Library Services and Construction Act, administrados por el Nassau Library System bajo la supervison de la Biblioteca Estatal de Nueva York.

addition, will need to find out more about themselves in order to better interact with the world of work. A surprising number will need to get more education or training. Some will need to gain skill in presenting themselves or will need help with identifying and solving specific problems that get in the way of finding a job. People will come to the job and career information center in need of support and assistance in coping with problems associated with unemployment or loss of a job. Often one person will have several different needs at the same time. Some needs, especially those which are only vaguely understood by the client, interfere with a person's ability to get and use information. Effective interviewing techniques can elicit specific needs.

Needs stimulate the search for information. The remainder of this chapter focuses on a group of needs commonly faced by job seekers and career changers. The needs of job seekers and career changers, discussed below, have been grouped into three general categories with several needs listed in each category. The major categories are:

1. The Need to Obtain Knowledge or Self-Knowledge;
2. Decisions to be Made and Problems to Solve, and
3. Actions to Prepare For.

The stylized format used to introduce each of the needs serves several purposes. It introduces each need, shows how it might be expressed, indicates how librarians can respond, and provides examples of how people have been helped by library staff. Each need description uses the following format:

Need Sketch

The NEED SKETCH provides a general description of each need, including a brief introduction to the kinds of situations that are associated with this need or condition. The thumbnail sketch often explains how people might use information to solve a particular problem.

How the Need May Be Expressed

Briefly discusses how an individual who has this need might approach staff. The questions included here are the kinds of questions which have been asked at other job and career information centers. A WORD OF CAUTION: Although specific questions are included in this chapter to illustrate needs, **do not expect people to**

come with straightforward questions. Considerable research by a number of people over a long period of time shows that people do not INITIALLY ask librarians questions that actually reflect their needs. As the trust level rises, questions will more likely reflect need. Chapters 4 and 5 help librarians obtain the skills needed to determine actual needs.

How Librarians Can Help

This links these needs to a series of strategies that a library might use to respond to the particular need. The suggestions under this heading can easily be developed into program objectives which can be used to shape a library's job and career center. These responses will depend on the needs of the community and the resources available. Strategies which generally require less effort and fewer resources are listed first.

The three stories told earlier in this chapter show some of the strategies which job and career center staff use to work with their clientele.

The story of Laurie , a displaced worker and a single mother, shows how her local librarian initially raised Laurie's awareness of what was possible at the library by going to the factory.The librarian used strategies designed to increase Laurie's access to information, and she provided reassurance as Laurie made a decision based on the new information she received at the library.

Librarians and counselors who worked with William used several different strategies on his behalf. They provided a workshop he needed, helped him with career counseling and other personal assistance strategies, and linked him with other services in the community.

Library staff worked to increase Raoul's access to resources in the library and in the community. They provided him with a wide variety of help in increasing his access to information and in solving several problems associated with his job search, including the fact that he had serious language difficulties and was new to the country and the city.

How Clients with This Need Have Been Helped

This heading provides very brief examples of how individuals and groups of people have been helped by librarians and counselors. Additional examples are found throughout the book.

Testimonials

Included here are very brief statements from people who have come to education and job information centers with specific needs. These testimonials, in the people's own words, give some idea of how they were helped. Many of the testimonials in this book came in the form of unsolicited letters, notes, and phone calls. However, do not leave testimonials to chance. Chapter 10, "Evaluating Job and Career Information Centers," presents methods that can be used to get testimonials and stories (these can then be passed on to the director, funders, the library board, and other interested parties).

THE NEED FOR KNOWLEDGE/SELF-KNOWLEDGE

SELF ASSESSMENT

"I feel better and have a clearer picture of myself and my goals."

"My career plans are easier now. Working with the staff at the job and career center helped me step out and look at my options with a different perspective."

The following comments are about information which increases knowledge for personal decision-making:

"I have learned about careers I wouldn't even have thought about–ones that seem to be suited to my own skills."

"I have learned about careers I wouldn't even have thought about-ones that seem to be suited to my own skills."

NEED: SELF-ASSESMENT

Need Sketch

Job seekers often need to find out more about themselves in order to better interact with the world of work. The process of self-assessment helps people think about how their interests, values, dreams, personality, skills, abilities, and experience, have an impact on job decisions. Self assessment helps people realistically match their interests and qualifications with education, training, and job opportunities. This need is overeaching. At the beginning stages of information seeking on any topic there is a great deal of uncertainty. How successful people are in realistically assessing themselves has a direct bearing on how well they are able to meet other needs associated with job seeking or making a career choice. Effective self-assessment will have a major impact on career decision making.

How the Need May Be Expressed

Seldom is this need expressed directly. People may not even realize that they need to go through the process of assessing their skills and options before they are in a position to use information effectively. Librarians who make career advising software available to their users are more likely to get questions about self-assessment. "Will I be able to become an computer technician?" or statements like, "I hate working indoors," or "I have trouble with numbers," or "I just don't know where to turn." These kinds of questions and statements show the need to mesh interests, skills and options.

How Librarians Can Help

Many people need help getting started with self assessment. Librarians can help them by providing bibliographies of valuable books and other resources.

Books such as *What Color Is Your Parachute* and *Joyce Lain Kennedy's Career Book* can help some individuals get started with self assessment. Some librarians have purchased self-assessment kits which are used by trained counselors in the library. Increasingly, managers of career information centers are purchasing career assessment software which has made responding to the need to provide assistance with self-assessment much easier. Many librarians have purchased such programs as SIGI Plus developed by the Educational Testing Service and DISCOVER, created by American College Testing. Librarians who use effective interviewing skills can help people become aware of the need to assess their skills and options as part of the information seeking process. In a few libraries there are career counselors who help individuals assess their skills and interests.

How Clients with This Need Have Been Helped

Hundreds of people have come to their local library job and career information center to use such interactive computer assessment pro-

FIGURE 3-2: **WEBS Provides Free . . . —Westchester Educational Brokerage System**

grams as SIGI Plus or DISCOVER. They typically spend an hour or two at the computer answering questions about their interests, priorities, and work values. At the end of such a session, they are provided with a computer printout which helps start them on a more extensive self-assessment process which often results in making job, career, and education decisions. They are encouraged to talk it over with a librarian or career counselor.

The two stories below show how two individuals who came to the library received help with self-assessment.

A food manager with a high school education felt that he had reached a dead end. He learned that his local public library had a career center and decided to give it a try. He visited the library, used the library's career advising software, talked over the printout with the job and career center librarian, and after some weeks of exploring a number of careers, decided to enroll in college and work toward a business degree.

A clerical worker who was unable to advance in the company where she had worked for a number of years came to the public library discouraged and was looking for a new job. The librarian suggested that she check out a book on thinking creatively about your career and schedule an appointment to enter her interests in the library's career advising program the following week. This marked the beginning of what this woman described later as a very stimulating time in her life. She made several appointments to work with the software, talk with the librarian about the printouts, and read about different career options from books the librarian recommended. She decided after several months to enroll in the local community college program on starting and running a business with an eye toward opening her own accessory shop.

Testimonials

> "My counselor made me aware of the many possibilities open to me." "The DISCOVER program showed me I have options I hadn't previously considered." "She tells you what you need to hear, not what you want to hear. She made me realize I'm not stuck."

NEED: TO OBTAIN INFORMATION TO INCREASE PERSONAL KNOWLEDGE

Need Sketch

Job and career information forms the basis for many education, job, and career decisions. The average person changes jobs at least five or six times when they are part of the full-time workforce. Often people have several different careers in a lifetime. Work itself is changing. As we move into the information age, many manufacturing and agricultural jobs have disappeared. Jobs and careers of the future will require a more educated workforce.

When someone seeks information about job opportunities, he\she may need to gain a better understanding of the changing world of work. Many kinds of jobs have been eliminated and people who held these jobs need new skills to find other work. In short, job and career information needs will vary considerably.

People may need to better understand the world of work. They may want to get up-to-date information about careers, explore possible career choices in depth, or find out about a specific job. They may need help in finding and contacting people in specific careers as sources of information. Work and education are very closely tied. When people seek information about jobs, they are likely to need information about education or training as well.

How the Need May Be Expressed

The most common questions are the ones that librarians have always received: "Do you have books on careers?" Questions may indicate a specific career: "Do you have any information on how to become a stock broker?" Job and career center staff members say that they now approach a question such as this one a little differently because they know that it may have an underlying kind of need other than that which is being expressed, for example, the need to make a job change.

How Libraries/Librarians Can Help

Librarians who seek to provide basic job information can start by developing a collection that is adequate and current. An additional step is to ensure that staff has taken steps to increase access to the library's resources by telling the public about them. They may purchase the state's occupational information system and other career software and provide career advising software. Most staff help people use these materials and develop guides to job, career, and education resources and conduct workshops on the world of work. Librarians develop and widely distribute brochures describing job and career center services. They negotiate questions to assure that they are providing the information actually needed. Career fairs raise awareness about a career which can then be followed up by an individual.Create specialty bibliographies (by different job families)

FIGURE 3-3: Career Information Sources—Chicago (IL) Public Library

CAREER INFORMATION SOURCES

Business Information Center
Business/Science/Technology Division

The Chicago Public Library
400 North Franklin Street, 4th Floor
Chicago, Illinois 60610
(312) 269-2814
Mon-Thurs 9-7
Friday 9-6
Saturday 9-5

OTHER DIVISIONS

The Fine Arts, Social Sciences, Audiovisual and Literature & Languages Divisions of The Chicago Public Library also order career material in their subject areas. The Government Publications Division receives some career related materials from federal, state and local government agencies. Periodicals are also kept in subject divisions. Career researchers will be interested in the General Information Services Division's collection of out-of-town telephone directories (including yellow pages) and its large out-of-town newspaper collection. College catalogs are available in the Social Sciences and Education reference area.

TALKS AND TOURS

Small groups can schedule talks or tours on career information. Staff members from the Business Information Center guide patrons in locating, evaluating and using career information sources.

CAREER INFORMATION SOURCES

The Business Information Center provides an extensive collection of materials for career planning and the job search process. Books, government documents, serials, and pamphlets are gathered together in one central location. Library resources may be used to find information on specific companies or information (developments, trends, compensation, etc.) about specific occupations and industries. The Division's collection of directories is useful in compiling lists of companies by geographic location or industry. Other materials are devoted to job hunting skills such as resume preparation and interviewing. These titles are just a few that may be of interest to you.

General Sources

Career Changing: The Worry-Free Guide
Dictionary of Occupational Titles
Discover What You're Good At
Encyclopedia of Careers
The Great Escape From Your Dead-End Job
The Hidden Job Market for the 80s
How to Get a Job in Chicago: The Insider's Guide
How to Write Better Resumes
Image Impact
Moonlighting: A Complete Guide to Over 200 Exciting Part-Time Jobs
Networking: The Great New Way for Women to Get Ahead
Occupational Outlook Handbook
Sweaty Palms: The Neglected Art of Being Interviewed
What Color is Your Parachute: A Practical Manual for Job Hunters and Career Changers

Examinations

Study guides are available for many Civil Service, entrance and licensing examinations. They are arranged in occupational groupings. Some of the fields covered are:

Agriculture, Agribusiness & Natural Resources
Business & Office Occupations
Communication & Media
Computer Occupations
Construction
Consumer & Homemaking Related Occupations
Environment
Health Occupations
Manufacturing
Marine Science
Marketing & Distribution
Military Careers
Personal Services
Public Service
Recreation & Hospitality
Transportation

Directories

Many U.S. and foreign industrial directories are available in the Business Information Center. By using the Standard Industrial Classification Code (SIC) specialized companies in a specific geographic location can be found. Some of our titles are...

Company Directories

Directory of Corporate Affiliations
Dun & Bradstreet Million Dollar Directory
Dun's Employment Opportunities Directory
Moody's Investor's Service Manuals
Standard & Poor's Register of Corporations
Thomas Register of American Manufacturers

Chicago Directories

The Becker Guide: A Guide to Publicly Held Corporations and Major Financial Institutions in the Chicago Area
Illinois Manufacturers Directory
Illinois Service Directory
Metropolitan Chicago Major Employers

Out-of-State Directories

Industrial directories for all states and many countries.
Directory of American Firms Operating in Foreign Countries
Dun & Bradstreet Principal International Businesses
Directory of International Corporate Affiliations

Specialized Directories

Accounting firms, consultants, executive search firms, advertising agencies, import-export firms, insurance companies, research laboratories, securities dealers, etc.

Professional Associations

Encyclopedia of Associations
National Trade & Professional Associations of the U.S. and Canada

Annual Reports

Since 1971, all corporate reports (10-K) and prospectuses filed with the Securities and Exchange Commission are available. Proxy statements and 8-K filings are also held. Annual reports to stockholders have been collected since 1980.

Industry Information

The Business/Science/Technology Division holdings include many industry surveys and forecasts, along with over 2,600 periodicals. The heavy concentration of trade journals make these a valuable source of want ads, as well as information about particular industries. Periodical indexes can be used to locate specific articles. Also available are very specialized indexes such as the Accountant's Index, Cumulative Index to Nursing Literature, Engineering Index, Computer Literature Index, etc.

General Indexes

Business Periodicals Index
The Business Index
F & S Index
Wall Street Journal Index

Surveys & Forecasts

Crandall's Business Index/Interindustry Forecast
Predicasts Basebook
Standard & Poor's Industry Surveys
U.S. Industrial Outlook

Some Sources of Want Ads

National Ad Search (Compiles executive, technical and management ads from 68 Sunday newspapers)
National Business Employment Weekly
Federal Career Opportunities

Career Information File

The Career Information File is a collection of pamphlets, brochures, and current information received from the major professional and trade associations,organizations and labor unions.

City of Chicago
Richard M. Daley, Mayor
Cindy Pritzker
President, Board of Directors
John B. Duff
Commissioner

The Chicago Public Library:
Committed to Quality Library Service

FIGURE 3-4: Careers in Science & Technology—Carnegie Library of Pittsburgh (PA)

CAREERS IN SCIENCE AND TECHNOLOGY:
BOOKS THAT CAN LEAD THE WAY

T 49.5 .O27 1986 — O'Brien, Mark — **HIGH-TECH JOBS FOR NON-TECH GRADS**

qTA 157 .R48 1985 — Reyes-Guerra, David — **THE ENGINEERING/HIGH-TECH STUDENT'S HANDBOOK**

QE 34 .R67 1983 — Rossbacher, Lisa — **CAREER OPPORTUNITIES IN GEOLOGY AND THE EARTH SCIENCES**

Q 147 .S48 1986x — Shapiro, Stanley — **EXPLORING CAREERS IN SCIENCE**

TL 850 .S54 1984 — Sheffield, Charles — **SPACE CAREERS**

T 21 .S67 1986x — Southworth, Scott — **EXPLORING HIGH-TECH CAREERS**

QA 76.25 .S66 1985 — Spencer, Jean — **EXPLORING CAREERS AS A COMPUTER TECHNICIAN**

QA 76.25 .S67 1984bx — Stair, Lila A. — **CAREERS IN COMPUTERS**

3

THE CARNEGIE
LIBRARY OF
PITTSBURGH

The books are available at the Job and Career Education Center, Main Library, The Carnegie Library of Pittsburgh.

(see Figures 3-4 and 3-5). Develop bibliographies in the languages that are most commonly spoken in the community.

How Clients with This Need Have Been Helped

Information gained at the library may open up new options ("Oh, I never even considered that!") or, conversely, may provide a dose of reality, ("That would mean five more years of education, that's out of the picture.")

School-age children and college students are likely to explore a variety of careers. Many adults need current information about requirements for particular jobs or careers. Some people will need to talk to a career counselor about options.

Laid off workers from industries like steel, fishing, and logging (who in all probability will not return to these jobs) have used the occupational information system developed by their states to explore other job options.

Prisoners nearing their release time have used computerized career guidance software packages to prepare them for the world of work outside of the prison walls.

High school seniors in a rural community used DISCOVER, the library's interactive career assessment software, as part of a senior paper assignment which asked students to explore a career. The career advising software helped the students match their interests and potential careers through the use of this user-friendly interactive software.

A woman asked about the educational requirements and pay scale for becoming a physical therapist. The librarian found information which indicated that a physical therapist required four years of education, but a physical therapy aide needed only one year of training and was permitted to work with patients while taking classes. The woman discovered a way to assess whether she liked the work as well as information about the job itself.

Testimonials

> "This place really drew me in. It is so inviting. I didn't realize that the library had all of these things to help me." "The library has made it easy to explore different job possibilities!" "I changed my mind on one career. I just didn't want to put that kind of time into preparing for it."

DECISIONS TO BE MADE/PROBLEMS TO SOLVE

The need to develop resume writing and interviewing skills "Thanks for your help. All that reading on informational interviews was the answer to getting the job . . . that and transferable skills and a good resume."

The need to develop basic or remedial skills, "I have gained a lot of confidence in my ability to make important decisions."

The need for self-esteem, support, and coping, "Your personal interest, concern and encouragement kept me going at a time of self-doubt and loss of hope." [Develop a paragraph which introduces decision making and problem solving].

NEED: TO MAKE DECISIONS

Need Sketch

Choosing a career or changing a job will require a number of decisions. Many job seekers need to be able to identify and solve a number of problems and obstacles which come up in the job seeking process. Job seekers and career changers often need help to with setting goals, making decisions, and taking action. Like self-assessment, this is an overarching need and will be seen in several of the others described in later pages. For example, people who decide to make a job change, open a small business, or return to school are making important decisions. They often remark that learning about new options at the library gave them the courage to make a decision and take action.

How the Need May Be Expressed

People who are in the process of making decisions and taking action are trying to solve problems. Often this need is expressed in a straightforward manner. A student may need information to make a decision on which university program to enroll in, "I need to choose between Stanford and Harvard." Some may state one need, "I need to write a resume," and after working on the problem for a while, the person decides that he\she needs entirely different kinds of information or assistance. A person may express his\her concern in the form of a problem, "I have lost my job," or "I feel stuck in my work." After some degree of trust is established, some people actually state a concern which is a reflection of a situation that requires some action. In short, even though this need may not be expressed directly, it can be very real and can interfere with a person's ability to get needed help.

How Librarians Can Help

Librarians need to let the person seeking assistance know that librarians do not just focus on books. They need to show that information can be valuable in the problem-solving process and that it is appropriate to focus on the problem that needs to be solved. Library staff can show their clientele that there are a range of community and library resources that are available to help in the problem solving process. Librarians should use neutral and open questions when interviewing their clientele. Job and career center staff often provide workshops on the job seeking process, including sections on setting goals and taking action.

How Clients with This Need Have Been Helped

Decision making goes hand in hand with self-assessment. People who use career guidance software (such as SIGI Plus) to assess their skills and interests, frequently make decisions (to enroll in college, embark on a new career, and so on) based on the knowledge gained in self-assessment.

People who have felt helpless and unable to get out of a poor situation (such as a dead-end job) have found that after talking with a career counselor at the library they had learned how to look at options and how to weigh them by factoring in their own interests and skills. Having done this, they were able to make a series of decisions that helped them out of the situation they had been in. Frequently people decide to gain additional skills to help them chart a better course for their work life.

A man who worked in a bicycle repair shop hated his job and desperately wanted to quit—he knew he wanted something more. He was depressed about his situation and unable to take action. The librarian encouraged him to look for training programs in the area. He decided to enroll in the local community college, soon moving into the "honors" program which was challenging and satisfying to him.

A high school student wanted to drop out of school. His mother sent him to the job and career center to take a sample GED test. He realized he didn't know as much as he thought he did and decided to stay in school.

FIGURE 3-5: SIGI Plus: A Computer-Based Career Guidance System

SIGI plus

A COMPUTER-BASED CAREER GUIDANCE SYSTEM

- **Learn what is needed to make career decisions**
- **Examine your present values, interests and skills**
- **Determine which careers match your values**
- **Compare careers**

A Free Library Service of the Westchester Library System
as part of its adult career and educational counseling service–
WEBS (Career & Educational Counseling Service).

Available at these libraries–

Harrison Public Library
Bruce Avenue
835-0324

Ossining Public Library
53 Croton Avenue
941-2416

Yonkers Public Library
Grinton I. Will Branch
1500 Central Park Avenue
337-1500

For more information about SIGI PLUS or WEBS
Ask any reference librarian or call the WEBS office
at 592-8214, Monday-Thursday, 9:00 a.m.–3:00 p.m.

WLS
A SERVICE OF THE
WESTCHESTER LIBRARY SYSTEM

Testimonials

"I feel good about the decisions I have made. They have more of a basis in fact now." "Going back to school was one of the hardest decisions I have ever made. After all, I am over thirty years old and have two kids. I really appreciate the help I got from the job and career center librarian in making it." "I came in not knowing what I was going to do with my life and left forty-five minutes later with a real sense of direction." "I am going back to school soon because of your program."

NEED: TO DEVELOP RESUME WRITING AND INTERVIEWING SKILLS

Need Sketch

The resume is the capsule summary of a person's skills, abilities, and experience. Most people, sooner or later, need to write a resume and the specifically targeted cover letter. The resume is a very important self-presentation tool. The well-crafted resume can be the key to a coveted interview; the poorly-written one can mean that a person isn't even considered, even though he or she may be the most qualified candidate.

The resume is a formidable obstacle for many people. Often people are shy about spelling out their abilities on paper. Many are unable to realize that experience and skills gained as the result of volunteer or other non-paying work (such as being a homemaker) can be a valuable addition to the resume. How to get started, how to select a format, what to put in, what to leave out, what to emphasize, and how to be succinct are among the decisions that many people have difficulty making.

The successful resume may get people in the door, but they may need help with their interview presentation skills. They may need to learn how to research an employer so that they are able to show that their qualifications match the needs of the employer.

How the Need May Be Expressed

One of the most frequently asked questions in the job and career center is, "Where are your resume books?" Given the concerns indicated above, the resume books may provide only part of the help that is needed. Some people may be more specific in their requests, focusing on the task at hand, "I need to write a resume." People may focus on their need to gain interviewing skills or to make an impression so that they can be paid at the high end of the salary range.

How Librarians Can Help

There are a number of ways librarians can help. Most librarians have for many years purchased a variety of books on resume writing and job interviewing. Many have purchased videos and audio tapes on interviewing skills. Often a clearly marked section of the library is set aside (frequently a combined job, career, and education section) where these books can be easily found. Librarians have developed bibliographies and pathfinders. Some critique resumes of people they have been working with. In some libraries, the questions come so frequently that librarians have developed guides to the resume writing/job interview process—some are photocopied and others have been professionally printed. Many of these same libraries offer workshops on resume writing and job interviewing at regular intervals. A number of librarians have purchased resume writing software to help people develop drafts of their resumes. Detailed booklets on resume writing with sample layouts included are also used. These may be provided as self-help brochures or in conjunction with a resume workshop.

How Clients with This Need Have Been Helped

A recently divorced woman who had a B.A. but hadn't worked in many years came to the job and career center as her first attempt to get help. She had no idea of how to develop a resume, or how to look for a job—she was feeling at a loss. The librarian helped her develop a resume and get a sense of control over what was happening in her life as she began to search for a job.

A nurse who no longer wanted to work in a hospital came to WORKPLACE with the idea of changing to a community-oriented nursing/counseling job. She worked with the librarian to rewrite her resume to highlight her counseling experience as well as nursing skills. Her resume was so good that she credits it with getting her an ideal job that seemed tailor made for her interests and skills.

An electronics technician who had relocated to be close to his ailing parents learned about WORKPLACE, a job and career information center in his local library in Pennsylvania. He worked with the local librarian who helped him use the resume writing software package on the center's computer. With the librarian's consultation, he composed an effective resume and cover letter which opened the doors to an interview at a high tech company in town. He used the library's interviewing videotapes to prepare for the interview and called the library later to tell them that he had landed the job.

FIGURE 3-6: Resume Writing Worksheets—Alpena County (MI) Library

RESUME WRITER'S WORKSHEETS

ALPENA COUNTY LIBRARY
JOB LAUNCH–EIC
211 N. FIRST
ALPENA, MICHIGAN 49707
(517) 356-6188

Name____________________
Address____________________
City, state, zip____________________
Phone #(s)____________________

OBJECTIVE____________________

HIGHLIGHTS OF QUALIFICATONS

- ____________________
- ____________________
- ____________________
- ____________________
- ____________________
- ____________________
- ____________________

EXPERIENCE:

dates______ company____________________
address & phone____________________
job title____________________
duties____________________

dates______ company____________________
address & phone____________________
job title____________________
duties____________________

ALPENA COUNTY LIBRARY
Job Launch (Employment Information Center)
211 N. First Ave.
Alpena, MI 49707

OUTLINE

I. Name: Use your formal name instead of a nickname.

Address: Avoid abbreviations & include zipcode. If your address is temporary (ie, moving or college student), use a relative's address or arrange for a Post Office box.

Telephone: Include area code. If your home phone is not always answered during the day, list a second number where you can be reached or a message can be received.

II. Job or career objective:

A short, concise sentence describing the position you desire.

III. Highlights or summary of your qualifications:

An overall summary of special skills, achievements & character qualities.

IV. Work/employment history:

List most recent jobs first, then work back. If your work experience is limited list volunteer work. Emphasize any skills learned that will relate to the job you want. Use "action words" to describe duties performed.

V. Education & training:

List formal education & any job related training, including military experience. List dates attended & degrees received. Academic achievement can be noted. Job related seminars & workshops might also be included.

An engineer with a Ph.D. felt that the help he received in a mock job interview session at the Camden County (NJ) Library resulted in a job offer $10,000 higher than expected.

Testimonials

"I found the [resume writing and interviewing skills] workshops particularly helpful. I'll feel more prepared when I begin my job search." "The counselor helped me polish my resume until it was dazzling. On my first interview, the company representative said, "After reading your qualifications, I just had to see you."

NEED: TO OBTAIN BASIC OR REMEDIAL SKILLS

Need Sketch

Certain groups of people have education problems which make looking for a job particularly difficult. Over a million workers are permanently dislocated each year and over 20 percent of these people lack a high school education. In all, 23 million adults in America are functionally illiterate. Only four in ten prison inmates have a high school diploma. Individuals who lack adequate skills are more likely to experience problems getting or keeping a job. They may have more need for support and coping assistance.

Laid-off workers and displaced homemakers frequently find that the best way to find more rewarding work is by upgrading their skills and knowledge.

How the Need May Be Expressed

The need for education or training information is not likely to be presented directly. A decision to get help with basic adult education, GED, to learn to read, or to gain English proficiency may come as the result of frustration at not being able to get a job. There may be referral from or to a literacy program in the library or community. Because the lack of these skills is a stigma, a librarian may only be able to find out about this need if he\she is trusted.

How Librarians Can Help

Librarians can people learn how to read by providing literacy programs in the library or referring individuals to them. They may buy job-related, high interest-low level materials that focus on workplace skills. It is particularly important to place these materials so that they are usable by those who need them. Staff provide bilingual materials which describe library services and community assistance for new U.S. citizens. They make contacts with leaders of ethnic communities, join a literacy coalition, or work with employees in the community on workplace literary programs.

Figure 3-7 from Chester County, PA, seeks to attract tutors to a local literacy program. Libraries which do not sponsor literacy programs should include community literacy resources in local community information directories or databases. Although librarians are not likely to develop their own literacy materials, they are likely to sponsor literacy programs. Often in conjunction with other agencies, they may develop materials designed to help people prepare for the GED.

How Clients with This Need Have Been Helped

Public libraries are truly bootstrap institutions. For over one hundred years, they have provided millions of people with the opportunity to gain insight and pursue their education.

A western Pennsylvania woman who got help at her public library WORKPLACE first attended an out-placement workshop at the factory where she had been working. The librarian explained in the workshop how workers could learn about other careers at the library. After going through a computer assisted self-assessment process, she decided to enroll in college to pursue a more rewarding career.

A man who had worked in a mill took a higher paying job in the forest until he had an accident. When he returned to the mill for less physical work, he was required to take an entry level test that he found he couldn't pass. He worked with the job and career center staff and the local community college to upgrade his reading, writing and math skills..

Testimonials

> "My sights were raised. I had been content with my factory job until it went out from under me. Now I can use more of my brain."

NEED: TO FIND SUPPORT AND COPING ASSISTANCE

Need Sketch

People who are out of work and who come to librarians for information about jobs may also need to cope with the emotional stress which accompanies job loss. They need to regain confidence in themselves, someone to talk to about their problem, a support

FIGURE 3-7: Literacy Program—Chester County (PA) Library

Place
Postage
Here

CHESTER
COUNTY
LIBRARY

Chester County Library Literacy Program
400 Exton Square Parkway
Exton, PA 19341

LITERACY PROGRAM

. . . The Volunteer Tutor

- attend a training workshop
- tutor twice a week at convenient times and sites
- receive continued support from program staff and through inservice meetings
- will be a part of Laubach Literacy Action
- gi. . and grow

Chester County Board of Commissioners
Earl M. Baker Robert J. Thompson Patricia M. Baldwin

Chester County Library and District Center
400 Exton Square Parkway
Exton, Pennsylvania 19341
(215)363 0884

group, or career or psychological counseling. They may need emergency assistance, including housing or food help.

How the Need May Be Expressed

Only gradually as the librarian employs one or more of the personal assistance strategies that focus on the problem, will these needs be expressed. These needs are generally learned in the course of assessment or diagnostic interviews. Before most people are able to even mention these needs, they must feel that they can trust the staff to respond appropriately to their revelations of vulnerability.

How Librarians Can Help

What librarians do here depends on the need and other resources in the community. There are people who need nothing more than a smile and an encouraging word when their confidence lags. Often this can be just responding positively to a telephone call or a surprise drop-in visit preceding a job interview or some other milestone. Reassurance may be all of the support needed at that moment to help boost their confidence.

Others more severely damaged by the loss of a job and all that it entails, will need referral to community resources equipped to provide the kind of assistance needed: Food, shelter, psychological counseling, or career counseling. When librarians conduct a need-centered community analysis and needs assessment, they identify a variety of groups in the community who will be able to provide a wide range of support and coping assistance.

Librarians should not provide assistance beyond their knowledge and experience. They maintain working contact with social service agencies. Often the most valuable coping assistance which can be provided is a knowledgable referral to an appropriate source of support.

How Clients with This Need Have Been Helped

Frequently people who have been laid off, or who for some other reason are in the process of changing jobs, or making a decision (which can take weeks or months) return to the librarian, career counselor, or other staff for reassurance before they attempt new things—going for a job interview or enrolling in college. They benefit from receiving moral support. Others have benefited from a referral to an appropriate agency in the community. Still others have gained support from job clubs which are sponsored by the library or other agency.

A woman who had been laid off from a real estate job and hadn't found other work was really desperate: "I need to pay the rent." Because her problems had such immediacy, the librarian helped her look into community agency options and approaches before beginning a more long-term program to find a job.

A woman who had lost her job in a factory and decided to return to school came for moral support to the job and career center where she had worked on the decision-making process. She had not traveled much, even in the area, and the thought of going to school 35 miles from home was disturbing to her. She came ostensibly for directions to the college parking lot but, was really seeking encouragement and advice on the admissions interview she was going to. She was excited about the prospect of going to college but fearful at the same time. The librarian helped her feel that she could take this big step safely and effectively.

A group of eight welfare recipients met for a total of 18 hours over a period of eight weeks in the West End Branch of The Carnegie Library of Pittsburgh. What started out as a quasi-requirement by the welfare department for the continuance of benefits turned out to be two-month-long support group. In spite of their problems, and the problems inherent in being heads of families on a welfare budget, this very special group of people had much to offer each other in the way of help and found support through this library program.

Testimonials

A steelworker who was trying to retool himself told a job and career center librarian: "You are the only government person who has ever told me what I CAN do, rather than what I can't do and has helped me figure out a way to do it." "It was most helpful in terms of giving me hope and a positive mental attitude.".

ACTIONS TO PREPARE FOR

Starting a business: A woman who started her own business with help from the information she got at her public library noted, "People in Nebraska are inventive, but we didn't have the information we needed to know how to run a business or market our products until this new library project, the job and career center, came along."

Preparing for a job change: "I was in a real dead end job. I am now working on a career plan. It's slow, but changing jobs was the first step in getting me where I need to be."

Conducting a job search: "The seminars taught me to be patient and don't settle for second best in a job."

Get more education: "I found the library's job and career program very helpful. I am planning to go back to school because of it."

NEED: TO START A BUSINESS

Need Sketch

Small business is the backbone of America. Most small entrepreneurs face a similar problem, they do not have all of the expertise they need in-house—they just can't afford it. Public libraries can help small business developers gain the expertise they don't have on board. Many public libraries are becoming major resources for their community's economic development due to the information that the library staff creates and disseminates.

Developing a small business is risky, and information and assistance in finding the right resources could spell the difference between success and failure. People who start businesses may need to find out what local, state, and national consulting is available for budding entrepreneurs; to develop a financial plan; to determine their market; to find out more about their product as well as their competition.

How the Need May Be Expressed

People may start by saying, "I need to find out how to get a business started. Do you have any books on this?" On the other hand, they may come in with a number of questions which focus on some aspect of opening a new business—for example, "What is the success rate for a small business," "Do you have information on small business development," "I need to find out about opportunities in the community," "I need to be able to contact helpful resources in the community," "How do I find out more about my local competition?" or "Where can I find out about licensing regulations?"

How Librarians Can Help

Librarians should develop a database of local economic development resources and provide access to economic development statistics. They usually take steps to raise awareness in the community of library resources and services speaking to such groups as county extension or the chamber of commerce. It is quite common for staff to join a service club. Librarians hold small business seminars and brown bag lunches and sponsor workshops on starting a small business or developing a business plan. A more complicated action may be to start a service aimed at economic development which includes a Government Procurement Center such as the one at the Toledo-Lucas County Public Library.

Job and career center staff engage in a range of collaborative activities. These are valuable, not only because they are cost-effective, but also because they also put librarians in touch with other agencies who are seeking to work toward the economic vitality of the community. For example, the Nassau Library in New York worked collaboratively with other agencies in the community to develop a conference on economic development. The University of Michigan Library, with funds from the Kellogg Foundation, worked with librarians in selected Michigan communities through M-LINK to provide economic development and educational information and expertise. Cooperating M-LINK libraries have worked closely with community agencies and groups to share this expertise.

Many job and career information center staff target services for special needs. Brooklyn Public Library has developed a business idea sheet for the teenage entrepreneur. Schenectady County, New York, has developed a workshop on how to start a business.

How Clients with This Need Have Been Helped

Due to the efforts of the Toledo-Lucas County Public Library's Government Procurement Center, small businessmen in Toledo, Ohio have procured contracts from the federal government worth over 100,000,000 since 1986.

An entrepreneur in Grand Marais, Minnesota regularly called on the public librarian for information that he used to improve the quality of his dog sleds, ultimately building one of the most competitive sleds in the world. His local librarian was given statewide recognition for her approach to service.

With help from their western Nebraska public library, a couple whose farm implement business failed during the recession in the mid 80s turned his woodworking hobby into a craft shop that now has 30 workers and was written up in the Wall Street Journal.

A middle-aged Filipino man in Skokie, Illinois had worked for the telephone company for 15 years. He wanted to start his own consulting company but realized that he needed information and

FIGURE 3-8: Business Resource Center—Bay County (MI) Library System

Bay County Library System

BUSINESS RESOURCE CENTER

"providing the business community of Bay County with resource information needed to develop, sustain, improve, and promote their interests."

- books, periodicals, pamphlets
- online database searching
- workshops and seminars
- instruction
- referral service

Call: (517) 893-5919

Bay County Library System
Bay City Branch Library
708 Center Avenue
Bay City, MI 48708

BAY COUNTY LIBRARY SYSTEM

Do you need help with .....

- **market research**
- **demographic information**
- **business plans**
- **IRS requirements**
- **franchise possibilities**
- **patent and trademark information**
- **incorporation procedures**
- **supply sources**
- **marketing and advertising**

Call (517) 893-5919

FIGURE 3-9: Using The 1990 Census Data—Flint (MI) Public Library

USING THE 1990 CENSUS DATA

A Workshop for Business Planners, Service Organizations, Students and Others on Using the 1990 Census of Population and Housing.

10 A.M.
TUESDAY
MARCH 9

7 P.M.
THURSDAY
APRIL 8

ROOM B-1
FLINT PUBLIC LIBRARY
1026 E. KEARSLEY ST.

FREE ADMISSION

Flint Public Library
A Service of the Flint Board of Education

2/93

FIGURE 3-10: How To Start Your Own Business—Schenectady County (NY) Public Library

Don't go into business without one...

A BUSINESS PLAN

DEVELOP ONE at the Chester County Library

LEARN TO MAKE MISTAKES ON PAPER...
NOT IN THE REAL WORLD

LEARN ABOUT:

FINANCIAL PLANNING FOR YOUR BUSINESS
EMPLOYING RESOURCES OF EXPERTISE
HOW MUCH MONEY YOU NEED FOR A LOAN
and much more

Presented by: SCORE*
*Service Corps of Retired Executives

SATURDAY, NOVEMBER 12 9:00 AM - 5:00 PM
STRUBLE ROOM

Workshop is limited to 20 participants
A $10.00 non-refundable fee is required
Advance reservations are required

This is a program of Workplace
a service of the Chester County Library

- -

Please fill out this form and return to: **CHESTER COUNTY LIBRARY, 400 EXTON SQUARE PARKWAY, EXTON, PA 19341, ATTN: WORKPLACE.** Make $10.00 check payable to the **CHESTER COUNTY LIBRARY.**

NAME______________________________

ADDRESS____________________________

PHONE________________

Workplace is a grant administered by the State Library of Pennsylvania through the Library Development Division with funds provided by the W.K. Kellogg Foundation

HOW TO START YOUR OWN BUSINESS

A MINORITY AND WOMEN BUSINESS ENTERPRISE WORKSHOP SERIES

FEBRUARY 9, 1989 - JUNE 29, 1989

Thursday, February 9, 1989 at 3 P.M. - Self Assessment
Thursday, February 23, 1989 at 7 P.M. - Money Matters
Thursday, March 9, 1989 at 3 P.M. - Business Plans
Thursday, March 23, 1989 at 7 P.M. - Financial Management
Thursday, April 13, 1989 at 3 P.M. - Accounting/Record Keeping
Thursday, April 27, 1989 at 7 P.M. - Legal Aspects
Thursday, May 11, 1989 at 3 P.M. - Special Requirements
Thursday, May 25, 1989 at 7 P.M. - Procuring Government Contracts
Thursday, June 1, 1989 at 3 P.M. - Writing Bid Specifications
Thursday, June 29, 1989 at 7 P.M. - N.Y. State Certification

Workshops are free of charge and open to the public.

All workshops will be held in the McChesney Room at the Schenectady County Public Library - Liberty and Clinton Streets.

Please call 382-5275 or 382-5147 to register, if you plan to attend.

Sponsored By:

The City of Schenectady Affirmative Action/Minority/Women Business Enterprise Office
The City of Schenectady Department of Development
Schenectady County Public Library's Education and Job Information Center
The New York State Department of Economic Development
Albany Small Business Association

microcomputer skills. He learned DOS at the public library and over a period of time gathered information on potential client companies.

Testimonials

A businessman who got help at the Prince George Public Library commented, "I thought that the library was the best place to start preparing for opening my own business. It turned out that it was the ALL AROUND best place to go.

"I came into the library with only vague ideas and the job and career center staff helped me percolate them down to something specific. I got help making connections with resources in the community and just generally seeing how to proceed."

NEED: TO PREPARE FOR A JOB CHANGE

Need Sketch

Frustration provides a strong impetus for change. People ready for a job change may be those who are overqualified for their jobs or frustrated with lack of opportunity for upward mobility, who find little support in the workplace, or whose skills and values do not match those of the environment. There is an immediacy to their need, but, at the same time, they often cannot leave their present job until they are able to line up a new one.

How the Need May Be Expressed

People are not likely to tell librarians immediately of their need to change jobs. Sometimes they ask for information on advancements in their field or other issues related to their job. People are not likely to discuss these kinds of matters with individuals they do not know (and, therefore, do not trust). However, during the course of a diagnostic (assessment) interview, that focuses on the problem and why information is needed, people will often give more detail about their situation. If someone needs to change jobs, is not the staff's responsibility to help them change jobs; however, job and career center staff can listen, learn more about the situation and help people find and use appropriate resources, alert them to job and career center services that will help, and refer them to other community resources.

How Librarians Help

The public library may provide a number of resources which can be used to explore job options. Staff may develop a directory of area employers or a job bulletin board. People who wish to make a job change may need to develop a new resume. Librarians can provide guides to resume development or a resume writing clinic. A job seeker may need to think about his own skills and interests. In that case, librarians may want to provide appropriate career advising assistance, such as career advising software, suggest joining a job club, and/or schedule an appointment with a career counselor.

How Clients with This Need Have Been Helped

People who have come to the library with this problem have often gained by making a decision or taking an action of some sort, like the following:

- A woman who, from high school graduation had been in a series of jobs, most recently a cook in a fast food restaurant, came to the public library and found that it had a career information center. After expressing some surprise that such a service existed in the library, she talked with the job and career librarian about her needs. The librarian suggested that she read a book on alternative career planning and that she schedule an appointment with the career advising software that was always heavily booked.
- A session on the computer helped her realize that her real interests lay in textiles. The librarian then recommended several books and articles about aspects of textile design. The librarian worked with her over a period of several weeks. After these discussions, she decided to look for a temporary job in an area closer to her interests and began planning a career in fashion.
- After 15 years in the field, a man decided he was tired of working in banking. He researched potential careers in the library and discovered that real estate management was an up-and-coming field to which he could adapt his experience. He comments, "It was wonderful to find so much material to help me."
- A young woman who had worked in an automobile factory for ten years and had been through a series of layoffs, decided that there just had to be something better. Drawn in by the library's very attractive job and career center, she

FIGURE 3-11: Directory Of Employment Agencies—Bethlehem (NY) Public Library

FIGURE 3-12: Free Career Workshops: Workplace Wednesdays—Free Library Of Philadelphia

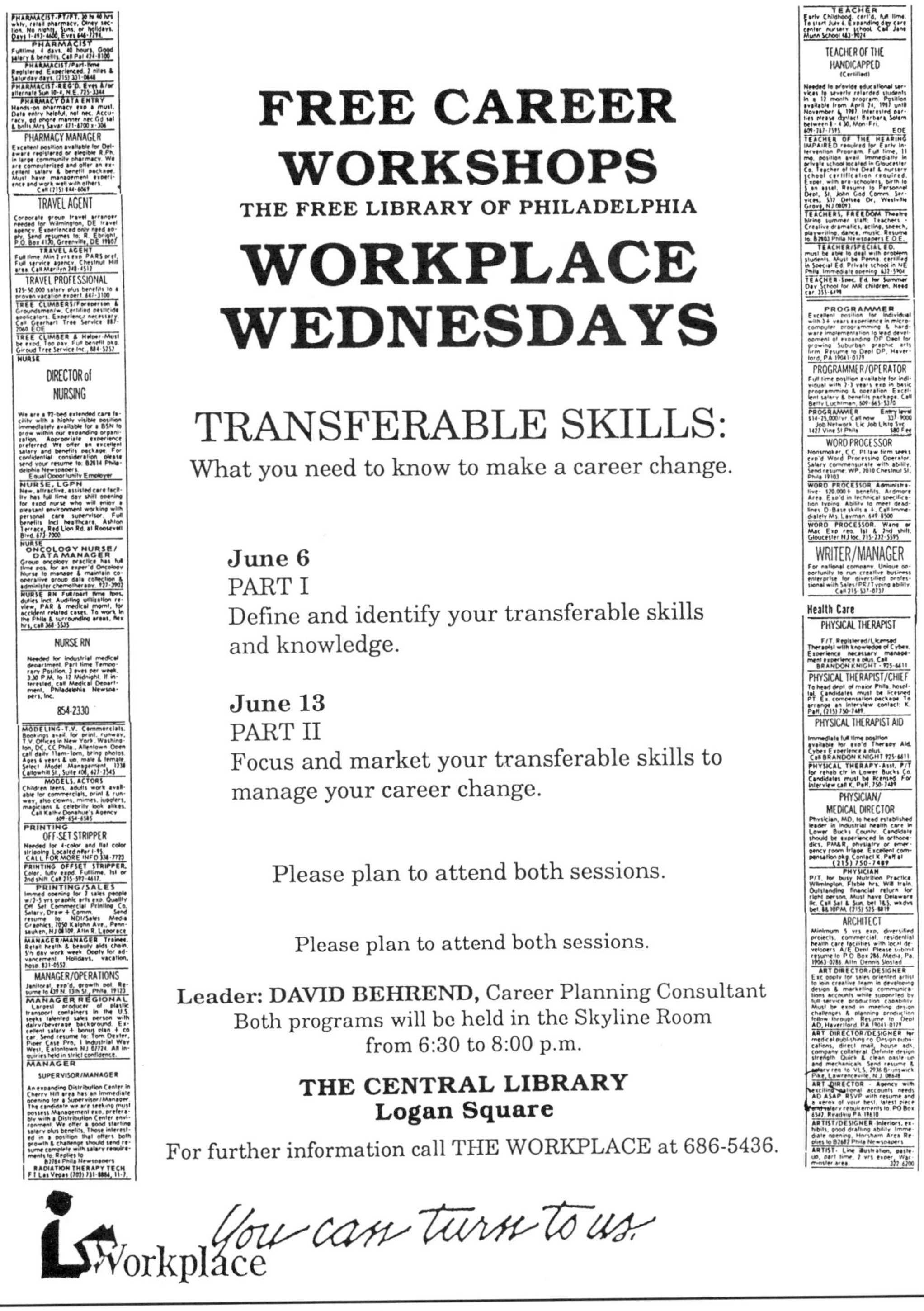

decided to talk with the lady behind the center's information desk. The librarian listened to her concerns and suggested that she schedule an appointment to use the library's career advisement software, and then discuss her options further. She worked with SIGI Plus, talked with the coordinator, and decided at the librarian's suggestion to enroll in a career decision class given at the local community college.

Testimonials

"Planning a new career makes it possible for me to hold on to my factory job long enough to get started. By next year I should be well on my way to a new job. I realized by coming here that there were options. I decided that it was best not to quit now and get just another job. It would have meant more of the same."

"It challenged me to make a career change that I feared doing. I'm very happy about my new job. This program is the best thing I've done for myself in the last five years."

NEED: TO CONDUCT A JOB SEARCH

Need Sketch

Some people who need job search information may be looking for their first job or attempting to get a better one. They may need help with two basic skills: Understanding the job search process and finding out how people discover job leads and successfully follow up on them. People who have been laid off, have left a job to relocate with a spouse, or have had some other major life change have additional problems to deal with as they conduct their job search. These job seekers may be attempting to meet several needs at the same time. For example, they may also need support and coping assistance as they go through the process. They may need to locate education or training opportunities or to learn how to write a resume or interview for a job. People without a job may need to take some action relatively quickly.

Job seekers need help targeting jobs that are a realistic match with their qualifications. They may need assistance using library resources to target employers who need people with their qualifications. The kinds of needs which are associated with searching for a job may include: learning the most effective strategies to use in the search process, finding out what jobs are available, or learning how to take a specific action, such as how to target or research employers, make and use contacts, fill out government forms, or get information about relocating to a better job market.

How the Need May Be Expressed

To mask the real need (to find a job), a person's opening question may be very general and framed in the following "librarian's terms:"

> "Do you have books on jobs?"
>
> "Where are your out-of-town newspapers?"

When library users realize that it is OK to ask more direct questions, they may ask something like, "What can I do with a degree in English?," "How can I prepare for a civil service exam?," "Do you have SF-171s?" Or, they may tell you a little about themselves, like, "I am new in town. How can I find out who is hiring?," "I need to write a cover letter," "I received my education in Mexico. How much is transferable to the job market here?"

How Librarians Can Help

In addition to providing books on jobs and careers, librarians often purchase newspapers from communities where job prospects are good. Some libraries provide specific job listings and/or develop resource books on job seeking skills. Many librarians conduct job-seeking workshops, provide interactive video tapes on the job-seeking process, or sponsor job clubs. Librarians may survey local employers to find out the kinds of skills that they are looking for or they may develop a local employer file or notebook. Realizing that people may not think of the library when they are looking for a job, librarians have made visits to factories which are closing or laying off workers and explain the library's job and career resources and services.

How Clients with This Need Have Been Helped

Hundreds of people each month are served by the workshops on the job search which are conducted by the Cuyahoga County (OH) Public Library's InfoPLACE service.

Many job seekers in Pennsylvania have been introduced to their library's services through visits by library staff to their workplace. For example, when a factory in a northeastern community was about to close down permanently, the director of Washington County Public Library's job and career information center scheduled a visit to the factory to explain the library's resources and services. Several workers, aware for the first time of these resources, used the public library to explore career options. The librarian showed them how to use career advising software and talked with them about career and job options. They benefited by learning about new options and by receiving moral support during their struggle to gain new employment.

A young woman who had just graduated from college with a degree in sociology moved to a community with a job and career information center. She discovered the center when she came to the library to check out a book. She was new in town and felt lost and confused about where to begin her job search. She talked with the career counselor in the library several times, read several books on careers recommended by a counselor (who worked five hours a week under contract with the library), and worked on her resume. These were all very helpful to her because she was in search of a direction for her life in a new community.

A man with a graduate degree in chemistry who had worked indexing and abstracting scientific articles in Russian and English in the Soviet Union came to the Skokie Public Library looking for potential employers in the Chicago area. His job search included finding out what he was qualified for and what could he do in the area.

Job seekers of Memphis/Shelby County (TN) are served by JOBLINC, a 35-foot bus that is a mobile job and career center. Instead of people coming to the library, this fully equipped job center makes stops at community centers, shopping malls and churches all over the county and serves 1200 people a month. The bus offers: Job listings, two computers with career and resume software, videorecording equipment, books and materials, and information on education, skills and community assistance.

Testimonials

"I was just a number at the employment agency, but the librarian worked with me to help me get prepared for the job search."

"This was the best advice and help I received during my job search. Without this I would probably still be looking for a job."

NEED: TO GET MORE EDUCATION OR TRAINING

Need Sketch

Work and education are very closely linked. Most adults have spent over a decade in school preparing for the world of work. Many adults have spent more than two decades in preparation for a career. Career choices are the result of education decisions. People who come to job and career centers for job information may do

FIGURE 3-13: JOBLINC Bus

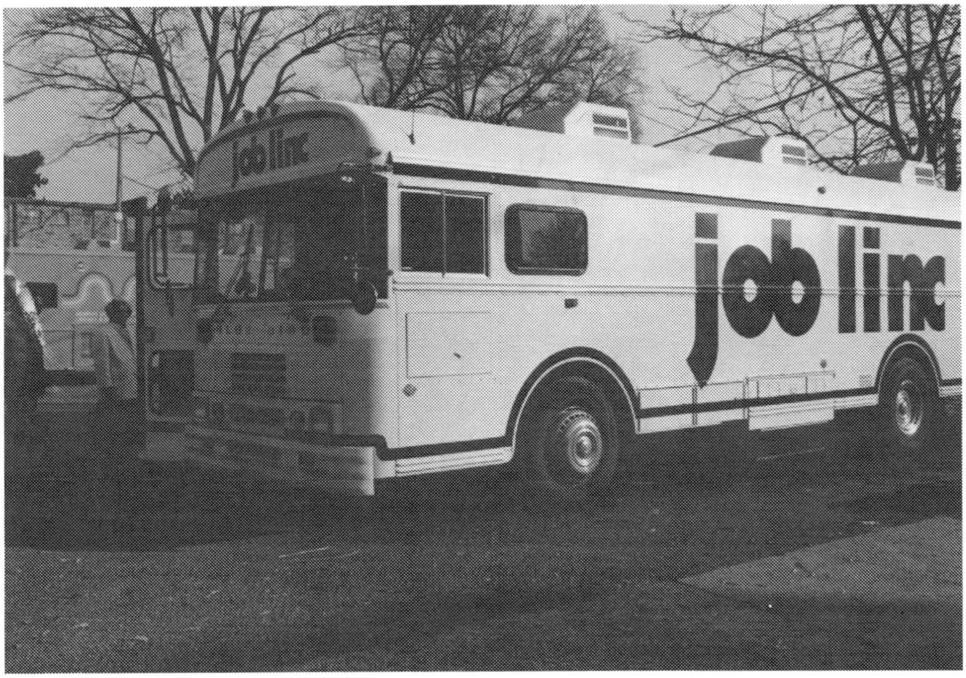

some self-assessment in the process and determine that they really do need more education or training.

How the Need May Be Expressed

Questions include, "How can I get information about a school of cosmetology?" or "I need to choose a major." or "I need financial aid information."

Job seekers may need information about programs and opportunities or to learn about different ways to earn a degree. Many times people do not come directly for education or training information, but decide that they need it after spending some time talking with the librarian about their needs and looking at their options.

The decision to get more education, whether this is for an advanced degree, a college education, or enrolling in a special training program is often accompanied by the question, "How am I going to pay for it?" "Are there scholarships or loans I am eligible for?" Financial aid information is often needed for this decision.

FIGURE 3-13: Inside Of The JOBLINC Bus With Career Counselors

Job/Career Information Series

EDUCATIONAL OPPORTUNITIES

EDUCATION INFORMATION CENTER
Peter White Public Library
217 N. Front St. • Marquette MI 49855

EDUCATION/JOB INFORMATION CENTERS
INLAND NORTHWEST EJIC

FINANCIAL AID BIBLIOGRAPHY

1989 INTERNSHIPS. 38,000 ON-THE-JOB TRAINING OPPORTUNITIES FOR COLLEGE STUDENTS AND ADULTS, edited by Katherine Jobst. SCLD-374/1988/IN

A's and B's. YOUR GUIDE TO ACADEMIC SCHOLARSHIPS, by Victoria A. Fabisch. SPL-378.3409 AS & BS

CHRONICLE STUDENT AID ANNUAL, published by Chronicle Guidance Publications. SPL-378.3097/CHRONIC

COLLEGE CHECK MATE: INNOVATIVE PLANS THAT MAKE YOU A WINNER, by Priscilla S. Goeller. SPL-378.30973/GOELLER

COLLEGE GRANTS FROM UNCLE SAM, by Anna Leider. SPL-378.3097/COLLEGE

CUTTING COLLEGE COSTS, by Bruce H. Donald. SPL-378.3809/DONALD/SCLD-378.3809/DONALD

DIRECTORY OF FINANCIAL AIDS FOR MINORITIES, by Gail Ann Schlachter. SPL-378.3025/SCHLACH

DIRECTORY OF FINANCIAL AIDS FOR WOMEN, by Gail Ann Schlachter. SPL-378.3025/DIRECT SCLD-378.3025/DIRECTO

DON'T MISS OUT: THE AMBITIOUS STUDENT'S GUIDE TO FINANCIAL AID, by Robert and Anna Leider. SPL-378.3097/LEIDER SCLD-378.3097/LEIDER

How Librarians Can Help

The public library is likely to have the best educational resources in the entire community. Let people in the community know about them. Sometimes these resources are difficult to use. Help people learn to use them. If appropriate, create databases of educational opportunities and financial aid in the area. Work with local colleges. Purchase your state's education and occupational information software. Provide help in finding scholarships. Develop a collaborative program with local educational institutions.

How Clients with This Need Have Been Helped

Getting information about jobs and careers frequently leads people to the realization that they need more education. Recently librarians have used new techniques to help people understand the need to get more education and have provided more direct assistance in helping them take action.

A young woman in Spokane, Washington. thought she would not be able to go to college because her family couldn't afford it. The staff member of the job and career information center helped her find financial aid and assisted her in completing the financial aid form. She received a scholarship. Encouraged by his daughter's success, her father began exploring his own higher education options and decided that he, too, would go to college.

Testimonials

"When I walked past the library, I used to just think books, books, books. I didn't know they could help me find schools. The counselor showed me a lot of catalogs for adult education courses I needed to improve my skills." "I have learned a lot about different colleges." "I became intrigued with programming computer simulations and I am now learning how to do that."

HOW PEOPLE HAVE BENEFITED FROM COMING TO THE JOB AND CAREER CENTER

Chapter 3 has focused on needs which people have brought to the staff who work in public library job and career information centers.

FIGURE 3-14: Educational Opportunities—Financial Aid Bibliography

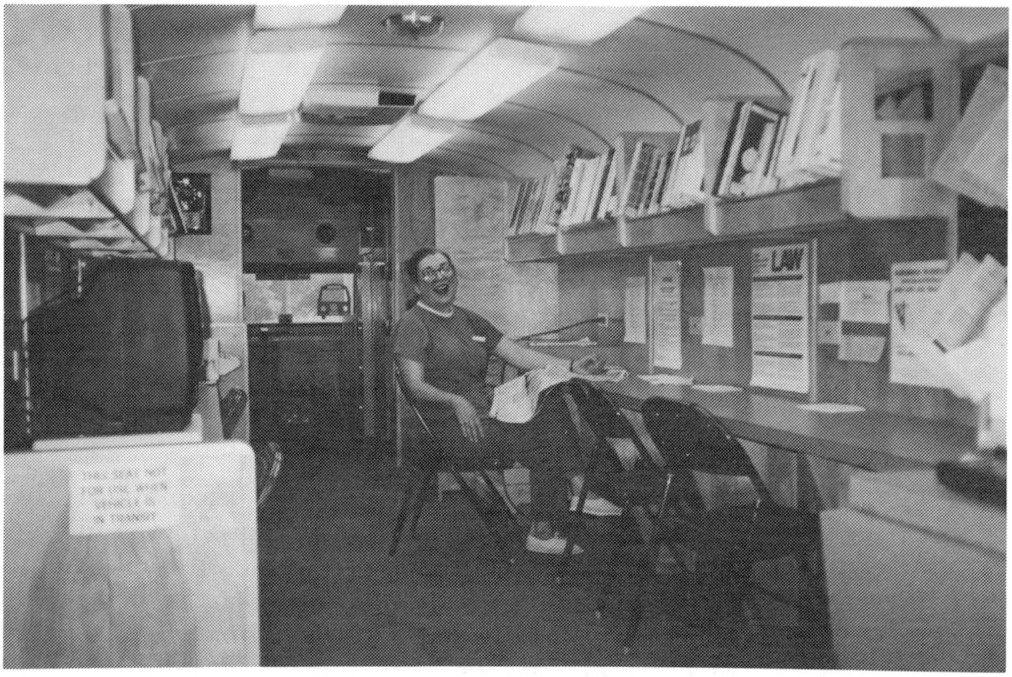

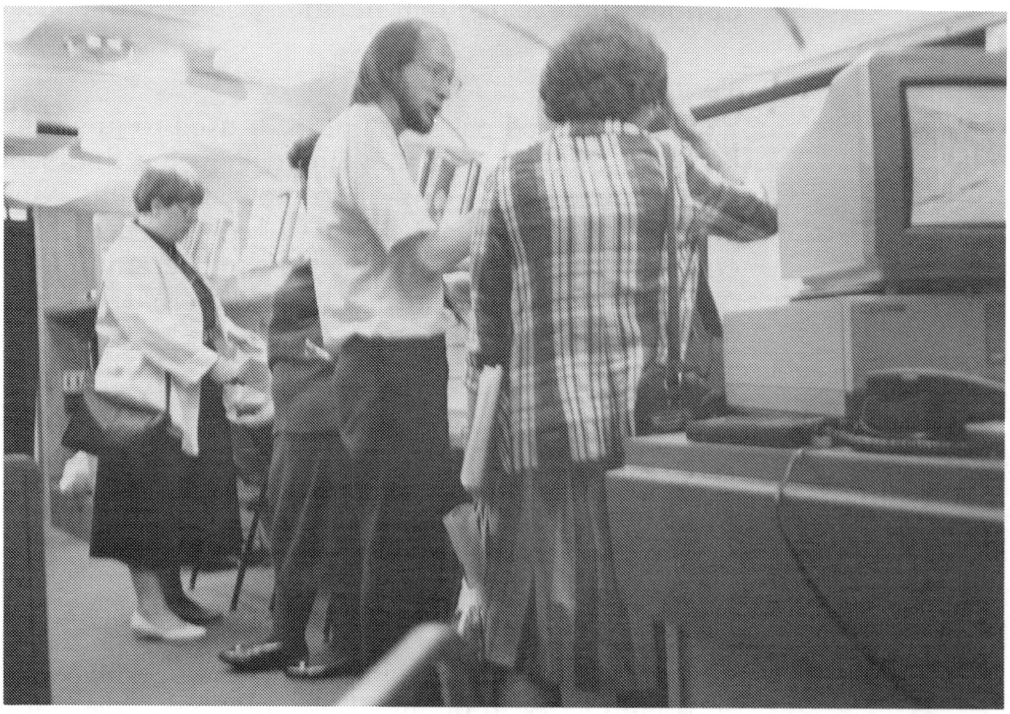

Using a stylistic format, the needs and the ways they might possibly be expressed were discussed. For each need this was followed by an examination of several strategies librarians might use to respond to the need. As a result of these strategies, the people described in this chapter received tangible benefits which were illustrated through a series of testimonials and anecdotal experiences. When grouped, the benefits fall into the categories below which result from a recent survey was conducted of the people who took advantage of these services in a number of libraries. In sum, people who come to library job and career information centers said that they:

- Appreciated the help of the staff during a trying time of life—when they were trying to cope with change, get a job, or take charge of their lives.
- Were more able to take control of their situation as the result of working with job and career center staff.
- Had increased their understanding of the possibilities, become more active, and taken steps toward increasing their basic reading skills.
- Were able to make more informed decisions than they had before talking with an job and career center staff member.
- Saw their options more clearly or were better able to identify their educational needs and plan their future more realistically.
- Gained self esteem.
- Developed new skills.

The following chapters describe the strategies librarians and career counselors use to help people who come to them for assistance in the job seeking or career change process.

RESOURCES

Durrance, Joan C. *Serving Job Seekers and Career Changers: A Planning Manual for Public Libraries*. Chicago: American Library Association, January 1993.

Durrance, Joan C. "Information Needs: Old Song, New Tune." In *Rethinking the Library in the Information Age: Issues in the Library Research—Proposals for the 1990s*, 159-77. Washington, D.C.: United States Department of Education, Office of ducation Research and Improvement, Office of Library Programs, October 1989.

Katz, Martin R. *Computer-Assisted Career Decision Making: The Guide in the Machine*. Hillsdale, NJ: Lawrence Erlbaum Associates, 1993.

4 STRATEGIES DESIGNED TO RAISE AWARENESS AND INCREASE ACCESS

A 1990 Gallup poll conducted for the National Career Development Association stated flatly that, "Americans need greater access to information about occupations." Unfortunately, studies show that in many cases, people just are not aware of the services that staff in job and career information centers provide. Librarians can increase the chance that people will get the information they need at the library by increasing the availability of resources, by taking steps to make more people aware of them, and by making resources accessible. People can't use services they don't know about.

STRATEGIES TO RAISE AWARENESS

Many people have no idea that the library can provide the information and assistance common to many job and career centers. When people in the community learn about the rich resources in the public library, they are often astounded. Many people have no idea that the library provides services such as those found in the job and career center. It is important to let people in the community know about the job and career center.

One very important way to reach job seekers is through the agencies they visit. Often employment professionals aren't aware of what is available at the public library. During the planning period, let community agency staff know about the resources the library already has and tell them that serving job seekers and career changers has been given a higher priority than in the past. Other professionals will be very pleased to find out what is available in the library.

Effective awareness efforts should be built around the following: the understanding that there is a need to raise awareness and that the message needs to be clear; the selection of target audience(s); and the method(s) which will be used to reach and communicate with people.

Approaches to raising awareness will reflect the kind of program being developed. Even the smallest program should have some kind of publicity. Marketing should grow as the program grows. Publicity and marketing for the job and career center is facilitated by the kind of community-centered planning that has been undertaken. Suzanne Walters's *Marketing: A How-to-Do-it Manual for Librarians* makes fine marketing suggestions.

Because most people are unaware of this service, developers of job and career information centers should develop specific objectives aimed at increasing the public's awareness of these services. Awareness objectives should include diverse methods of reaching potential clientele. Plans should be flexible and changed as services develop. Methods used to increase the visibility of the job and career center will vary depending on the marketing plan.

Below, and throughout the next several chapters, I have placed a set of objectives with each strategy. These objectives are designed to focus the discussion. Staff may choose to develop additional objectives and specific activities appropriate for the local community for each of the strategies. Chapter 9, "Evaluation," will examine ways to measure your objectives.

POSSIBLE OBJECTIVES THAT RAISE AWARENESS AND INCREASE VISIBILITY IN THE COMMUNITY

Develop a Clear, Understandable Message

Need-based services will not be used unless people know about them. Strategies designed to raise awareness let people know what resources and services are available. Perceptions that people have of library roles can change overnight when they become more aware of what is possible. Think about different kinds of strategies to raise awareness, so that people who are experiencing this need might think about the library as one place to get help.

At the very basic level of raising awareness, librarians should be able to explain what the job and career center does. Staff should be able to prepare written information sheets which introduce your services and talk with people about the library's resources and services. Public presentation skills are valuable. Staff need to be able to analyze the environment, decide who to reach, develop ways to reach target audiences, use a variety of appropriate promotion and distribution means, and determine whether the target group is being served.

Identify and Reach Several Specific Target Audiences

Successful job and career center staff attempt from the planning stages of service development to identify those individuals and groups in the community who will most benefit from coming to a library job and career center. Not everyone in the community needs these services, but those who do—for example, homemakers returning to the job market, people who have been laid-off, individuals who are new to the community, immigrants, people who are

FIGURE 4-1: Job Information Center—Hempstead (NY) Public Library

THE JOB INFORMATION CENTER (JIC)

The JOB INFORMATION CENTER (JIC) located in the Hempstead Public Library is available to all Nassau County residents.

At the JIC you will find all kinds of material which will help you make important decisions. If you are thinking of going back to school, changing careers, or looking for a different job, the friendly staff at the JIC is waiting to help you.

Career Counselors can help you decide on the career that is best for you. Meet with a trained counselor who will help you evaluate your skills and background.

...e an ...with **SIGI PLUS,** an ...ive career guidance program ...n a computer! Appointments with SIGI PLUS and career counselors are always confidential.

The JIC also holds workshops throughout the year. Attend a workshop and learn how to write a resume, or learn how to improve your job interviewing skills. If you're interested about getting into a particular field, check with us to find out if we have a workshop coming up. You may have come up with a good idea for a new workshop.

JIC librarians can show you the many materials we have available to assist you in your job search...

- Out-of-town newspapers
- Periodicals which contain job listings

...e sent to us ...State Department

- ...ooks which list companies around the country

We can also show you books on how to write a resume and cover letter.

Going back to school? We have guides to colleges, graduate schools, and vocational schools, as well as catalogs for individual schools.

We also have books on a variety of careers. Find out more about the career you are interested in.

The JIC also has a video cassette collection. You must be a registered video cassette borrower at Hempstead Public Library to withdraw any of these tapes. If you are not, your home library can interloan JIC video cassettes from us. Ask to see our list of JIC Videos.

HOURS:

Monday-Thursday	**10 am - 9 pm**
Friday	**10 am - 6 pm**
Saturday	**9 am - 5pm***

*July-Labor Day Closed Saturday

FIGURE 4-2: WORKPLACE Flyer—Free Library Of Philadelphia (PA)

Workplace GOAL - To help adults make informed decisions about jobs, careers, and education.

The WORKPLACE helps adults identify the steps needed to reach their career goals, assess and market their skills and knowledge, and explore the working world. The WORKPLACE offers workshops on all phases of the employment process, provides information on career fields and specific jobs, and gathers information on local agencies, training programs, and educational opportunities that can benefit job seekers.

Workplace USERS - Any adult who is

- Exploring careers
- Planning a career change
- Re-entering the workforce
- Conducting a job search
- Seeking information on educational or training opportunities
- Looking for information about local and national companies and businesses
- Preparing a resume
- Looking for agencies to help with career planning or training.

Workplace RESOURCES -

Print:
Career and employment information in books, magazines, and newspapers
Civil Service announcements
Directories of businesses, professional and trade organizations

Computer:
Vocational tests
Financial aid information
Word processing programs for preparing resumés

Video:
Videotapes about job interviewing, work attitudes, and career advancement

NOTE: Resources for use in The WORKPLACE

Workplace SERVICES -

- Help in using all resources of The WORKPLACE
- Guidance in locating other career resources in The Free Library of Philadelphia
- Workshops and programs on all aspects of career development
- Referrals to other agencies that can assist you in achieving your job and career goals

Workplace is funded under a contract with the State Library of Pennsylvania, Department of Education. The W. K. Kellogg Foundation provided grant funds for the Pennsylvania WORKPLACE programs.

Workplace HOURS -

The books and other print materials may be used any time the Central Library is open:

9:00 am - 9:00 pm -- Monday, Tuesday, Wednesday
9:00 am - 6:00 pm -- Thursday and Friday
9:00 am - 5:00 pm -- Saturday
1:00 pm - 5:00 pm -- Sunday (September - May)

Please make an appointment to use the computer and video resources. Call 686-5436 or sign up at the desk in the Education, Philosophy and Religion Department.

Workplace SCHEDULE OF WORKSHOPS -

For a current schedule, send a stamped, self-addressed envelope to:

WORKPLACE
Education, Philosophy and Religion Department
The Free Library of Philadelphia
Logan Square
Philadelphia, PA 19103

TELL YOUR FRIENDS! A - 4 - 88

Workplace
Education, Philosophy and Religion Department
The Free Library of Philadelphia
Logan Square
Philadelphia, PA 19103

WORKPLACE

JOB AND CAREER INFORMATION CENTER FOR ADULTS
Education, Philosophy and Religion Department - Central Library
The Free Library of Philadelphia
Logan Square
686-5436

attempting to get off welfare, students who are about to make education and career decisions, and others—should be targeted. Experienced job and career center staff have found that community contacts and linkages, make it possible for library staff to work with other professionals and groups who are working with the same target audience. These approaches which are discussed in Chapter 8, "Strategies Designed to Create Links and Make Referrals" and Chapter 10, "Marketing and Evaluation."

Become More Involved in the Community

Community contacts will build referrals to the service. Tie services to important local events by being involved in community activities and issues. Be aware of employment trends, such as a potential factory closing where staff may be able to assist a large number of displaced workers through an employer. Participate in local job programs with other agencies and businesses.

Make Presentations to Groups

Talk to local civic and business groups about how the library is responding to community economic concerns. Stay informed about community changes and opportunities for collaboration.

Periodically Sponsor Special Events in the Job and Career Center Such as an Open House

Introduce the service to the public, to library personnel, to fellow agency contacts, community and business leaders, and financial supporters through an informative open house. Invitations to special functions or a demonstration of new resources such as career software should be sent to the library board. A job fair developed cooperatively with other agencies can reach audiences who don't normally use the library. Use the opportunity to thank agencies for past support and to strengthen ties with them. Show people what your job and career center is really doing.

Participate in Public Events

Job center staff frequently attend or help sponsor local fairs. Develop a poster session or a portable job and career center information booth to explain the services you can provide. Because staff can't personally attend everything, job and career center staff may make stand-alone exhibits with photos, brochures, and self-help handouts.

FIGURE 4-3: You're Invited To An Open-House!—The Carnegie Library Of Pittsburgh (PA)

You're Invited
to an

OPEN HOUSE!

at

Workplace

at the
Hazelwood Branch
of
The Carnegie Library of Pittsburgh

THE CARNEGIE
LIBRARY OF
PITTSBURGH

Develop Handouts and Distribute Them Outside of the Library

Printed materials such as bookmarks (see Figure 4-4), brochures, mailers and business cards are common methods of dispersing information about job and career center services. These can be produced in a variety of ways and be distributed in the library or through various means throughout the community. [Provide identification information about the job and career center (including address and phone) on all materials.] A brochure that describes the library's job and career center and the services provided by its staff is essential. It will tell citizens what to expect. The goals of Carnegie Library of Pittsburgh's WORKPLACE are included in its general brochure.

WORKPLACE exists to help adults make job, career and education decisions. Through computerized decision-making systems, WORKPLACE helps job seekers clarify their needs, assess their skills, explore today's world of work, and make career and job decisions. WORKPLACE offers workshops on all phases of the job search; it provides information on specific jobs, and gathers in one location information on area agencies, programs, and educational opportunities that benefit the job seeker.

Graphic materials and objects such as posters, buttons and calendars can be used to announce special events or to raise awareness about general services that you provide. Posters placed in high traffic public locations inside and outside the library can be an effective awareness tool (see Figure 4-5).

Inform the Local Media about Services for Job Seekers and Career Changers

Prepare press releases or public service announcements (PSAs) for the local newspaper, cable access TV, and radio stations to announce workshops, special events, new computer programs, staff additions, upcoming promotions, and other job and career center news. Every time these appear, the job and career center name and services are promoted.

Contact local publications—for example, newspapers—and suggest that they might want to cover a special event or feature a story about the benefits of the service to the community. Frequently local newspapers need interesting, and what they consider unusual, feature articles on special events and items of public interest. Arrange for an interview to talk about the services or for general press coverage of a special event or workshop.

FIGURE 4-4: Assorted Bookmarks—Multiple Sites

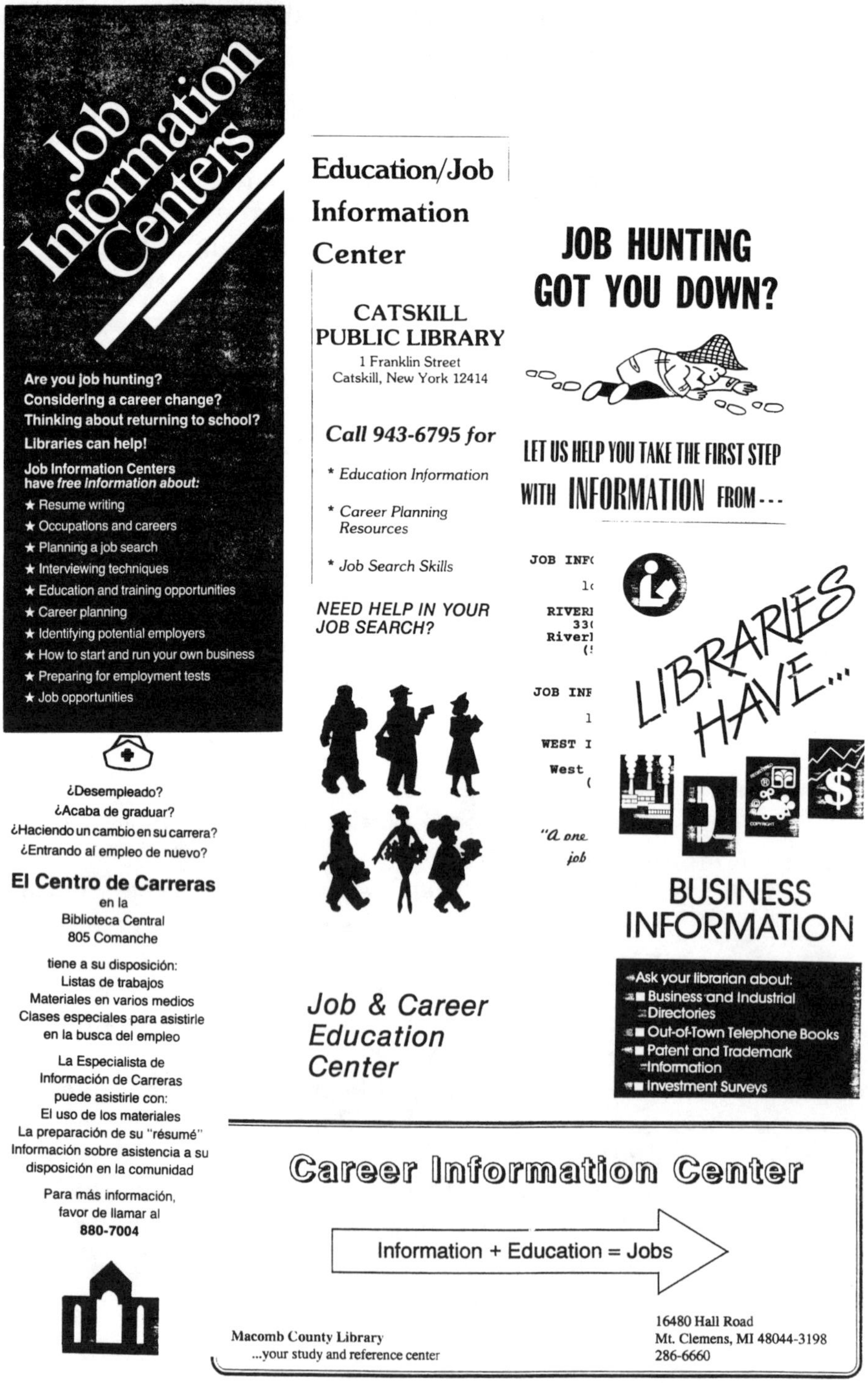

FIGURE 4-5: Be Wise . . . Inquire!—Howland (NY) Public Library

EDUCATION/JOB INFORMATION CENTER

BE WISE . . .
INQUIRE!
FREE:

- ★ *Career Information*
- ★ *Resume Writing*
- ★ *Job Information*
- ★ *Job Hunting*
- ★ *Financial Aid Assistance*

HOWLAND PUBLIC LIBRARY

313 Main Street - Beacon, New York 12508

Call for Appointment: 914-831-4323

Designed, typeset and printed at the Mid-Hudson Library System, Resource Center for Library Materials and Services 2P.JIC 006A.10-90.50

Write for the Local Paper

Consider writing an article for the local paper, particularly one distributed in the immediate neighborhood or service area. Offer to develop a regular newspaper column to address local job and education issues, stressing the ways that the job and career center can help. The Regional Learning Service in Syracuse (NY) places a 'help column' called "Learn to Work" in the Sunday paper near the want ads. Place announcements in the want ads section of the local paper. This is an excellent method for reaching job seekers and job changers.

Reach Non-Print Media

Use radio and TV public service announcements; get on a radio or TV talk show. Radio and television reaches non-readers. Let local media know about staff involvement in special activities and library responses community concerns. Offer to participate in radio and TV talk shows which highlight the needs addressed by the services your job and career center provides.

Note: Be prepared for a large response to these mass media awareness techniques. Keep all library staff members informed of promotional efforts so they may be prepared for additional inquiries.

Develop a Job and Career Center Newsletter and Include Articles in Other Newsletters

Include information about the job and career center in the library newsletter and in the newsletters of related organizations. Newsletters can be circulated to numerous service agencies within the community, or can be tailored for a specific audience such as local businesses. Distribution of an informative newsletter for public use with articles on how to locate job information or how to avoid interviewing pitfalls can provide needed information and promote library services as well. Compare the cost of time and resources producing it in-house with those of having an outside firm typeset and produce it.

FIGURE 4-6: "Learn To Work" Newspaper Article—Herald American, October 14, 1990

LEARN TO WORK

Occupational therapist helps disabled to restore job skills

Q. I am interested in finding out more about occupational therapists. What are their responsibilities and how much do they make? Also, what local schools offer programs?

A. An occupational therapist works with physically, mentally, or developmentally disabled clients. The occupational therapist uses activities and equipment to help clients develop or restore function and achieve the highest level of function in a job. (Don't confuse an occupational therapist with a physical therapist, who helps restore physical functions through exercise and therapy.)

An occupational therapist evaluates a client's disabilities and plans treatment; teaches a client ways to overcome a physical handicap and/or an emotional disability; and designs equipment to lessen disability due to illness, injury or birth defect.

The beginning salary is $22,000 to $25,000 a year. The employment outlook is excellent. This occupation is expected to grow much faster than average due to expanded insurance coverage of occupational therapy services; substantial growth in the aging population; and the emphasis on out-patient clinics and home health programs.

A bachelor's degree, which includes clinical practice, in occupational therapy is required. Keuka College, Utica College of Syracuse University, Syracuse University and State University of New York at Buffalo offer occupational therapist programs. Call the education hotline, 448-4633, for addresses and phone numbers.

Q. How does one earn the FCC general class license?

A. Since deregulation, the rules for licensure have been liberalized by the Federal Communication Commission. The FCC no longer issues the first or third-class operator licenses.

But the second-class operator license still is required for people in charge of transmitter readings. The exam is given at FCC centers around the country. To apply, contact: Federal Communication Communication Commission, 111 W. Huron St., Buffalo, N.Y. 14202.

Learn to Work is produced by the Education Information Center. Readers may submit questions to HELP, Education Information Center, 405 Oak St., N.Y. 13203. Questions will be answered in this column as space permits. Others will be answered by mail.

STRATEGIES DESIGNED TO INCREASE ACCESS THROUGH OUTREACH

POSIBLE OBJECTIVES WHICH TAKE THE SERVICE TO THE PEOPLE

A valuable strategy for getting the message out is to take the program to where the need is. This greatly increases access for the target population. Set up job and career center "mini-centers" wherever potential target groups congregate. Make presentations about job and career center services at factories or other businesses that are laying off employees. Give lectures at ESL classes or programs for displaced homemakers. Taking the service to the people reaches people who might not otherwise be served and it increases the visibility of the job and career center to new audiences.

Outreach strategies should be designed to reach individuals who may not be able to read promotional brochures and posters.

Work Cooperatively With Relevant Agencies

Consider arrangements with employment centers, programs for welfare recipients, and businesses etc., to set up a mini-center on a regular basis. Provide job and career center services at the same time and same place each week or month. Use a laptop computer with a modem to link to library-based and Internet resources. Bring along career advisory software to demonstrate what is possible. Have representative, popular, and timely materials on hand for people to look at and use. Job and career center brochures should be taken to all events.

In rural areas, it may be possible to take a 'circuit rider' approach, in which you might travel to several small communities on a regular basis to provide job and career center services. These communities may not have their own library or access to job and career center information unless you can bring it to them.

Add a Job Information Center Presence to the Bookmobile

Add job and career center materials, a laptop computer, and a modem to the bookmobile or establish a bookmobile which focuses solely on job, career, and education information. A JOB-MOBILE, similar to a bookmobile can include a collection of job, career, and education books and resources, including a laptop computer and career software. Consider a regular schedule and also attend special events, such as city festivals, county fairs, or high school career days. In the Memphis-Shelby County (TN) Public Library, the job and career center is permanently housed in a large bus called JOBLINC, (JOB Library Information Center) which travels throughout the area.

Develop Workshops To-Go

Don't be afraid to move your workshops out of the library; many people do not know that the library provides job and career center services and you can create opportunities for assistance that may be more suitable for the public by working in a more visible location. Some job and career center staff conduct pre-registered or drop-in WORKSHOPS outside the library. Look for non-library locations with public transportation access convenient for your target audience. Promote and conduct resume critiquing at a community center.

Start a Hotline

A hotline may contain recorded information about relevant information. The Regional Learning Service in Syracuse (NY) helps maintain a hotline with area educational opportunities as well as community Information and Referral data.

STRATEGIES DESIGNED TO INCREASE ACCESS TO RESOURCES

Most public libraries already provide a wide range of educational and employment materials. These resources are unique to the community. No other agency shares the library's mandate to identify and organize books, newspapers, magazines, videos, computer programs, and other resources for public use. It is the responsibility of library staff to develop an approach designed to increase the public's knowledge of and access to these valuable resources. Social service agency staff are often bewildered with the array of materials that are available in a local public library. One agency director commented, "We can't keep up with the relevant technical and printed materials related to employment and training and we rely heavily on the public library for this information."

Developing a job and career center provides librarians with the opportunity to look carefully at a wide range of educational and employment materials. Given the rich resources that libraries are in their communities, the resources in the library are already probably the strongest in the community. No other agency shares the public library's mandate to provide information to all citizens in the community. Librarians have a responsibility to increase the public's awareness of and access to these valuable resources.

POSSIBLE OBJECTIVES DESIGNED TO PROVIDE ACCESS TO CURRENT AND APPROPRIATE EDUCATION, CAREER, AND JOB RESOURCES

Select a Wide Range of Materials

See Serving Job Seekers and Career Changers for detail about selecting and evaluating resources. Identify key resources using that guide and others listed at the end of this chapter. Consider different reading levels and languages when selecting resources. Bring the library resources together. Consider adding a color or other code to books as a user finding aid.

Purchase and Market Career Advising Software

Consider purchasing software and videos to provide additional help for the job and career center clientele. There are a number of materials and resources from which to choose. Some materials, such as interactive career assessment software (such as SIGI Plus by Educational Testing Service and DISCOVER by American College Testing) and interactive training videos for the job seeking process (such as the Karli tapes), are very expensive. Don't eliminate consideration of resources just because of the cost. The purchase of one piece of software that will be in constant use for the entire year may be a better use of selection dollars than fifty books which not adequate for the job. Look for new money sources for expensive resources such as computer software and business sources.

Develop Bibliographies, Path-Finders, and Other Materials which Increase Access to the Library's Resources

Let people know what you have. Bibliographies which focus on the need are the most effective. These materials double as instructional tools. See Chapter 7 for a number of examples of bibliographies.

FIGURE 4-7: Booklist/Women: Careering, Re-Careering, Or Re-Schooling—Brooklyn Public Library

Education & Job Information Center

BOOKLIST

WOMEN: CAREERING, RE-CAREERING OR RE-SCHOOLING?

Look for these books in the Education and Job Information Center, Brooklyn Public Library, Grand Army Plaza. Telephone 718-780-7777.

OWNING YOUR OWN BUSINESS

The Work-at-Home Sourcebook
Lynie Arden

101 Best Businesses to Start
Sharon Kahn

Women Business Owners — Selling to the Federal Government
Small Business Administration

Starting a Mini-Business: A Guidebook for Seniors
Nancy Olsen

How to Write a Winning Proposal
Virginia Larsen

WORK/LIFE SUCCESS

The Assertive Woman
Stanlee Phelps & Nancy Austin

Feel the Fear and Do It Anyway
Susan Jeffers

Janice LaRouche's Strategies for Women at Work
Janice LaRouche & Regina Ryan

Your Perfect Right — A Guide for Assertive Living
Robert Albert & Michael Emmons

You're the Boss — A Guide to Managing People with Understanding & Effectiveness
Natasha Josefowitz

Network Your Way to Job & Career Success
Ronald Krannich & Caryl Krannich

Women's Organizations — A New York City Directory
New York Commisssion on the Status of Women

RESUME & INTERVIEW

Resumes That Knock 'em Dead
Martin John Yate

Revising Your Resume
Nancy Schuman & William Lewis

The Perfect Resume
Tom Jackson

Knock 'em Dead with Great Answers to Tough Interview Questions
Martin John Yate

The Complete Q & A Job Interview Book
Jeffrey G. Allen

JOB HUNTING

How to Get a Job in New York — The Insider's Guide
Thomas Camden & Susan Fleming-Holland

Metropolitan New York Job Bank
Bob Adams, Inc.

The Best Companies for Women
Baila Zeitz & Lorraine Dusky

The Best U.S. Cities for Working Women
Andresky Fraser

Women's Job Search Strategy
Betty Windy Boyd

Hunting the Headhunters — A Woman's Guide
Diane Cole

WORKING PARENTS

The Working Parents' Survival Guide
Sally Wendkos Olds

Super Working Mom's Handbook
Roseann Hirsch

The Child Support Survivors Guide
Barry T. Schnell

Kids Culture Catalog — A Teacher & Parent Guide to Education Programs of NYC's Cultural Resources
Alliance for the Arts

CAREER CHOICE AND CHANGE

Joyce Lain Kennedy's Career Book
Joyce Lain Kennedy

Coming Alive from Nine to Five — The Career Search Handbook
Betty Neville Michelozzi

Where Do I Go from Here with My Life
John Crystal & Richard Bolles

Black Woman's Career Guide
Beatryce Nivens

Exploring Non-Traditional Jobs
Rose Neufeld

Do What You Love — The Money Will Follow
Marsha Sinetar

Careering and Recareering for the 1990's
Ronald L. Krannich

EDUCATION PLANNING

How to Get College Credit for What You Have Learned as a Homemaker & Volunteer
Ruth B. Edstrom

The Essential Handbook for Returning Women Students
Brooklyn College Women's Center

Campus-Free College Degrees
Marcie Kisner Thorsen

Bear's Guide to Earning Non-Traditional College Degrees
John Bear

Peterson's Graduate Directories
Peterson's Guide to Two Year Colleges

Index to Majors & The College Handbook
Maureen Matheson, Ed.

American Trade School Directory
Croner Publications

Regents College Degrees
University of the State of New York

College Planning/Search Book
ACT American College Testing Program

The One-Hour College Applicant
Lois Rochester & Judy Mandell

FINANCIAL AID

Directory of Financial Aid for Women
Gail Ann Schlachter

Directory of Financial Aid For Minorities
Gail Ann Schlachter

Better Late Than Never — Financial Aid for Re-Entry Women
WEAL Women's Equity Action League

Government Assistance Almanac
J. Robert Dumouchel

The "How To" Grants Manual — Successful Grantseeking Techniques
David G. Bauer

TEST PREPARATION

Contemporary's New GED
Patricia Mulcrone

Arco's Preparation for the SAT

Barron's How to Prepare for the CLEP — College Level Exam Program

Cracking the LSAT
Princeton Review

MAGAZINES

Career Woman
Executive Female
Savvy Woman
Working Woman
Working Mother
The NY Job List
Opportunities in Non-Profit Organizations
Job Opportunities Bulletin
Day Care Council of New York

Provide Access to Career Information in Electronic Formats through the Internet and Other Major Online Networks or CD-Rom

With the explosion of electronic information, it is now possible for librarians to provide access to job listins online through new services developed by governments and the private sector. States provide occupational information through a network of state occupational information systems coordinated by the National Occupational Information Committee. State Occupational Information Coordinating Committees (SOICCs)—made up of state vocational education boards, vocational rehabilitation agencies and employment security agencies, job training coordinating councils and economic development agencies—use emerging technologies to provide career information resources for citizens of each state. Most states have developed a state Occupational Information System (OIS), which is typically a computerized database. Providing access to the OIS adds valuable information for public library job and career center clientele.

The format for this information varies from microfiche, to CD-ROM, to online. For information about any state's Occupational Information System, contact the national NOICC:

NOICC Offices

2100 M Street NW, Suite 156

Washington DC

(202)653-5665

Facilitate the Placement of Resumes on National Computerized Databases

The private sector is taking the lead in electronic linking of jobs and the resumes of job seekers. This section does not endorse the following products; it is included to show the kind of programs which take advantage of the power of computerized information. With these services individuals add their resumes to very large national databases. As of this writing, confidentiallity varies with the system and librarians who seek to add these services should inquire about what steps have been taken to assure the confidentiality of the individual who adds a resume to the system. Because these databases are searchable, large numbers of jobs or resumes don't clog the system. An employer who seeks a candidate who speaks Spanish and program in C, can search through the thousands of resumes very quickly.

The Online Career Center (OCC), a menu-driven gopher server, is available to job seekers and employers on the Internet. OCC provides a database of job listings, resume files, and company profiles. Searchable files include job opportunities, which are entered by employers and resumes are entered by job seekers. OCC is financed by membership and annual fees paid by employers. Therefore, employment opportunities are likely to be in larger firms. Job seekers may post resumes. Librarians could provide a pointer to it on a library gopher or might post the Internet address which is "gopher.msen.com". Information about this service may be obatined from "occ-info@mail.msen.com". Occ does not charge for access to the database through Internet. Job centers that seek to make this database available would need to provide access to the Internet.

KiNexus (a Chigcago-based firm) is a national subscription database of resumes available on Prodigy and in CD-Rom format. Most of its subscribers are employers who review the tens of thousands of resumes and make direct contact with those who closely match their neeeds. The Schaumberg Township District Library (STDL) in February of 1993, became the first public library to provide public access to this resume database. For $175 a month, Schaumberg receives a CD-ROM with thousands of resumes of registered job seekers which employers can search. Job seekers can post their resumes to the system at the public library by purchasing a pre-formatted disk for a nominal fee. The disk puts a reume inot common form preferred by kiNexus and employers. Information provided in the resume worksheet includes: Career objectives, work experience, personal attributes, personal achievements, and academic achievements; language facility, degree information, job, industry , and geopgraphic [proference, employment position sought, work history, computer skills, and personal inoframation such as name, address, and telephone number etc. The STDL asks each candidate to sign a waiver which releases the library fronm liability associated with adding an individual's name to the database.

POSSIBLE OBJECTIVES TO INCREASE THE VISIBILITY OF THESE RESOURCES IN THE LIBRARY

There are a number of activities (as seen by the objectives below) that staff can undertake to increase the visibility of the job, career, and education resources in the library.

Develop a Name for the Service that People will Readily Understand

A number of library job centers are referred to throughout this guide by their names. These names help people understand the services which are offered. Most libraries have named their services, even if they are housed in a small corner. In fact, most job centers make it a practice to identify the service and the people who are operating it. Research has shown that this makes a big difference in patron ability to use the service. Library staff should recognize the need for good signage to show people the location of the job and career resources. Many people who see the signs and notice that the area has been set aside for this special purpose are at first surprised, and then delighted.

Provide Space that People will Recognize as the Place to Find and Use Job/Career Information

Set aside space for a job and career center. Think about providing different kinds of space including tables for people to work at, a place for a computer, a place to talk privately, if possible. Consider the proximity of the space to the photocopying machine. Clearly send the message, "This is a job and career information center and you are welcome to use it even if you don't know much about how a library works."

Help People Use the Resources

Staff should be very familiar with job and education resources in the library and in the community. Staff should be willing to help people get the most out of library resources, and be able to show people how to use resources in formats (such as computer or video) that may be hard for some people to use, and explain to people about the job and career center services.

Advise People Regarding Specific Resources

When people ask for one kind of resource, show them that there are other, related materials in the collection. To help people become familiar with the resources in general, conduct guided tours of the center.

Develop Bulletin Boards and Give Away Displays

Prepare exhibits or displays. Provide plenty of space for job notices, educational opportunities, workshop information, etc. Use bulletin board space to alert library patrons about the kinds of services offered. Put posters describing the service on the bulletin board. Include give away space for the bibliographies and skill building materials (resume writing guides, etc.). Often bulletin boards are cluttered, but the give the impression of well-used space.

RESOURCES

[American Library Association]. *ALA Graphics Catalog*. Chicago: American Library Association, 1989.

Crawford, Walt. *Desktop Publishing for Librarians*. Boston: G.K. Hall & Co., 1990.

Durrance et al., *Job Seekers and Career Changers: A Planning Manual for Public Libraries*. Chicago: American Library Associaion, 1993.

Nebraska Library Commission. *Nebraska Education Information Center Network. 1987 Annual Report to the W.K. Kellogg Foundation*. Lincoln, Nebraska: Nebraska Library Commission, 1987.

Savage, Kathleen. *Serving Job Seekers and Career Changers: a Critical Bibliography for Public Libraries*. Chicago: Public Library Association, 1993.

Savage, Kathleen. *Vocational Careers Sourcebook and Professional Careers Sourcebook*. Detroit: Gale Research.

Walters, Suzanne. *Marketing: A How-to-Do-it Manual for Librarians*. New York: Neal-Schuman Publishers, 1992.

5 PERSONAL ASSISTANCE STRATEGIES DESIGNED TO INCREASE ACCESS TO INFORMATION

Research has increasingly shown that librarians must pay closer attention to the need behind the question in order to assist people effectively. Increasingly, librarians have at their disposal a variety of personal assistance strategies that can be used to identify and respond to individual needs. The personal assistance strategies discussed in this chapter and in later ones are used by many librarians. Although in practice personal assistance strategies are used together, this chapter and the next several separate them to show the range of approaches that can be used in working with an individual. Present professional practice serves to blur the distinctions and many librarians fail to realize that they regularly engage in a variety of strategies.

Strategies designed to increase access to information are used to:

1. make the information in the library more accessible and,
2. help librarians change the way that people think about interacting with library staff.

When barriers—those erected by patrons and by librarians—have been lowered, people are more likely to bring to trusted staff questions that are really important to them. These strategies are crucial to laying the groundwork that will meet needs.

This chapter focuses on personal assistance strategies which will help staff increase the public's access to information. They include:

1. Welcoming techniques,
2. The reference interview, and
3. Advising about resources or information.

Each strategy in this chapter is accompanied by a group of specific activities, listed here as objectives, which can be used to carry out the strategy.

Welcoming strategies set the stage for all interpersonal (personal assistance) strategies. Because many people's perceptions of libraries and librarians are fairly limited, welcoming strategies should be used to helping people feel comfortable enough to ask questions.

The reference interview is seen by many librarians as the key intervention strategy in librarianship. Reference interviews, by and large, result either in providing patrons with (or in referring them to) resources or in providing them information contained in resources. An effective reference interview starts with welcoming strategies. It then incorporates the effective use of open and closed questions and effective listening skills to determine (diagnose) the need. This is followed by one or more intervention strategies involving some sort of search strategy and the provision of a specific resource, or a group of resources or information (an intervention). Finally, by asking if the question has been answered, the effective librarian closes the reference interview by attempting to determine if she intervened appropriately. (Gers and Seward.)

Strategies which increase access to information and materials are part of the family of personal assistance strategies. They flow naturally from welcoming to negotiating questions to focusing more directly on the problem which brought the question in the first place. Advising on materials or information, also discussed in this chapter, is used if the librarian determines that the questioner needs more assistance in understanding and using the materials or information presented. Other categories of intervention strategies, problem assistance, instruction, and linking will be discussed in later chapters.

WELCOMING STRATEGIES

POSSIBLE WELCOMING OBJECTIVES

How people perceive library staff strongly influences whether they trust them enough to ask a question that might, in their opinion, make them sound stupid or uninformed. Because of the limited perceptions that people have about library services, librarians need to take extra steps to turn users who know that you can check books out of the library into users who are comfortable asking librarians to help them get needed information.

Develop an Awareness of Barriers that Interfere with Information Seeking

Research in the 1980s has confirmed what many librarians instinctively feel—many patrons feel uncomfortable in libraries. One researcher identified what has come to be called "library anxiety." (Mellon) For whatever reasons—and researchers aren't yet sure why—many people are intimidated by libraries and often feel "dumb" even to the point of believing that everybody ("but me") knows how to use libraries.

In addition to the anxiety many people experience using libraries, Carol Kuhlthau has found that students experience a variety of emotional states (including confusion, anxiety, and apprehension) when faced with a major school assignment. (Kuhlthau) Librarians need to gain a better understanding of the barriers faced by citizens and become informed about people's limited perceptions about libraries and librarians. In addition they need to take steps to change these perceptions. (Durrance, 1988)

Use Techniques that Assure People that It Is OK to Ask Questions

Many people perceive libraries as fairly hostile environments. If college students experience "library anxiety," we can expect that people who lack academic skills enter libraries with trepidation (if they enter at all). (Mellon) Therefore, librarians must use techniques which assure people who timidly venture into libraries, many with very old and out-dated perceptions about libraries, that it is okay to ask librarians questions.

The activity that the librarian is engaged in when she is approached with a question makes a difference. Interactions with librarians who are either free when approached by the questioner or who are working with another patron were far more likely to be successful than those in which the librarians are talking with another staff member or doing work at the desk when approached. Welcoming skills are particularly necessary when a patron interrupts a librarian who is either talking to a co-worker or who is working on a project at the desk. (Durrance, 1989).

Ways to increase the effectiveness of this skill are included in many books on communication in the workplace and in the training packages of a number of corporations whose employees work regularly with the public. Communicating Professionally includes sections on non-verbal behavior and establishing contact. Exercises are included. The Atlanta Public Library used a local department store trainer to provide staff with these basics, although going to a retailer for these skills should not be necessary.

Show Approachability

Over and over again people sing the praises of library staff who make them feel comfortable. The way librarians establish contact with patrons can start making them feel comfortable and at ease from the very beginning. Use of this technique may give people the courage to ask a question. Although most people know that they can get books at the library, fewer know that they can ask questions, and even fewer are aware that they can get help solving a problem. (Durrance, 1988).

Many people won't approach a stranger if they aren't sure whether the person is willing or able to help them. Showing approachability, sets the stage for being asked a relevant question. These techniques, which involve body language, eye contact, and an appearance of warmth, will help overcome human hesitancy to approach a stranger with a problem or question.

Librarians can welcome the questioner by looking up, smiling, and showing interest when approached. The initial contact, including body language, and the important first words spoken set the tone for the diagnostic interview.

Librarians may unintentionally treat some people differently. They may discover that they feel uncomfortable around individuals with disabilities, people of color, or the homeless. When this happens, librarians are likely to treat those individuals differently than others, starting with body language.

Sharpen the Ability to Establish Rapport with People Who Seek Assistance

Ross and Dewdney is an excellent guide for improving a variety of communication approaches It emphasizes the importance of establishing an atmosphere that encourages people to think of librarians as key links to information. (Ross and Dewdney) They use the term, "establishing rapport." Effective use of these basic strategies sends a message that they have come to the right place to get assistance.

Librarians who spend too many hours at the desk, or whose workload is too heavy may lose the ability to use this skill. A lack of empathy for what it is like to be at the other end of the interview may also lead to what can be perceived by patrons as behavior that cuts them off. This kind of behavior has been observed frequently as part of an ongoing study of the reference interaction. (Durrance, 1989).

Develop Effective Listening Skills

The ability of the librarian to become an effective listener is a valuable welcoming strategy. Effective listeners practice active listening, which precludes responding too quickly with a ready answer. This strategy is a strong underpinning of the reference interview. Reference interviews are likely to fail when librarians lack this skill. Ross and Dewdney (p. 33) say that the biggest barriers to effective listening include the following:

- Perceiving selectively
- Making assumptions
- Giving unsolicited advice
- Being judgmental or critical
- Being defensive or arguing

Listening skills can be improved by being attuned to any tendency to putting up the kinds of listening barriers mentioned above. Listen to what is being said; remember that similar questions may require different responses. Librarians should send appropriate verbal and non-verbal cues—for example, as nodding their heads, pausing, and using encouraging words—to show that they are listening. Ross and Dewdney have exercises to help improve listening skills. (Ross and Dewdney) Benjamin's *The Helping Interview* includes a discussion of effective listening skills. (Benjamin)

REFERENCE INTERVIEW PART I: DIAGNOSTIC STRATEGIES

Most people who write about the reference interview fail to show that the array of professional approaches available to librarians is diverse. All interpersonal skills are frequently discussed as "the reference interview." In reality, the reference interview—only one of the personal assistance strategies—is a grab-bag of diverse approaches.

This discussion examines the reference interview from several perspectives. First of all, the reference interview can be thought of as two sets of techniques—those which separate librarians' actions into the following:

1. Those that are primarily assessment or diagnostic, and focus on question negotiation. These techniques include actions which are focused on finding out what the real question is and deciding what information is needed; and
2. Intervention—for example, techniques which focus on taking action to respond to the need. Intervention can be considered

to be such actions as the search strategy, providing the information, or putting the resource in the patron's hands.

In the reference interaction, as seen in the following discussion, the librarian has a fairly wide range of possible intervention approaches. Not too many years ago, librarians said that answering reference questions was an art which could not be reduced to a set of techniques. From that time, librarians have learned that one of the best ways to improve the reference interview is through the use of effective questioning techniques. When used effectively, the reference interview can be an excellent technique to correctly answer patron questions.

Breaking the reference interview into diagnosis and intervention provides a vehicle to examine the varied intervention approaches that are used in this set of strategies. Often a librarian will determine (diagnose) that a specific source will not be sufficient for the need, or that the patron is unable to use the "best" resource. When this occurs, she will need to shift gears and use other personal assistance strategies that may take a little longer and approach the problem differently.

POSSIBLE OBJECTIVES FOR USING THE REFERENCE INTERVIEW AS A DIAGNOSTIC TOOL

Possible objectives for using the reference interview as a diagnostic tool can be drawn from the following section which focuses on barriers to success and effectiveness diagnostic techniques.

Avoid Poorly Selected First Words

The effective reference interview is one in which the actual need is determined (diagnosed). The first words spoken by a librarian can prove to be crucially important to the success of the reference interview. In general, the first words out of a staff member's mouth should be welcoming. Avoid starting a reference interview with a closed statement. There is now considerable research which shows that when a librarian starts a reference interview with closed questions—for example, "Did you look in the card catalog?;" "Is this a school question?;" "Do you want something you can take home?;" "Do you want a adult or a children's book?" or "Have you looked for that in the magazine section?"—the interview has a good chance of failing. (Dervin and Dewdney; Durrance, 1989; Gers and Seward; Ross; Ross and Dewdney)

My research shows that initial statements (the first words out of a staff member's mouth) that appear to be orders, "Look in the card catalog" or sound judgmental, "That question is too general," or "I don't think we can help you," have a negative effect on the questioner. Train staff to avoid starting an interview with a closed question.

Show Interest in the Question

Effective interpersonal communication skills greatly enhance the success of the reference interview. Librarians who are friendly, interested in the question, and make the questioner feel comfortable are judged by patrons to be the most effective in conducting reference interviews. Whereas librarians have a high regard for being non-judgmental about a question, patrons may mis-read this trait to be a lack of interest in the question and in him or herself. (Durrance, 1989)

Develop Skills in the Effective Use of Open and Neutral Questions

Only about 55% of reference interviews result in providing a correct answer to patrons' questions. Often when librarians fail to provide correct answers, it is because they have not learned how to use open and closed questions and determine the information need. The effective use of open questions (strategies that librarians can use to increase their ability to accurately assess the need for the information), as well as asking a follow-up question will increase the success of the reference interview. (Ross and Dewdney; Gers and Seward.)

Reference interviews which start with open questions are likely to be more successful than those that start with closed questions or statements. Interviews which start with an open question, such as, "What kind of information do you need?" or "Tell me more," or "What kind of career change?" or "What is it you need the information for?," are more likely to be successful because these types of questions fairly quickly result in identifying the real need. Ross and Dewdney provide an in-depth discussion of the reference interview (among other topics) and include a number of exercises that can be used to increase the effectiveness of the reference interview. That manual shows librarians how to use open and "neutral" questions, (open but structured questions). (Dervin and Dewdney, Ross and Dewdney.) Practice the use of open and neutral questions and using statements effectively with a partner.

Sometimes in the course of asking open questions in the reference interview, the librarian discovers that finding out more about the need will be valuable in guiding the information search. Questions will then focus on helping the client focus step back and think more fully about problem. Chapter 6 will present more details on how to find out more about the need.

Clarify the Question to Prevent Premature Diagnosis

A valuable diagnostic strategy which grows out of the effective use of open and closed questions is clarifying the question so that it is adequately understood. This strategy is variously known as negotiating or clarifying the question (question negotiation is often synonymous with the reference interview).

Accurate diagnosis is essential to appropriate intervention. The process of finding out about the need should start early in the interaction between librarian and patron. It may begin in response to a patron's question such as, "Where are your books on resumes?" Even as a librarian moves to take the patron toward the resume books, (s)he may start the diagnosis by inquiring about the use that will be made of the information requested, by using such techniques as open or neutral questions ("Can you tell me how you will be using this information?") and showing interest in the responses.

After the librarian has determined what she thinks is the real question, she then shifts into the second set of reference interview strategies—questions which focus on intervention. There are a number of actions a librarian might take. See Ross and Dewdney's discussion of Premature Diagnosis. (Ross and Dewdney, pp. 42-43.)

THE REFERENCE INTERVIEW PART II: INTERVENTION STRATEGIES

Research shows that many librarians answer the questions they have been asked (rather than negotiating the question). (Dewdney; Durrance) When a librarian immediately answers the question that has been asked she has, of course, skipped the diagnosis stage and moved immediately to intervention. In the reference interaction, even when there is no diagnosis, there is a range of possible intervention strategies.

Each of the typical reference intervention approaches below can result in quite different outcomes to the reference interview. When intervening in the reference interview a librarian may, among other approaches, put what she considers to be the "right" source in the hands of the patron or she may point to the resource across the room. On the other hand she may advise the patron on two apparently similar resources, or refer the patron to another staff member, or another location (among many possible intervention choices). Choosing among other reference interview intervention strategies, the librarian may answer the question that was asked, lead the patron to a group of resources, or provide information based on negotiating the question. She may check to see if the resource or information provided was appropriate.

POSSIBLE OBJECTIVES THAT ILLUSTRATE INTERVENTION SKILLS OF REFERENCE LIBRARIANS

Avoid Intervention Approaches that Cut Off Communication

Below is a discussion of several intervention strategies which library staff do use to respond to reference questions. They illustrate the wide range of approaches that librarians take in a reference interaction. Be cautious in using them. They are likely to result in a failed interaction.

Don't recommend that the questioner check the catalog.

Often librarians are guilty of starting the reference interview with the words, "Did you check the catalog?" Patrons who are not sure if it is okay to ask a librarian a question take this response to be a real put-off. Librarians who use this approach make the assumption that all users can capably manipulate the library's bibliographic apparatus. Avoid using this intervention, a closed question. Replace it with something like, "What have you done so far," and you have returned to the diagnostic stage.

Don't answer the question that was asked without negotiating it.

In one study Pat Dewdney found that: 1. 60 percent of library users frame their question to accommodate their perceptions of what librarians need (as in "Where are your BOOKS on resumes"?); and 2. most of the time librarians answer the question that has been asked rather than negotiating to find out what the questioner actually requires. (Dewdney)

If a librarian assumes that all that is necessary is to answer the question that was asked, there is a good chance that the questioner's real need will not be met. If, for example, a librarian responds to a request for resume books with: "Here they are. Can I show you a particular kind of book?," it may appear on the surface that the answer more than adequately met the need. However, if the real need was not directly expressed and the patron actually needed help with a problem such as the job seeking process, the interaction is a failure and the need has not been met because it was not identified. Such an intervention lacked a proper diagnosis.

Other red-flag intervention strategies include:

Avoid choosing a resource or a group of resources based on the initial question.

Avoid the temptation to point to a likely resource across the room.

The negative strategies discussed above are not people centered. They are question centered and they give the appearance that the professional is too busy to be bothered with finding out whether the response he/she has chosen fits the need of the questioner.

The intervention strategies sketched out below are designed to respond more effectively to patron questions. Of course, not all will be used with each questioner; they offer a range of typical appropriate responses and can be used as the basis for service objectives. Most need little explanation because they are widely used in practice. They are isolated here to remind librarians of the wide range of intervention approaches available and used.

Develop a Search Strategy Based on an Effective Diagnosis

This strategy and all of the strategies discussed below are likely to improve the reference interview when they are based on the effective use of diagnostic techniques discussed earlier. The strategy chosen will vary based on what has been learned during the diagnostic stage.

Take the Patron to the Likely Resource or a Group of Resources

The perceptions of library users are frequently that there are two kinds of librarians "the pointers" and "those who like to help." The latter are librarians who come out "from behind the desk to guide patrons to materials." (Mellon, p. 11). This technique is often used when continuing the diagnosis. This may occur when on the way to the appropriate location. Often, at the same time, the librarian is advising the questioner on the nature of these particular resources.

Provide Information Based on Negotiating the Question—i.e., a Skillful Diagnosis

Remember that the question belongs to the patron and not the librarian and that the same question can have a number of different responses, depending on what the needs of the questioner are.

Conduct a Reality Check when Carrying Out the Search Strategy

As skilled librarians know, the intervention stage in a reference interview frequently reverts back to the diagnostic stage as librarians act (made additional interventions) based on additional knowledge gained in the process of the reference interview.

Advise or Instruct the Patron on Two Apparently Similar Resources

Reference librarians often use this technique. However because strategies have been grouped in this book, this strategy is discussed more fully in the next section.

Refer the Questioner to a More Appropriate Staff Member, Department, or Community Resource

Referral is often given without the accompanying responsibility to assure that it is appropriate. Referral should not be a way of getting off the hook. Follow-up to make sure that the referral was appropriate. Referral is examined in more detail in Chapter 8.

Inform the Questioner of the Approaches that are Being Taken and Be Sure that the Questioner Understands Them

My research has found that often librarians neglect to tell patrons what they are doing as they are providing reference assistance. Because patrons are not informed, they do not know what to do. Use the techniques to foster inclusion recommended by Ross and Dewdney.

Check to See If the Resource or Information Provided or Approach taken Was Appropriate

The follow-up question (such as "Is that what you needed?") is a technique that if used properly will assure both the librarian and the questioner that the chosen intervention has been effective. It is included here because it is the final diagnostic strategy. Should the librarian find that, no, the response had not met the need, then the librarian shifts back into the diagnostic mode.

There is a general progression from the reference interview into other strategies, including advice giving, instruction, and assistance with some aspect of the problem. In the course of the diagnosis, the librarian may decide that it is appropriate to use another strategy to increase the client's access to resources or information. Advising, offering a professional opinion or giving a professional judgment about something, has been used as a technique by librarians because nearly the turn of the century. It has been used primarily with resources. It can also be effectively employed to meet the needs of job seekers.

STRATEGIES USED TO ADVISE ABOUT RESOURCES OR INFORMATION

Job and career information centers are not the first public library services to use advising based on a professional judgment as a technique. Literacy, adult independent learner programs, and community information services all require the ability to advise and consult with clientele who are solving particular problems. Typically, librarians give advice in three areas:

1. Recommendations about materials;
2. Advice regarding referral to community resources; and
3. Consulting with clientele about such actions as resume writing and interviewing.

The first one is discussed here; two and three are discussed later in the book.

POSSIBLE OBJECTIVES TO IMPROVE THE ADVISING SKILLS OF REFERENCE LIBRARIANS

Develop Advising Skills and Approaches

Early Reader's Advisors, like many contemporary job and career center staff, preferred to use a quiet area away from the busy reference desk that would facilitate the discussion of the reader's interests, background, and study plans. Like Reader's Advisors, job and career center librarians need extensive knowledge of the library's collections, knowledge of reading levels and differing abilities of people, "understanding of and interest in people, and the ability to make patrons feel comfortable when expressing their interests and concerns, motivations, and abilities. Sensitivity, tact, warmth, and enthusiasm", considered to be desirable characteristics of Readers' Advisors are also needed by job and career center staff. (Birge, p. 23; Heim and Monroe.)

Librarians have used advising as a technique as far back as the 1920s. The "Reader's Advisor" was a position developed in a number of public libraries "in response to the growing numbers of unskilled rural and foreign workers" who were migrating to the nation's industrial centers. (Birge, p. 18). Reader's Advisors work closely with the people who come to them for assistance in using the public library as a 'People's University.' These services have been oriented toward helping people create and work over a period of time through self-education plans with the aid of the librarian and have been seen as quite different from the "more impersonal, more superficial" reference services which were "directed primarily to ascertaining an individual fact or filling an immediate need in a single, rapid transaction." (Birge, p. 19)

Provide Advice on Library Materials

Users of job and career centers frequently need advice on which tools to use. Librarians feel comfortable using their knowledge of library materials to make recommendations on reading choices based on their expertise. Advice regarding the library's resources can unlock mysteries for job and career center clientele. Use judgment in advising; for example, judiciously suggest using a job-seeking videotape for someone with low reading skills. The following more specific objectives help fulfill the general one described above.

Advise the Questioner on a Group of Resources

Library users are often confused by the proliferation and the different formats of library materials. Some need to understand what a particular category of resources can do for them. Others will need help in identifying a resource (such as a resume book) which best suits their situation and reading ability. A public library, depending on its size, may have five, ten, or a hundred resume writing books and software programs that assist in resume writing. Suppose, in working with a factory worker, that he decides to change jobs and needs to write his first resume. That individual would certainly benefit from advice on the best resume book for his need.

Advise the Questioner on the Use of a Single Resource

Many patrons need assistance in using electronic resources, computer programs, and other format-specific resources. This is often accomplished in a brief introduction session, although librarians have developed instructional programs such as those described in Chapter 7.

Advise on a Sequence for Using Resources, Usually from General to Specific

Often when students are writing papers on career topics (or other topics), they need to start with more general resources before they move directly into a highly detailed resource. (See Kuhlthau, p. 142) This intervention (instruction) may increase an individual's access to materials they had previously been unable to use at all.

Develop Bibliographies and Pathfinders that Help People Use Library Resources

Librarians often anticipate need by developing guides to the use of materials, often those of a particular topic of interest or importance to a large number of people.

These strategies build on welcoming strategies, the reference interview, and advising. They focus on the situation that the individual is dealing with—a problem which must be solved (or a series of problems that need solving) like writing a resume, preparing for a job interview, conducting a job search, starting a business, etc. Although many reference librarians have adopted approaches that help them learn about the situation or the problem the person they are interviewing is working on, others do not. For this reason, and to continue presenting a wide range of strategies in related groupings, the next chapter focuses on strategies librarians use to better understand the need behind the question.

RESOURCES

Benjamin, Alfred. *The Helping Interview*, 3d ed. Boston: Houghton Mifflin, 1981.

Birge, Lynn E. *Serving Adult Learners: A Public Library Tradition.* Chicago: American Library Association, 1981.

Durrance, Joan C. "Information Needs: Old Song, New Tune." In *Rethinking the Library in the Information Age: Issues in Library Research—Proposals for the 1990s*, 159-77. Washington, D.C.: United States Department of Education Office of Education Research and Improvement, Office of Library Programs, October 1989.

Durrance, Joan C. "Reference Success: Does the 55% Rule Tell The Whole Story?" *Library Journal*, April 15, 1989. pp 31-36.

Dervin, Brenda, and Patricia Dewdney. "Neutral Questioning: A New Approach to the Reference Interview." *RQ* (Summer 1986): 506-513.

Gers, Ralph, and Lillie J. Seward. "Improving Reference Performance." *Library Journal* 110 (November 1985): 32-35.

Kuhlthau, Carol Collier, Seeking Meaning: A Process Approach to Library and Information Services. Norwood, NJ: Ablex Publishing Company, 1993.

Mellon, Constance. "Library Anxiety: A Grounded Theory and its Development." *RQ* (March 1986): 160-165.

Monroe, Margaret Ellen. Partners for Lifelong Learning: Public Libraries & Adult Education. Washington, D.C.: Office of Library Programs, U.S. Dept. of Education, Office of Educational Research and Improvement: United States Government Printing Office, 1991.

Ross, Catherine Sheldrick, and Patricia Dewdney. *Communicating Professionally: A How-To-Do-It Manual for Library Applications*. New York: Neal-Schuman, 1989.

6 PERSONAL ASSISTANCE STRATEGIES THAT PROMOTE SELF-ASSESSMENT, PROBLEM-CENTERED DIAGNOSIS AND INTERVENTION

Strategies that promote problem-centered diagnosis and intervention will help staff get people started on the process of helping people with self-assessment. This process focuses on individuals and helps them assess their needs and options and take steps toward problem solving. These strategies can also be used to help clientele get additional assistance in the community. Effective use of strategies that focus on the need will put people at ease and make them feel comfortable about seeking assistance. Problem-centered strategies are particularly valuable in working with people who are looking for a job, beginning self-assessment, trying to make a decision, or need support and coping assistance. Using these strategies can be rewarding professionally. People who have been helped with job related problems are often very grateful and ebullient in their praise of the staff who assisted them.

Helping people with a problem requires that librarians start with the need in approaching the client. Although most reference interviews last three minutes or less, often these strategies involve working with people for longer periods of time to focus on various aspects of a problem, such as developing a resume, researching a career, or self-assessment. They may also involve meeting with a client several times, often by appointment. These strategies require staff, training, facilities and resources. The effort expended in using these strategies yields a greater ability to meet needs and results in greater library recognition in the community.

STRATEGIES WHICH FOCUS ON PROBLEM-CENTERED DIAGNOSIS

Librarians can use interviewing techniques to find out more about a person's need. The difference between the approach used in the reference interview and the one used here is the emphasis. When seeking to find out more about the need or problem, the librarian uses interviewing techniques that focus on the problem which has brought the individual to the librarian (rather than the question which has been asked). Often at this stage people discuss their personal situation and may disclose information about themselves which is relevant to the need. ("I just won a merit scholarship! Now I need to decide on a college," or "I can't read," or "I need an emergency loan.")

POSSIBLE OBJECTIVES WHICH AID IN

Find Out What the Client Needs by Focusing on the Problem behind the Question Asked

People don't need information for its own sake. Although librarians value information, it only has value as a way of helping somebody do something. Most people look for information as a means to an end. The "end" is often an activity such as writing a term paper, buying a new car, or finding a better job. Adults in job transition may engage in a number of activities, such as making a job change, starting a business, applying for a job, or preparing for a job interview. Focusing on the need behind the question will avoid the false steps that come when assumptions are made about what is needed based on the question asked.

Experienced staff say that finding out more about the person's situation, and then assessing it, is an essential beginning point for working with someone who will need help over a period of time. This comment from a seasoned librarian shows how finding out more about the need changed her approach to serving people.

> "I was a good reference librarian. I used to pride myself on being able to quickly and effectively match people and our resource materials. Since working as a career information librarian, I have changed my whole interview style. I really need to find out more about the person and their need before I can effectively work with them."

Finding out more about the problem or situation will help librarians provide what an individual actually needs. Failure to learn why information is needed may lead to faulty assumptions and poor responses by librarians. New questioning techniques, especially the use of neutral questions have been developed to help librarians find out more about the need behind the question. (Dervin and Dewdney; Ross and Dewdney).

Develop Listening Skills to Aid in Diagnosis

Develop empathetic listening techniques. The Helping Interview by Alfred Benjamin provides an excellent background guide to the various parts of the professional interview. It was written with several professions in mind. Some form of the helping (or problem-solving) interview is used by counselors, social workers, psychologists, and others. The Helping Interview introduces the principles involved in empathic listening. Developing empathic listening skills can help librarians determine client needs.

Because the ability to listen effectively and be a good communicator are needed by other professionals as well, perhaps an agency or group in your community has already developed a workshop which librarians can attend. Librarians at TIP, Detroit Public Library's community information service, for example, attend workshops designed to increase empathic listening developed at a local social service agency.

Build Trust

A sense of trust, which is essential to the development of a client-professional relationship, may be established during this process. When librarians show that they are able to listen and understand a problem or situation, their clientele may disclose personal information about themselves—for example, "I lost my job," or "My husband left me." These are confidential revelations which are only made to trusted individuals. If such information is given, it may reveal an additional need—referral to an appropriate agency or the need for support and encouragement.

Develop Excellent Interviewing Skills as an Aid to Diagnosis

Patrons may ask questions of librarians the way they think librarians want them asked, making it more difficult to determine the actual need. We don't know why this is, only that it happens. Perhaps an individual thinks, "This is a library and libraries are collections of books. I should phrase my question so that the librarian knows that I know what I am talking about." Skilled librarians have long known of the necessity to negotiate the question.

One skilled practitioner puts it this way;

"Sometimes we need to backtrack a patron. They may think that all we have are the books. I need to know more about what they need. We talk about their problem first. After we focus on the problem, I am then able to better assess what we can or can't do. Taking their needs into consideration, I explain what we can do to help. They then learn that we offer a variety of services that can help them tackle that job change. If they decide that they want to spend more time on the process, we sit down and I try to find out more about what they need.

The following questions collected by Pat Dewdney illustrate this point. The first sentence is the question or statement that was asked by the patron. The second (in parenthesis) is what was actually needed.

1. I'm looking for books on ethnic arts and crafts. (Really wanted to prepare for a job interview).
2. Where could I find information about a particular company-what they make? (Wanted to prepare for a job interview).
3. Do you have business directories? (Is looking for a job and wants to send out his resume).

Develop strong interviewing skills. Many librarians have learned from conducting effective reference interviews that knowing why somebody needs the information can make a tremendous difference in the approach they use. (Dervin and Dewdney) Finding out about the need is part of most initial interviews conducted by other helping professionals.

Neutral questions (open questions designed to find out more about the need), such as "What are you trying to find out?" "How do you plan to use this information?" or "How will this help you?" have been found by Dervin to be particularly effective in ferreting out the real need. Neutral questions are devices for finding out what uses people will make of the information they receive. (Dervin and Dewdney; Ross and Dewdney)

Develop Methods to Continue Diagnosis over Time

Responding to the need requires understanding it. Job and career center staff actively try to find out more about the need behind the question. Determining (diagnosing) the need may come about over time. Practitioners, often unconsciously, are developing sets of protocols and mechanisms to diagnose needs. Job and career center staff find that often they can more effectively determine the need over time. At most centers there is a certain amount of on-going interaction. Staff learn the names of clients so that they can remember them when they return for additional work. They make appointments for sessions with self-assessment software as well as discussing progress and change in needs.

A young woman who had worked in an automobile factory for ten years and had been through a series of layoffs, decided that there just had to be something better. Drawn in by the library's very attractive job and career center, she decided to talk with the lady behind the center's information desk. The librarian listened to her concerns and suggested that she schedule an appointment to use the library's career advisement software, and then discuss her options further. She worked with SIGI Plus, talked with the coordinator and decided, at the librarian's suggestion, to enroll in a career decision class given at the local community college.

When is the diagnosis complete? Finding out about the need may consist only of a single interview. More likely, the need will gradually unfold in successive discussions between the patron and the librarian. In the process, the librarian may also learn of some handicap, learning disability, attitude, reading or other problem which might effect the approach used or the materials or resources recommended.

STRATEGIES WHICH FACILITATE PROBLEM-CENTERED INTERVENTION

Job and career center staff do not prescribe—they assist, they advise, they make opportunities available based on their understanding of the unique situation that has been presented. For example, if a librarian realizes that a middle-aged laid-off auto worker does not know how to match his skills with those needed for another field, she may intervene by recommending the use of self-assessment software. Often librarians suggest a helpful book such as *What Color is Your Parachute* or *Joyce Lain Kennedy's Career Book*, but not all clientele are able to use these resources. Likewise, if the librarian understands that when a middle-aged man or woman has lost a job, he or she may as well have lost confidence, the librarian—in the process of assisting—can provide moral support and encouragement. This might be a simple encouraging word or providing a boost of confidence to someone who calls just before a job interview to talk about progress.

Librarians may help clients think about themselves and their options. Many use self-assessment inventories or interactive computer career guidance programs. Some provide or refer their clients to career counseling which consists of in-depth interviews with qualified career counselors. Some librarians have experimented successfully with bringing in career counselors for a few hours a week. Others have hired full time career counselors who work closely with librarians to assist job seekers and career changers.

In summary, library staff who understand a client's need (i.e., who have diagnosed it) may assist the client in taking action. Intervention is the act of taking action which helps the client solve the problem. It may involve, assisting with self-assessment, advising on options, referring a client to a workshop, or engaging in some other problem-centered activity.

POSSIBLE PROBLEM CENTERED INTERVENTION OBJECTIVES

Help the Client with Self-Assessment

It is not possible to help some people get and use information until they have been able to take stock of their situation. That is often the first step in taking charge of solving their own problems. Someone who has a fair idea of where they are going and how to get the needed information has already overcome a number of obstacles.

When appropriate, help people step back and assess the situation. It may be necessary for librarians or counselors to help the client better understand his or her own interests, values, skills, and abilities. Facilitating self assessment may require the use of various tools that facilitate this process (such as career guidance software with self-assessment modules or self-assessment workbooks) and well-honed interpersonal skills.

Purchase Self-Assessment Tools

Self-assessment tools can help people match their interests and values with the world of work. A variety of resources are available to help people assess themselves and their situations. Two kinds of self-assessment tools frequently found in public libraries are as follows:

1. Self-assessment inventories: For many years career counselors have used pencil and paper assessment inventories to help their clients think through their interests, preferences, abilities, and values—elements which are essential to guiding their clients toward choosing a career or job that is a good fit. The more a client knows about what he or she wants, the better it can be communicated to you. These are frequently used by counselors and librarians, and given as hand-outs to their clientele.

2. Interactive career guidance software: In recent years computer programs have been developed which greatly facilitate the assessment process. Two of the most effective are SIGI

Plus, developed by the Educational Testing Service, and DISCOVER, created by American College Testing Service. Both of these programs have multiple modules (including self assessment, profiles of occupations and careers and the skills, knowledge, and preparation needed, decision making assistance, etc.). A number of librarians have purchased career assessment software in recent years.

Develop an Understanding of the Use of Interactive Career Assessment Software

As job and career center staff incorporate software such as this into their services for job seekers and career planners, they frequently begin to add workshops to show how self assessment fits into the career decision making process. Public libraries that have well-developed self-assessment programs linked to career counseling, include Westchester County, NY, Cuyahoga County, OH, Longview, WA and Flint, MI.

People who have been helped by job and career center staff frequently point out that they learned a lot about themselves by going through a career self-assessment module in SIGI Plus or DISCOVER, and by going over these results with a career counselor or the librarian. These computer software programs have made it possible for librarians to work with patrons on self-assessment in a way which a few years ago would have been unthinkable. User-friendly computer programs facilitate the self-assessment process through the use of structured questions that focus on values, interests, skills, and preferences.

Having gone through the self-assessment segment, the user's profile is matched with job and career profiles. At the end of each computer session, the user will obtain an individual printout based on his answers to the preference questions. Staff use these printouts as a basis for advising their clients on approaches and resources needed to pursue a particular course of action. Computer software like SIGI Plus and DISCOVER is valuable for adults and high school students.

Even rural communities have been able to bring this resource to their communities. For example, the Alliance Public Library in rural western Nebraska through a grant from the W. K. Kellogg Foundation developed a job and career center. Among the resources purchased was DISCOVER. After the town librarian alerted the high school English teacher to its new resources, the teacher decided to change the senior term paper and turn it into an exploration of a career. She told the seniors to use this opportunity to explore a career, find its pros and cons, and then indicate after this in-depth exploration whether they would pursue this career. Library staff put all of the materials on reserve, had the seniors visit the library as a class, and encouraged each senior to make an appointment to use DISCOVER. Students and the teacher appeared pleased with the results. One student was especially pleased to find out that he and his life-long career choice were incompatible after he researched it and used DISCOVER to identify his own interests and approach. One of the library staff commented, "That's why the computer program is so helpful. It asks questions about their own interests and about themselves."

Libraries that make heavy use of career assessment software include Everett (WA) Public Library and Carnegie Library of Pittsburgh (PA). See profiles of these libraries as well as profiles of Anita Johansen and Vera Green.

Use Advice as Appropriate

In the last chapter we discussed advising that focused primarily on materials and information. In that chapter it was suggested that librarians may, for example, advise on which of several resources will work best. In this chapter we focus on advice regarding the problem. Job and career center librarians who provide advice and encouragement in the problem solving process must be sure that they have determined the need adequately first.

Note: There is a clear distinction between facilitating the problem-solving process and solving a problem for the client. Librarians don't solve problems for clients; they do provide advice on needed information, instruction, counseling, referral, etc.

Job and career center staff provide advice on the process and action. Librarians who provide computerized self-assessment services, advise their clientele on elements in a resume or a computer printout. They help clients decide which services to use, making sure that the client is in charge of the process. Staff do not make clients dependent on them for decision making.

> Joe had worked in an auto parts store for twenty years. The store went out of business, and Joe was out of a job. He discovered the job and career information center when he came to the library looking for a book on how to write a resume. He had never been unemployed before and was very discouraged. The center coordinator talked with him

> and suggested several books to read. At the center, Joe worked with a counselor to develop a resume, and over several weeks returned several times to let her know how his search was going. Some time later Joe found another job. He said of his experience at the library, "This is a good service. It's been a god-send for me. We are very fortunate to have them here."

Staff provide options and advice on specific actions which are taken in the process of breaking a large problem into its smaller parts. If, for example, in the course of working with job center staff, an individual decides to develop a resume, the librarian may have or know of several different options to assist that individual. If that is the case, she may advise the client on the several options—including attending a resume clinic, learning to resume software, checking out a resume book, or going to someone who may critique a resume he has written. Advice would proceed from knowledge of the individual's needs and situation.

Staff provide advice on community resources: The need-centered job and career center has a staff that has made appropriate community contacts which can be used to refer clientele who need a range of community services. For example, staff working with a factory worker who realizes that he really needs more training in order to move up in his job, and can advise that client about the training opportunities in the community. That advice can be used to help him weigh several options.

> Charles R., a man in his mid-thirties, came to WORKPLACE for assistance in finding a job as an electronics technician. He was new in the area and was having trouble getting a job. He talked with a librarian about his situation that included a recent job loss in another city and the death of a parent. The librarian at WORKPLACE worked with him as he researched high-tech firms in the community. The librarian also helped him compose a resume by using a computer resume-writing program, he critiqued his resume, and helped him as he developed a job search strategy. After four months, Charles got an interview with a company he was really interested in. He came in to get advice before going to the interview. The librarian recommended a videotape to help him prepare for the interview. A few days after the interview Charles called to tell the librarian that he had been hired.

If advice is not appropriate, the staff member may engage in another strategy, instruction (see Chapter 7), and formally teach him and a group of others how to develop a resume and appropriate job-seeking strategies or recommend other workshops.

Provide Appropriate Career Counseling Assistance

Career counseling is different from the advising discussed above. In recent years a number of libraries have experimented with bringing certified career counselors into public libraries. Counselors may be full time or part time, and work directly for the library or as consultants. Librarians who do not use counselors either as consultants or staff, may want to learn how and when to refer to a career counselor.

Some libraries have made career counseling by qualified counselors a regular part of the service by hiring a full time or part time career counselor, or have worked with a counseling agency to set up a satellite office in the library, using counseling interns.

Counselors work with librarians in a number of communities, including: Nassau, Westchester, and Schenectady counties in New York. Counselors coordinate the job and career centers in the public libraries in Marquette and Flint in Michigan; Everett, Longview, and Spokane in Washington; and Cuyahoga County in Ohio.

In these libraries career counselors provide counseling sessions in the library and work closely with librarians. Counseling often consists of several one hour sessions over several weeks. They consist of working on assessment, goal setting, developing a plan of action, and working with the excellent resource materials that are in the library's collection. The following profiles illustrate different approaches that can be used to bring career counseling services to library users.

CAREER COUNSELING AND THE NASSAU COUNTY LIBRARY

At the Nassau County Library System on Long Island, NY, librarians contract with career counselors for a specified number of appointments per week. Librarians who work with patrons and find that they would benefit from career counseling, schedule an appointment with a career counselor who will meet with a client two to three times. Confidential records are kept for people who use this service. Counselors and librarians work very closely together. Usually after a counseling session, the counselor will bring a client over to the career center librarian who will work with the client to obtain resources that can help with the problem solving process. This system has been in operation at Nassau for more than

FIGURE 6-1: WEBS Career Development Seminars

WEBS
Career & Educational
Counseling Service

Come to a two-hour registration and information session to learn about
8-Week FREE

CAREER DEVELOPMENT SEMINARS

to help you make a career decision

- Understand your interests, values, skills
- Gather career and educational information
- Weigh your options
- Learn job search strategies

INFORMATION SESSION SITES:

Pre-register for one of the following dates by calling:
592-8791
(Monday, Wednesday and Thursday)

GREENBURGH PUBLIC LIBRARY
Tuesday, September 8, 6:45 p.m.
Tuesday, September 22, 6:45 p.m.

JOHN C. HART MEMORIAL LIBRARY*
(YORKTOWN)
Wednesday, September 2, 6:45 p.m.
Wednesday, September 9, 6:45 p.m.

MOUNT KISCO PUBLIC LIBRARY*
Tuesday, September 15, 9:00 a.m.
Tuesday, September 22, 9:00 a.m.

MOUNT PLEASANT PUBLIC LIBRARY
Thursday, September 10, 6:45 p.m.
Thursday, September 17, 6:45 p.m.

NEW ROCHELLE PUBLIC LIBRARY**
Monday, September 14, 6:45 p.m.
Monday, September 21, 6:45 p.m.

OSSINING PUBLIC LIBRARY*
Tuesday, September 22, 7:00 p.m.
Tuesday, September 29, 7:00 p.m.

WHITE PLAINS PUBLIC LIBRARY**
Monday, September 14, 7:00 p.m.
Monday, September 21, 7:00 p.m.

YONKERS PUBLIC LIBRARY
GRINTON I. WILL BRANCH
Tuesday, September 8, 7:00 p.m.
Tuesday, September 22, 7:00 p.m.

These information sessions are for registration. Eight-session career seminars will begin in October.

This project is supported by LSCA Title I funds
granted by the State of New York

Co-sponsors: Putnam/Northern Westchester BOCES*
The Westchester Community Foundation**

WLS
A SERVICE OF THE
WESTCHESTER
LIBRARY SYSTEM

1992

a decade. During that time, the system has developed joint in-service training programs which involve counselors and librarians. These programs, which focus on a variety of topics and resources, encourage professional cooperation between counselors and librarians.

This program is coordinated by a career counselor with a master's degree who works part time at system headquarters and reports to a librarian, Coordinator of Special Services, Dorothy Puryear. The system uses LSCA funds and other grant money to support this program in eight public libraries in the system. Through a cost-share partnership developed between system headquarters and the participating libraries, funds are made available to libraries on a dollar for dollar match.

CAREER COUNSELING AND THE CUYAHOGA COUNTY PUBLIC LIBRARY

InfoPLACE in Cuyahoga County, OH was started by Jeanne Patterson who had both a master's degree in library science and one in counseling. InfoPLACE has two full time and two part time career counselors. These counselors during a recent month held 272 one-hour counseling appointments which are usually made two weeks in advance. Career counselors at InfoPLACE spend a good part of their time helping clients learn to use the library's resources. Individual counseling is supplemented by a set of workshops that focus on various aspects of job and career seeking. One six-hour workshop focuses specifically on Career Decision Making. These workshops are held at different branch libraries.

This story of Carol shows how Cuyahoga's program works.

> Several years ago Carol, a single parent who was working part-time in a small church as an education director, came to an InfoPLACE career decision workshop after seeing the local library branch's workshop announcement in her neighborhood newspaper. Her children were in their early teens and Carol felt that she now had the freedom to think about her own future. She also needed to be able to support herself when child support payments ended in a few years.
>
> Carol took the six hour, three evening workshop, conducted by an InfoPLACE counselor, very seriously. She worked through all of the self assessments and met several times with an InfoPLACE counselor. The counselor assisted Carol in thinking through the process, obtaining

interviews with people working in several careers she was considering, and helped her make contacts with graduate schools for the careers requiring an advanced degree. Carol worked with an InfoPLACE librarian who helped her in gathering information from library resources. Carol decided on social work, found she could get good financial aid at Case Western Reserve University's School of Applied Social Sciences, and could "make it" if she went half-time and kept her part time job.

Four years later, the counselor was surprised and delighted to have another appointment with Carol. She wanted to share all of her good news. She was just two months away from receiving her Master's degree, had straight A's, and had received several honors and awards. She was just completing a hospital social work internship at the Cleveland Clinic. Her supervisor there told Carol that her work was outstanding and that she was trying to find or create a permanent position for her. But Carol wasn't taking any chances and wanted the counselor's help with both a resume and targeting other potential employers.

CAREER COUNSELING AT THE LONGVIEW PUBLIC LIBRARY

Career counseling is an integral part of the job and career center program at Longview (WA) Public Library. The job and career center is staffed by a career counselor, Judy Fuller, who had extensive counseling experience at a small liberal arts college prior to creating the program at Longview Public Library. Because Ms. Fuller is also director of special projects and has other duties at the library, much of her time at the job and career center is spent with people who have made appointments to see her. She has approximately 15 counseling appointments per week. Typically she will see a client three times. As an initial part of her work with each client, she conducts an intake interview to determine more about each situation and to determine what is needed. She then works with each client on the specific needs that have been identified. The counseling appointments are frequently information-based, and she helps clients use the library resources. Clients are often referred to other community resources such as the local college's ABE program.

Leslie, a young woman in her early thirties with a degree in sociology, discovered the job and career center when she came to the Longview Public Library to get a book. She was new to the city, unemployed, and feeling lost and con-

> fused. She visited the counselor several times; during this time, the counselor helped her think through options, worked with her on a resume, suggested books for her to read, gave her names of people to contact, and talked with her about interviewing. Leslie found a job after some weeks and was quite satisfied with the assistance she had received.

Provide Support And Reassurance

People who are looking for work or who are changing careers will need moral support along the way. Career center staff have learned to pay close attention to the need for support and encouragement for some people. Change is always difficult, and work is an anchor for many people. A job seeker may become nervous as the job interview approaches. Staff are not afraid to show that they understand the process that the individual is going through.

> A woman looking for a job after a factory closed decided that she wanted to go to college. Although she was excited about her decision, at the same time she was apprehensive about this major life change. She, like many people in this rural area, had not traveled much—even in the area—and the prospect of commuting thirty-five miles to college had been disturbing to her. In addition, she had to overcome her concern that she was too old to go to college. She came to the job and career center to get directions to the college for her admissions interview. The librarian gave her encouragement and guidance on how to approach the admissions interview. As she left, the librarian suggested that she come back and let her know how things turned out.

During a period of loss of self-esteem, some people may need a temporary boost of confidence. As job and career center clientele come to see librarians as trusted professionals, occasionally they may come for additional support. This should be anticipated. Strategies used by librarians to reassure people who need it include being prepared to spend a minute or two with someone who calls to say that she has a job interview and is nervous, and the librarian asking to be told how it turned out. It may mean providing moral support prior to a big interview or reassuring an adult who has decided to enroll in college, but has difficulty believing that she will actually be able to do it. Sometimes more extensive support is needed which will take more time and effort.

> A single parent on welfare had been coming to the center for assistance of one kind or another for about a month when she was observed by a project evaluator. When she first came in she was very angry and vented her anger when she first talked with the job and career center coordinator, "They (DSS) don't think I am really looking for a job." The coordinator got a job history from her and helped her develop two resumes. Later the coordinator said, "She needs a lot of praise. She has no self esteem. I helped her create a "brag file." As a result of working with the job and career center staff, she has developed a goal. She decided to become a legal secretary."

Support and reassurance helps people move to self-sufficiency. However, librarians should seek to empower their clientele—not make them dependent. Make sure you refer those who need more help to counseling services in the community.

Often effective support can come from other job seekers. Support can be facilitated in a workshop setting or by encouraging job and career center clientele to join or form a job support group, often called a job club, that can be run by job seekers. The librarian's role will vary. Librarians can provide a space for regular meetings, help facilitate the organization of the club, bring in speakers, facilitate the meetings, or aid members to become their own facilitator.

This chapter and Chapter 5 have examined a variety of personal assistance strategies designed to increase access to information and to assist in the problem solving process. Librarians also have at their disposal a range of strategies which can be used to instruct their clientele as individuals or in groups. The next chapter examines a group of instructional strategies.

RESOURCES

Benjamin, Alfred. *The Helping Interview*, 3d ed. Boston: Houghton Mifflin, 1981.

Bolles, Richard N. *What color Is Your Parachute? A Practical Manual for Job-Hunters & Career Changers*, 1993 ed. Berkeley, California: Ten Speed Press, 1993.

Dervin, Brenda, and Patricia Dewdney. "Neutral Questioning: A New Approach to the Reference Interview." *RQ* (Summer 1986): 506-513.

Kennedy, Joyce Lain. *Joyce Lain Kennedy's Career Book*, 2nd ed. Lincolnwood, Ill,: VGM Career Horizons, 1993.

Ross, Catherine Sheldrick, and Patricia Dewdney. *Communicating Professionally: A How-To-Do-It Manual for Library Applications*. New York: Neal-Schuman, 1989.

7 STRATEGIES: TO PROVIDE INSTRUCTION AND INSTRUCTIONAL MATERIALS

Instruction is an outgrowth of good use of personal assistance techniques. When librarians raise awareness of the library as a place to get help with the career planning process, when they show through welcoming and the reference interview that librarians are information specialists, they increase the demand for service. As a result of increasing expectations, librarians often start using instructional materials, programming and instruction as a way to respond to this increased demand.

INSTRUCTIONAL STRATEGIES, PART 1: MATERIALS DEVELOPMENT

Librarians may choose to create bibliographies and pathfinders for their career materials. They may develop job notebooks or lists of newspapers and periodicals that contain job listings. Librarians, often in conjunction with other agencies in the community, create pamphlets and booklets on frequently requested topics such as developing an effective resume. These materials, which are either given away or sold at a nominal fee, are heavily used by job center clientele. Although they are time-consuming to develop, they actually may save time by avoiding some repetitive explanations.

Library materials and tools can send a strong message to people looking for job, career, and education information that people at the library understand their needs. Staff developed materials can be a direct response to needs that have been identified through the pressures of daily service

Most materials that librarians develop can be used in two ways as stand-alone materials which can be displayed in the library or in the community and as hand-outs at workshops. Note that give-away materials should be attractive and include library identification and information about how to make contact with the job and career center.

POSSIBLE OBJECTIVES TO GUIDE MATERIALS DEVELOPMENT

Create Materials for Multiple Uses

A bibliography or a guide to resume writing, for example, can be displayed with resource materials to be picked up and used as needed, given to a patron as part of a response to a question about resume writing, or included in the packet given out to participants in a workshop on resume writing. Patrons can take away instructional materials from the library to consult later or use on an ongoing basis. Remember that although self-help materials are important, they are NOT substitutes for the personal assistance provided to job seekers.

Develop Materials which Help People take Advantage of Library Resources

Begin with familiar materials such as bibliographies, pathfinders, pamphlets, and handouts. The following items are typical bibliographies that have been developed by job and career center staff in several libraries. Bibliographies come in a number of forms: bookmarks, flyers, one or two page handouts and booklets even columns in newspapers and library newsletters are frequently developed by librarians to identify the kind of materials and resources which are available for career decision makers. When creating these types of bibliographies, remember that more is not better. Provide a few titles and suggest that to get more suggestions, people should talk with a librarian.

Develop Materials which Help People Understand and Use Library Services

People will not use library services if they are unaware of their existence. Most job center staff develop brochures to explain job and career center services which are quite different than many people expect from a public library. Chapter 2 provides a number of service profiles; a number of them include materials from their own brochures. Most often these brochures include a service mission statement and a description of specific services which are offered.

Develop Materials that Directly Respond to Needs

People who feel that they must change jobs are often stymied and not sure where to turn. Libraries that choose to respond to the needs for assessment and decision-making often also help people who are thinking about a job change. A bibliography may be useful for some people (see Figure 7-1)

Increasingly librarians are developing materials to help people use information as they start their own business. General bibliographies on starting a small business have often been replaced by targeted bibliographies and resource guides (see Figure 7-2).

Provide Materials in Languages Other than English if Appropriate for the Community

In the past two decades more new immigrants have come to our country because the turn of the century. Most of these people have language difficulties for the first few years. Language difficulties often interfere with job seeking. Librarians can help respond to their needs by providing in appropriate languages library guides and other materials to help the job seeker. For example, a Spanish-language pamphlet developed by the New York State Department of Labor is a valuable addition to job center materials in New York State Libraries(see Figure 7-3).

Partnerships with native speakers in the community are an effective way of reaching out. Likewise, employing staff with language facility can assist new immigrants. People in Brooklyn, for example, speak approximately 100 languages, but staff can navigate in about 50 languages. A list of staff with their language facility is kept on file at the library.

Develop Handouts for Often-Requested Help such as Writing a Resume or Steps in the Job Search

The are a number of excellent examples of how librarians have responded to the need for assistance in gaining access to resume writing and interviewing by preparing materials to help people gain additional resume writing and interviewing skills. Frequently these are one to two page handouts or short pamphlets on developing a resume and cover letter or interviewing (see Figure 7-5).

Librarian-developed booklets can present information on library and community resources, as well as agencies and services for special needs. Some guidessuch as the Job-Seeker Survival Kit from Hempstead Public Library which covers resumes, cover letters, interviewing, salary negotiation, resignation, and unemploymentare extensive (see Figure 7-6).

The professionally printed Resume Guide prepared by Cuyahoga County's InfoPLACE staff has been so successful in Cleveland that it is now available for purchase through the Public Library Association (see Figure 7-7).

FIGURE 7-1: Discovering The Hidden Job Market—Flint (MI) Public Library And Career Change Bibliography—Spokane (WA) Public Library

DISCOVERING THE HIDDEN JOB MARKET

A listing from the COPE Center of the Flint Public Library

HIDDEN JOB MARKET RESOURCES

A listing from the COPE Center of the Flint Public Library

COPE 371.43/Co — Cooper, Violet Moreton
How to find those Hidden Jobs. Career Managements Association, 1986.

COPE 650.19/Ja — Jackson, Tom
Guerrilla Tactics in the job market. Bantam Books, 1978

COPE 371.43/Ja — Jackson, Tom
Hidden Job Market: a system to beat the system. New York Times Book Co., 1976

COPE 371.45/Ro — Rogers, Bob
Secrets of the Hidden Job Market. Betterway Pub., 1986

FBI 331.4/We — Welch, Mary Scott
Networking: the great new way for women to get ahead. Harcourt Brace, 1980

BOOKS WITH HIDDEN JOB MARKET CHAPTERS

COPE 371.45/Al — Allen, Jeffrey
Finding the right job at midlife. Simon & Schuster, 1985

FBI 331.2/Ap — Applegath, John
Working free: practical alternatives to the 9 to 5 job. AMA, 1982

COPE 371.43/Az — Azrin, Nathan H.
Finding a job. Ten Speed Press, 1982

COPE 371.43/Ba — Bastress, Frances
The relocating spouse's guide to employment: options and strategies in the U.S. and abroad. Woodley Pub., 1986

COPE 371.43/Be — Bernard, Susan
Job search strategy for college grads. Bob Adams, 1984

COPE 371.43/Bi — Birsner, E. Patricia
Job hunting for the 40+ executive. Facts on File Pub., 1985

COPE 371.45/Ca — Carney, Tom
Job smarts: how to play the career game and win. Facts on File, 1984

COPE 371.44/Ch — Chapman, Elwood N.
I got the job. Crisp Pub., 1988

CAREER CHANGE BIBLIOGRAPHY

EDUCATION/JOB INFORMATION CENTERS

EJIC

INLAND NORTHWEST

SPOKANE PUBLIC LIBRARY

Look under the following subjects to find books and periodicals on career change.

- Age and employment
- Applications for positions
- Career change
- Career development
- Career plateaus
- Competition
- Corporate reorganization
- Executives
- Job hunting
- Job satisfaction
- Job security
- Married people—employment
- Middle managers
- Occupational mobility
- Organizational Change
- Personality and occupation
- Recruiting of executives
- Self-actualization (psychology)
- Success in business
- Veterans
- Vocational guidance
- Vocational interest
- Women executives

FIGURE 7-2: Industry And Marketing Information And Company Information—Schaumburg Township (IL) District Library

Business Information Center

The business collection is the largest reference and circulating book collection in a public library in the suburbs of Chicago. All reference librarians on duty are professionally trained to assist with business questions. They also handle questions on the telephone. The following are a few examples of the type of information frequently requested:

- Basic company information including addresses, officers, products, annual sales, number of employees, and other items.
- Statistics on the manufacture or sales of various items.
- Information on investments, including stock prices.
- Decisions made in specific tax court cases, labor arbitration cases, Supreme Court cases, and others.
- Company information on businesses operating in foreign countries.
- Detailed information on computers, peripherals, and software.
- Advertising rates and circulation statistics for magazines and newspapers.

THE SCHAUMBURG TOWNSHIP DISTRICT LIBRARY maintains an extensive collection of publications to assist the business person in searching for industry information. The following includes selected major sources that are available at the library. For further information and assistance, inquire at the Reference Desk.

Industry Outlooks

STANDARD & POOR'S INDUSTRY SURVEYS — R 332.67 STA
A two-volume examination of the prospects, trends and problems of major domestic industries. "Comparative Company Analysis" sections compare sales, earnings, profit margins and other statistical data on major public companies within selected industries. Published quarterly.

U.S. INDUSTRIAL OUTLOOK — R 330.973 UNI
Economic data and analyses of more than 300 industries. Short-and long-term economic forecasts as well as historical data are included. Published annually.

VALUE LINE INVESTMENT SURVEY — Business Index Table
One of the most popular investment advisory newsletters in the nation. Approximately 1,700 stocks are regularly surveyed. Industry information as well as specifics on companies within each industry are provided. Updated regularly.

THE WALL STREET TRANSCRIPT — Magazine Desk
The best source of investment information from brokerage reports. Each issue also contains an in-depth overview and forecast of a selected industry and a discussion of leading firms in the field.

Statistical Sources

COUNTY BUSINESS PATTERNS — R 339.4 UNI
State-by-state compilation of industry statistics arranged by county. Statistics for the U.S. as a whole are also included. Gives detailed industry breakdowns with total number of employees, first quarter and annual payroll and number of establishments by employee size. Published annually.

CRANDALL'S BUSINESS INDEX — Business Index Table
Another statistical compilation giving current and historical data on economic indicators, industries and business. Statistics frequently presented by month or quarter. Updated monthly.

State Manufacturing Directories

The Library has manufacturing directories covering all the states, as well as service (non-manufacturing) directories for Illinois and a few other states. All state manufacturing directories are located at R670.025, except those for Illinois which are located on the Business Index Table. The state manufacturing directories differ in coverage but generally include company address, telephone number, products, number of employees and executives' names. Alphabetic, geographic and product indexes are often included.

For the state of Illinois the Library owns:

ILLINOIS MANUFACTURERS DIRECTORY – Business Index Table

HARRIS ILLINOIS INDUSTRIAL DIRECTORY – Business Index Table

CONTACTS INFLUENTIAL (Central Chicago, Metropolitan North, South and West) – Reference Desk

ILLINOIS SERVICES DIRECTORY – Business Index Table

ILLINOIS BUSINESS DIRECTORY – Business Index Table

FIRST CHICAGO GUIDE (formerly **BECKER GUIDE**) – Reference Desk

METROPOLITAN CHICAGO MAJOR EMPLOYERS – Business Index Table

LOCAL TELEPHONE BOOKS (The Library holds all the telephone directories for Illinois and New York State, as well as telephone directories for most major U.S. cities.) – Periodicals Desk

Don't Forget That

DON'T FORGET THAT COMPANY INFORMATION may be also be available through the Library's online database searching. Please visit the Reference Desk and discuss the possibility of having an online search conducted. A search of $30 or less per month is available free to Schaumburg Township Public Library card holders.

For Additional Help

FOR ADDITIONAL HELP IN LOCATING company information or other reference needs inquire at the Reference Desk.

FIGURE 7-3: Como Prepararse Para Entrevistas De Empleo

PREPARESE

Antes de comenzar a trabajar usted tendrá una entrevista. La entrevista es probablemente el paso más importante para obtener un trabajo. Para ayudarle, este folleto tiene algunas recomendaciones que le preparan para ese paso decisivo en su futuro.

CONOZCASE

¿Cúales son sus intereses y calificaciones? Esté preparado para hablar de sus intereses y calificaciones en una forma breve, inteligente y clara durante la entrevista. Su futuro empleador querrá saber esta información.

CONOZCA ALGO DE LA COMPANIA

Antes de hacer una cita para una entrevista de trabajo, averigüe todo lo que pueda acerca de la compañía. Mientras más familiarizado esté con la compañía, mejor podrá ofrecer sus servicios a su futuro empleador.

TOME EN CUENTA SU APARIENCIA PERSONAL

Antes de salir para la entrevista asegúrese que está limpio, bien peinado y los zapatos lustrados. No use maquillaje exagerado, joyas que llamen la atención o demasiado perfume. Vístase apropiadamente: dé la impresión que está listo para trabajar.

VAYA SOLO A LA ENTREVISTA

El empleador está interesado en usted: en la forma en que usted se presenta. No le interesa saber lo que sus familiares o amigos opinan de sus calificaciones. Así que vaya solo a la entrevista y el empleador decidirá si usted califica.

LLEGUE TEMPRANO

Llegue a la entrevista algunos minutos antes de la hora indicada. Preséntese en una forma directa. Déjele saber a la recepcionista quién es usted y a quién viene a ver.

ESTE ALERTA DURANTE LA ENTREVISTA

Siéntese derecho, mire al entrevistador a los ojos y manténgase alerta durante la entrevista. Manténgase calmado y conteste las preguntas de su posible empleador en una manera formal.

PIENSE ANTES DE CONTESTAR

Piense antes de contestar las preguntas. Sea educado, preciso, honesto y franco. El empleador está especialmente interesado en la experiencia y adiestramiento que lo califican para el empleo. Prepárese a contestar preguntas como las siguientes:

- ¿En qué clase de empleos ha trabajado?
- ¿Cómo hacia el trabajo?
- ¿Usaba algún tipo de herramientas o equipo especial?
- ¿Cuánto ganaba?
- ¿Ha trabajado de voluntario alguna vez: trabajó sin paga, en una iglesía, escuela o en casa?
- ¿Tiene algún pasatiempo que le pueda ayudar en su trabajo?

LLEVE LA HOJA DE DATOS

Es muy importante tener una lista indicando sus trabajos anteriores, fechas de empleo, salarios y las razones por las cuales dejó el trabajo. Usted puede obtener un formulario preparado por la oficina de servicios de empleos con ese propósito. Sea breve y preciso al preparar el formulario. Algunos empleos requieren la preparación de un resumé formal. Estos son algunos de los puntos que debe incluir en la hoja de datos

- Nombre y dirección de sus empleos anteriores.
- Fechas de empleo.
- Referencias por lo menos de dos personas que lo conozcan.
- Nombre y dirección de las escuelas a las cuales asistió y el tipo de diploma o certificado que recibió.
- Incluya los cursos que puedan estar relacionados con el trabajo.
- Actividades escolares en las cuales usted participó.
- Junto con la hoja de datos lleve los papeles importantes tales como: Prueba de edad, tarjeta de inscripción del servicio militar, permiso de trabajo, tarjeta del seguro social, certificado de salud, licencia de manejar, etc. Si usted es veterano o es miembro de alguna unión, lleve los papeles de dimisión de las fuerzas armadas (DD214) o la tarjeta de identificación de la unión.

SEA AMABLE

Sea diplomático, educado y amable. Escuche todo lo que su posible empleador tenga que decir. No discuta. Conteste todas las preguntas en una forma precisa y con tacto.

DEJE SUS PROBLEMAS EN SU CASA

No le cuente sus problemas al empleador; a él no le interesan sus problemas personales o familiares. El sólo está interesado en usted como posible empleado.

BUSQUE CONSEJOS

Cuando haya terminado la entrevista, aún cuando usted cree que no ha obtenido el empleo, sea cortés y amigable. Busque la ayuda del empleador, pregunte sobre otros empleos que pudieran surgir en un futuro. Dé una buena impresión y puede ser que lo vuelvan a llamar.

AYUDA DEL DEPARTAMENTO DE TRABAJO

La oficina de Servicios de Empleo del Departamento de Trabajo del Estado de Nueva York está preparado para ayudarle con:

- Entrevistas de trabajo
- Asesoría vocacional
- Exámenes vocacionales
- El mejoramiento de sus oportunidades de conseguir un empleo.

NEW YORK LABOR Helping NY work

P340 (5-91)S

COMO
PREPARARSE
PARA
ENTREVISTAS DE EMPLEO

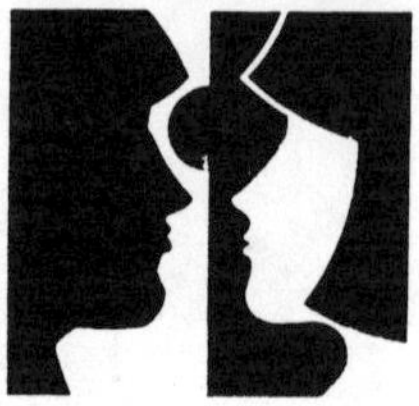

STATE OF NEW YORK
Mario M. Cuomo, Governor

DEPARTMENT OF LABOR
Thomas F. Hartnett, Commissioner

FIGURE 7-4: Korean Parent Workshop—Los Angeles (CA) Public Library

Los Angeles Public Library

Los Angeles Public Library

PARTNERSHIPS FOR CHANGE

Is a program of the California State Library and supported by the Library Services and Construction Act

PRESENTS

KOREAN PARENT WORKSHOP

한국 학부형을 위한 연수회

대학 진학 준비와 안내 ★

College Preparation and Information

시일: MAY 10, 1991
5월10일, 금요일 오후 7~9 시

강사: Suzie K. Oh 와 Jung Hae Kim
(교육전문가) (라성통합교육국 장학사)

★ 부모들이 알아두어야 할 필수사항,
대학 진학을 위한 각종시험,
자녀들이 학교때준비해야할일들
적성에 맞는 대학선택요령

장소: 피오 피고 도서관

PIO PICO BRANCH
Los Angeles Public Library
2631 W. Olympic Blvd.

For more information, call (213) 381-1453

MR. JAE MIN ROH, LIBRARIAN

Los Angeles Public Library

FIGURE 7-5: An Amalgam Of Resume Writing Handouts Developed By Three Different Library Systems

FIGURE 7-6: Job-Seeker Survival Kit—Hempstead (NY) Public Library

FIGURE 7-7: The Resume Guide—Cuyahoga County (OH) Public Library

The Resume Guide

By the InfoPLACE Counseling Staff

CUYAHOGA COUNTY PUBLIC LIBRARY
InfoPLACE
Your place for career information

Cuyahoga County Public Library

TABLE OF CONTENTS

Many librarians prepare materials which cover several job and career-related needs at the same time. Materials most frequently prepared include bibliographies, directories, and guides that include tips on several aspects of the process.

Develop Worksheets and Other Self-Help Tools to Assist Job and Career Center Patrons

Librarians also develop worksheets (such as those found in What Color is Your Parachute) for use in career decision workshops or as self-help tools. These can be used either as separate hand-out sheets or put together with other materials into booklet form. Cuyahoga County Public Library's InfoPLACE's Sourcebook for Career Planning and Job Search is given free to individuals in consultation sessions and workshops and is available in large quantities for distribution at branch libraries (see Figure 7-8).

Provide Guides to Financial Aid Information and Educational Resources

Some of the questions most frequently asked by adults and students in libraries are for information about colleges, universities, and other educational and training opportunities. Librarians anticipate these requests by preparing bibliographies and guides to educational resources in the library and in the community, by developing financial aid resource guides and directories (see Figure 7-9).

INSTRUCTIONAL STRATEGIES, PART 2: INSTRUCTION, PROGRAMMING, AND WORKSHOPS

As librarians develop need-centered services, they often develop instructional programs that help people learn how to do something they haven't done before, (such as writing a resume or researching an employer); or learn how to do something better (such as interviewing). Testimonial letters from individuals who have attended skill building workshopsfor example, those on resume writing and job interviewing skills, or basic reading, show what a difference these programs make in the life of an individual

FIGURE 7-8: Sourcebook—Cuyahoga County (OH) Public Library

The Sourcebook

for Career Planning and Job Search

CUYAHOGA COUNTY PUBLIC LIBRARY
InfoPLACE
Your place for career information

Cuyahoga County Public Library

ASSESS YOURSELF: WHO AM I?

VALUES

Defining your values, both life values and work values, is an important element of the career decision-making process. Remember the Socratic adage, "Know Thyself." Analyzing your values is a key to self-knowledge. Choosing a career or job consistent with your values gives you meaning, commitment and an internal sense of peace.

LIFE VALUES

First of all, what values are most important in your overall vision of life? How would you prioritize career against other life values? Is a career of top priority or is it one element of a balanced life where family, community service and personal time are of equal or greater priority? Career counselors define this concept as Career Saliency — the relative importance of a career to your overall life plan.

JOB____LIFE WORK
Work = In the way of life   Work = A way of life

How would you define work? Plot yourself on the above graph.

WORK VALUES

Are you seeking a field where the "bottom line" is profit and everything else is secondary? Or are you the type of person motivated by altruism — doing something for society, being more humanitarian than materialistic? Or are you somewhere in between? Neither of these alternatives is right or wrong per se — both ask you to define priorities based on your work values. The InfoPLACE career counselors have developed a list of 18 work values:

How would you rank these values in order of importance from 1-18?

_____ Clearly defined tasks and expectations
_____ High level of autonomy/independence
_____ Lots of variety on the job
_____ Excellent salary and benefits
_____ Work which contributes to humanity
_____ Work which permits me to make beautiful things and contribute beauty
_____ Opportunity for advancement
_____ Prestige/status
_____ Work which is intellectually challenging
_____ Producing a tangible product or visible result
_____ Job security
_____ Co-workers with mutual interests or shared values
_____ Opportunity to develop new skills on the job
_____ Chance to use creativity
_____ Working as a part of a team
_____ Excellent relationship with boss
_____ Position of authority/leadership/supervision
_____ Time flexibility/set your own hours

Assessing your life and work values helps you determine what you care about and is an essential part of determining your vision of a satisfying career. Ideally, the career or job you choose should be consistent with these values.

SKILLS

Skills make the world go round. Skill assessment enables you to gain a sense of what you can do and have done. Coupled with assessing your interests and values it can lead you toward defining what you want to do.

Can you build, maintain and repair things? Conduct research? Write budgets? Perform on stage or play a musical instrument? Teach, persuade, and motivate people, individually or in groups? Keep the world glued together with your typing, filing, office management skills?

The InfoPLACE Career Decision Workshop delves into assessing and analyzing three types of skills:

- **Technical/Special Knowledge skills** — Skills related to mastering a particular body of knowledge in a specific type of work, profession or leisure activity
- **Functional/Transferable skills** — Skills gained from any specific experience which can be transferred from one field, profession or occupation to another
- **Self Management skills** — Skills that are personal qualities (i.e. flexibility, cost-consciousness) which describe your personal work style

The U.S. Department of Labor has developed a useful 3-factor breakdown of the world at work to aid you in exploring your skills. Would you prefer working with DATA, for example — analyzing quantitative material, doing research and developing complex theories; or would you prefer working with PEOPLE — coaching, leading, persuading, as part of a team or as a manager; or perhaps working with THINGS — repairing machinery, building houses, being a skilled tradesman as a carpenter, electrician or machinist.

InfoPLACE and others have suggested adding a fourth category to the U.S. Department categories. Working with IDEAS — are you skilled at visualizing? Composing? Creating? Can you have an impact on data, people, things by using your ideas to solve social problems, create industrial designs, devise new processes and systems, weave new and complex opinions and theories?

Work values, life values, skills — all these factors deal with you as a complex human being. The InfoPLACE Career Decision Workshops provide a detailed in-depth assessment of these areas through the use of individual exercises, group interaction, and standardized inventories of vocational interests and personalities.

FIGURE 7-9: Financial Aid Resources—Flint (MI) Public Library

FINANCIAL AID RESOURCES

A compilation of Grants, Scholarships and Awards available to residents of Genesee, Lapeer and Shiawassee Counties.

Flint Public Library

A Service of the Flint Board of Education
Flint, Michigan 48502

Programming involves a variety of group activities which are not really instructional. Programming is closely associated with instruction. It may include sponsoring a job club which permits clients who are involved in workshops to have the opportunity to informally solve problems jointly or with the assistance of a career counselor. Programming may also involve sponsoring or participating in exhibitions or conferences, such as a small business fair. Outreach and marketing are often associated with programming.

Programs include workshops as well as a variety of activities that provide valuable assistance to job seekers. Programming requires the availability of meeting space. Programs are often developed in cooperation with other community agencies. Programs such as job fairs and job clubs are particularly common. Job fairs bring together a number of area employers to show what kinds of opportunities are available. Job clubs bring together individuals who are looking for work to talk with each other, and often a counselor as well, about job-seeking strategies and to provide mutual support (see Figure 7-10).

Librarians want their patrons to make the best use of library resources. Instruction is a strategy which helps library users learn to exploit resources more effectively, or use materials that they don't understand. If there is interactive career assessment software, instruction is almost invariably needed to get people started, even on the most user-friendly programs.

Librarians who provide instruction should be sensitive to the needs of the adult learner, particularly adults who lack basic skills or who are culturally different than the librarian. Those who develop workshops should be able to speak in front of groups. They should have the ability to identify other professionals in the community who can contribute to the workshops. Those who use audiovisual materials or computers in their workshops should learn to be at least amateur troubleshooters.

Job and career center sponsored workshops are staffed either by library staff or by staff from agencies in the community. At most workshops job and career center staff don't do all or even most of the speaking. They often use resource people from the agencies that are also used as key referrals. Staff who have not developed workshops before may wish to read a good book which includes workshop planning such as one of the following authors: Conroy, O'Donnell, Warncke, or Ross and Dewdney.

FIGURE 7-10: Attention Job Hunters! Job Club—Hempstead (NY) Public Library

Attention Job Hunters!

The Job Information Center at Hempstead Public Library announces October and November meetings of the JOB CLUB

October 29: Job Interviewing Part I -
Refining Your Job Interviewing Skills

November 5: Job Interviewing Part II -
Dressing for the Job Interview

November 12 & 19: Job Interviewing Part III/IV -
Put Your Interviewing Skills to the Test (See Yourself on Video)

Meetings begin at 6:30 PM
Please call or visit to register:
481-6990; 115 Nichols Ct., Hempstead, NY

Supported by Federal Library Services and Construction Act, Title I funds, granted by the State Library of New York to Nassau Library System

POSSIBLE INSTRUCTION OBJECTIVES AND ACTIVITIES

Develop Skills Needed to Plan and Implement Need-Based Programs

As soon as the word gets out that the library provides effective services for the job seeker and the career changer, business becomes so brisk that group instruction follows fairly quickly as an effective way to respond to the need. In many libraries, workshops which can handle a dozen people have replaced individual instruction sessions. Librarians who use group instruction have found that it is a cost-effective way of reaching a number of people at once. The number and kind of programs staff choose to develop will depend on the needs of the community. Some libraries run weekly programs on commonly needed topics (such as resume writing). Some libraries have no group instruction programs at all.

Develop Need-Based Instruction

Education and training needs vary with the individual. People may need to develop basic functional literacy skills. They may need to review and improve math or science skills. Often these are taught on a one-to-one basis, frequently involving a tutor. Literacy programs are extremely valuable because they help people gain skills that will prepare them for more meaningful employment.

Provide Instruction for Those Who Need Extra Help

Librarians may assist with special skills development, such as computer literacy. Frequently, the public library is the first opportunity for individuals to get hands-on experience with a computer. Offering special computer workshops may expand those opportunities for a wider range of people (see Figure 7-11).

Librarians responding to the need for support and coping assistance have developed materials and programs on selected WORKPLACE problems. Job clubs provide another kind of support system for people in the process of job hunting. They are often very effective because they bring together people in similar situations who can support each other.

Figure 7-12, "Follow the Road to Success," was prepared by the staff at the Clinton-Essex-Franklin job and career center for prerelease inmates who are in the seven area state correctional facilities. It contains a variety of job-seeking information including a directory of resources, discussion of the job market, the job search process, resume writing, filling out applications, and job interviewing.

FIGURE 7-11: Become Computer Literate—Buffalo & Erie County (NY) Public Library

BECOME COMPUTER LITERATE

Sign up now for the APPLE II COURSES OF YOUR CHOICE:

BASIC:
A. LITERACY
B. HANDS - ON
Apple IIe Demo Disk
AppleWorks Demo Disk

ELEMENTARY APPLEWORKS: (User needs own 5.25 disk)
1. Database
2. WordProcessing
3. Spreadsheet

ELEMENTARY DESKTOP PUBLISHING:
4. Print Shop
5. Publish It! 3

ADVANCED APPLEWORKS:
6. Timeout Modules
7. Mail Merge
8. Timeout Super Fonts

All classes are open to the public at no cost, **EVERY THURSDAY EVENING.**

Basic computer classes are conducted every Thurs. between 6 - 7 p.m.

An Elementary & Advanced subject is conducted between 7:00 - 8:00 P.M.

Taught by a member of the Apple Byters Corps Inc.
Buffalo State College

PETER C. CORNELL
LIFELONG LEARNING CENTER
BUFFALO & ERIE COUNTY PUBLIC LIBRARY
LAFAYETTE SQUARE, BUFFALO, N.Y. 14203

Funded in part by an LSCA Title I Grant

FIGURE 7-12: "Follow The Road to Success"—Clinton-Essex-Franklin (NY) Library System

Prepared by the
Job & Education Information Center
of the
Clinton-Essex-Franklin Library System

Audio and videotapes can be especially valuable for people who have trouble with the written word. Often videotapes cover several different aspects of the job process in one tape. Librarians have developed lists of job and career videos available at the library (see Figure 7-13). Some videos are targeted for people with specific needs, such as those who have been on welfare or who have recently lost a job.

Workshops frequently are developed to respond to several different needs at the same time. For example, InfoPLACE's Job Search Process Workshop covers the hidden job market, interviewing skills, researching potential employers, resume writing, and library resources. It is held over a period of weeks. Likewise, Chester County's "Need a Job?" series is held over four week period. To assure continued attendance from people who are often not motivated to complete a task, a nominal fee is assessed and refunded upon completion of the workshop (see Figure 7-14).

Teach Individuals and Groups How To Use Resources more Effectively

Write instructions for using sources or computer software. Give people advice on using resources. Help people feel comfortable using difficult to use resources.

Many librarians develop tools to explain how to use such career assessment software as DISCOVER and SIGI Plus. These computer programs have modules that help people explore their own interests, abilities, and values, and match them to career options. (Other less expensive software may provide information about career options, but most often lacks an assessment component). Figure 7-15 provides detail about the nine modules, including "Learning About Yourself," which are included in DISCOVER.

Hold Workshops that will Help People Improve Their Knowledge of a Process or Gain Needed Skills

Most job and career center staff hold workshops on topics like as resume writing and interviewing skills. Typical topics include workshops on:

- researching employers and the job search process;
- developing an effective resume;
- effective job interviewing;
- how to locate job openings;
- marketing yourself in a competitive job market;

FIGURE 7-13: Videocassette Collection—Hempstead (NY) Public Library

Videocassette Collection

JOB AND EDUCATION INFORMATION CENTER

HEMPSTEAD PUBLIC LIBRARY

115 Nichols Court
Hempstead N.Y. 11550
(516) 481-6990

Videocassette Collection
of the
Job & Education Information Center

(An annotated guide compiled by Caren Cramer)

Welcome to the videocassette collection of the Job and Education Information Center at the Hempstead Public Library. Whether you are a job-seeker, a student, a program director, or an individual who is investigating career and/or business opportunities, this collection can serve as a valuable resource for you. The videocassettes are available for loan to registered videocassette borrowers of the Hempstead Public Library and to member libraries for adult programs. For your convenience, this bibliography is arranged into the following subject areas:

Developing Job Search Skills - This subject area includes information about resume writing, interviewing, job search skills, and on-the-job skills.

Finding Out About Careers - These videocassettes investigate career fields and offer pertinent information about a variety of careers.

Increasing Your Business Know-How - This subject area includes information about how to start a business as well as how to operate more effectively in an already existing business.

Preparing For College - In this section, students preparing for the college selection process will find college tours, financial aid guidance, and "how to apply" information.

Improving Your Test Scores - These videocassettes cover a number of standardized tests and test-taking strategies for high school, undergraduate, graduate, and professional study.

With special thanks to the staff of the Job and Education Information Center for selection and acquisition of the collection and for the preparation of this guide. September, 1990.

Supported by Federal Library Services and Construction Act, Title 1 funds, granted by the State Library of New York to Nassau Library System.

FIGURE 7-14: Need A Job?—Chester County (PA) Library

Come to a workshop at the

Phoenixville Public Library

LEARN HOW TO:

- **Transfer Job Skills**
- **Write A Resume**
- **Interview Better**

Presenter: Samuel Rocray

Saturday, October 1	9:00-12:00	- Personal Assessment
Saturday, October 8	9:00-12:00	- Resumes: Part I
Saturday, October 15	9:00-12:00	- Resumes: Part II
Saturday, October 22	9:00-12:00	- Interviewing

This four part workshop is limited to 20 participants
A $5.00 refundable fee is required and will be returned to those who complete all 4 sessions.

This is a program of **Workplace**
a service of the Chester County Library

Please fill out this form and return to: **CHESTER COUNTY LIBRARY, 400 EXTON SQUARE PARKWAY, EXTON, PA 19341, ATTN: WORKPLACE.** Make $5.00 check payable to the **CHESTER COUNTY LIBRARY.** I understand this fee will be returned when I complete all 4 sessions.

NAME____

ADDRESS______________________________________

PHONE__________________ Position currently held__________

Position desired__________________

Workplace is a grant administered by the State Library of Pennsylvania through the Library Development Division with funds provided by the W.K. Kellogg Foundation

FIGURE 7-15: DISCOVER—Camden County (NJ) Library

DISCOVER

Unlock the secrets of ...

- Career Exploration
- The World of Work
- Your Potential

with this eye-opening new way to chart your future.

Job & Career Information Center
Camden County Library
Laurel Road
Voorhees, New Jersey 08043
(609) 772-1636

What is DISCOVER?

DISCOVER is an easy-to-use, computer-based career planning program that will provide you with information about yourself, occupations, schools and financial aid. It will help you use this information to make decisions about your future.

With DISCOVER, you are in control. Ask us how you can benefit.

Module 1: Beginning the Career Journey

If you are just beginning to explore, or you want to find out where you are in the process of career planning, Module 1 is a good place to start. In this module you can complete the Career Journey Inventory (CJI) to assess your personal level of career development at the computer, or you may choose to enter your results from having taken it in the Career Planning Workbook. Based on this inventory, the system suggests modules for your use.

Module 2: Learning About the World of Work

This part of **DISCOVER** introduces you to the World-of-Work Map, an easy way to organize the approximately 13,000 occupations in the United States. If you have studied this map before, you can take the short review option. Module 2 also allows you to explore occupations and/or programs of study based upon your choice of World-of-Work regions, families, or clusters.

Module 3: Learning About Yourself

In this part of **DISCOVER**, you may learn more about yourself by completing inventories of interests, abilities, values, or experiences at the computer, or by entering scores from having taken these in the Career Planning Workbook. You may also enter the results of inventories and tests you have taken in print form - namely, the Self Directed Search (SDS), Strong-Campbell (SCII), the Kuder, Career Decision Making System (CDM), the Differential Aptitude Tests (DAT), the Career Assessment Inventory (CAI), the Ohio Vocational Interest Survey (OVIS), and others. Any combination of these activities gives you the information about yourself which you need in order to go on to Module 4.

Module 4: Finding Occupations

Once you have learned more about yourself and where you fit on the World-of-Work Map, this module helps you find occupations which you should seriously explore. You choose one of five levels of education so that the list provided for you is realistic. You may also ask the computer why some occupations you thought were good ones do not show up on your list. In addition to getting a list of occupations related to your interests, abilities, values, and/or experiences, you may also search for occupations by specific job characteristics or by program of study (High School version only).

Module 5: Learning About Occupations

This module provides detailed information about more than 450 occupations, including those on your personal list. If you do not have a list from Module 4, you may enter numbers of occupations from this Guide (see Appendix A). For each occupation you research, you may select up to 15 topics for further information, including work tasks, ways to get training, salary range, employment outlook, and where to get more information. You may also narrow your list of occupations to a manageable number. You leave this module with ten or fewer top-priority occupations.

Module 6: Making Educational Choices

This module helps you move farther along in your career journey by helping you choose a path of training for your future occupation. It also displays majors or programs of study related to your top priority occupations.

Module 7: Planning Next Steps

Once you have specific occupations in mind and have selected a path of training and a major, you are ready to plan your next steps. This module helps you

- find and get detailed information about two-and-four-year colleges, graduate schools, and military programs
- identify sources of financial aid
- learn about job-seeking skills.

You use the computer as a powerful tool to combine many characteristics you want in a school, search a national data file, and come up with a list. You can then get extensive information about each school. If you need financial assistance, you can learn about national financial aid programs and complete a form to calculate your "unmet need" for a year of schooling. You may use another part of this module to improve your job-seeking skills and organize your thinking about the kind of job you want. You can create a cover letter, resume, or complete a job application.

Module 8: Planning Your Career

You are aware that your life contains a varied and changing combination of roles. This module gives you a new definition of "career" that includes the roles you play every day. In planning your career, you are able to "draw" your present "Career Rainbow", think about your future and the roles you would like to play, and plan action steps toward your future career.

Module 9: Making Transitions

This module helps you understand what a transition is, see your life and career as a series of transitions, determine the "temperature" of a transition, and learn how to weather a transition with a minimum amount of stress. To measure the "temperature" of a transition, you enter a personal one that you may be experiencing or anticipating, and you respond to 18 questions about it. If its "temperature" is high, you learn how to reduce the temperature of the transition and plan meaningful action steps.

- civil service jobs and how to get them;
- opportunities for self employment;
- the local labor market; entrepreneurship; computer basics workshops, or
- how to use the library's resources for a job search.

They may also provide basic skills instruction for job seekers. Job center staff may, in conjunction with a literacy program provide job related literacy skills and preparation for the GED.

The following examples are of skill-building workshops given or hosted by public library staff:

Career Opportunities Workshops: Workshops and job fairs can introduce people to a wide range of career opportunities (see Figure 7-16).

Career Decision Workshops: Librarians in New York (and a number of other locations) have, for many years, developed materials and planned workshops and programs designed to help people with the career decision making process. Often these programs come in a series and are held over a period of several weeks. For example, flyers such as the one from the Hempstead (NY) Public Library describes library career decision workshops (see Figure 7-17).

InfoPLACE staff have developed a Career Decision Workshop which includes: self assessment, goal setting, researching occupations, library resources, and career planning tips. Each year InfoPLACE offers 25 six-hour Career Decision Workshops and 25 six-hour Job Search Workshops. They are rotated among the 21 branches and regionals which have adequate meeting rooms.

Resume Writing Workshops: Westchester County New York and many other libraries respond to frequent requests for help with resume writing and interviewing with regular workshops on these topics-sometimes as often as once a week. A resume writing workshop might includes topics like alternative resume styles, developing your own resume, and resume critiquing. Interviewing workshops focus on preparing for the job interview, the kinds of questions frequently asked, how to respond to questions, and overcoming common errors in the job interview. These workshops often include role-playing exercises and videotaping so that participants can see themselves in action (see Figure 7-18).

FIGURE 7-16: Careers In The Health Care Industry And Careers In The Computer Industry—Hempstead (NY) Public Library

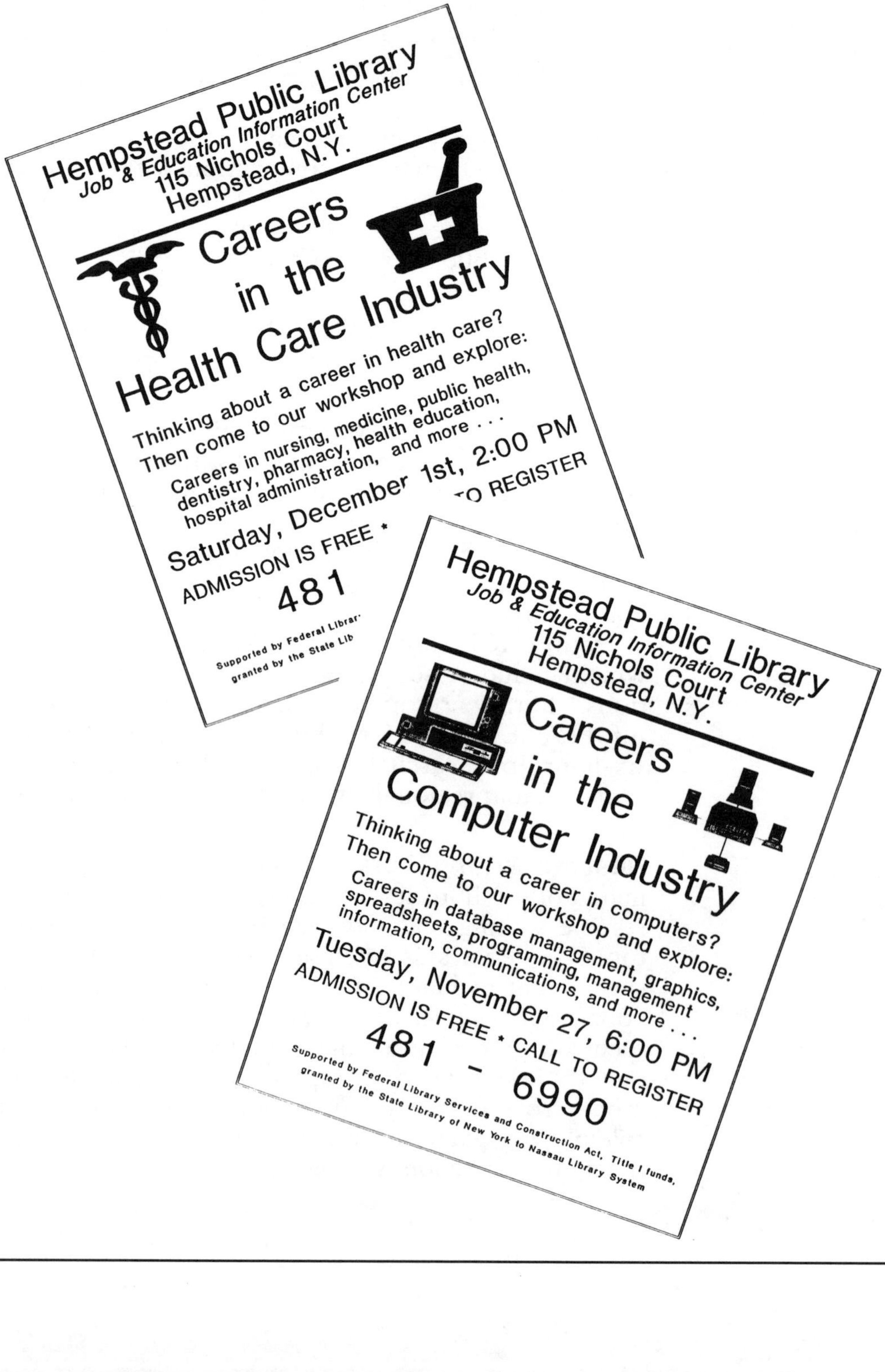

FIGURE 7-17: Career Planning Workshop—Hempstead (NY) Public Library

Hempstead Public Library

Job & Education Information Center

115 Nichols Court
Hempstead, N.Y.

Career Planning Workshop

- Prepare for Job Searching in 1991
- Investigate career development resources
- Develop your personal marketing strategy
- Explore job trends for OPTIMAL PLANNING

Thursday, January 17, 6:00 PM

ADMISSION IS FREE * CALL TO REGISTER

481 - 6990

Supported by Federal Library Services and Construction Act, Title I funds, granted by the State Library of New York to Nassau Library System

FIGURE 7-18: The Job Hunt—Westchester (NY) Library System

WEBS

Career & Educational
Counseling Service

THE JOB HUNT

- **Locate job openings**
- **Market yourself effectively**
- **Write a dynamite resume**
- **Prepare for job interviews**

A free 2-session workshop at the following sites:

Yonkers Public Library (Grinton I. Will Branch) Thursday July 20 and 27 7:00–9:00 p.m.

or

Mt. Kisco Public Library Thursday August 3 and 10 7:00–9:00 p.m.

Call WEBS at 592-8214 to register. Limited to 25 participants.

A SERVICE OF THE
WESTCHESTER LIBRARY SYSTEM

WEBS is one of several EICs
(Education Information Centers)
in New York State.

Self-Assessment Workshops: Workshops on self assessment are a regular part of the programs of some job and career centers. They are often a part of programs on career decision making.

Librarians have developed workshops, often in collaboration with other groups such as SCORE, Chamber of Commerce, etc., on topics like starting a business or developing a business plan.

Workshops sponsored by the library, often in conjunction with employers or other service agencies, are an effective way of providing job-seeking skills and information (see Figure 7-19). Cuyahoga County's InfoPLACE offers a Job Search Process Workshop that includes: the hidden job market, interviewing skills, researching potential employers, resume writing, and library resources.

Help People Improve Their Knowledge of a Process, or Gain Needed Skills on a One-to-One Basis

Any activity that is suitable for a workshop is also suitable for individual instruction. Start slowly by working with individuals on resumes, interviewing, etc. Many job and career center staff set aside certain times each week to critique resumesoften by using SCORE or other volunteers (see Figure 7-20).

RESOURCES

Brottman, May and Mary Loe. *LIRT Library Instruction Handbook*. Littleton, CO: Libraries Unlimited, 1990.

Conroy, Barbara. *Library Staff Development and Continuing Education: Principles and Practices*. Littleton, CO: Libraries Unlimited, 1978.

Crawford, Walt. *Desktop Publishing for Librarians*. Boston: G.K. Hall & Co., 1990.

O'Donnell, Peggy. *Public Library Development Program Manual for Trainers*. Chicago: American Library Association, 1988.

Ross, Catherine Sheldrick and Patricia Dewdney. *Communicating Professionally: A How-To-Do-It Manual for Library Applications*. New York: Neal-Schuman, 1989.

Warncke, Ruth. *Planning Library Workshops and Institutes*. Chicago: American Library Association, 1976.

FIGURE 7-19: Job & Career Workshops—Schenectady County (NY) Public Library

JOB and CAREER WORKSHOPS

Pre-registration required for all of the following due to limited space. Held in the Board Room at the Central library. No charge. Call 382-3500 or stop at the Central library to register.

Tuesdays March 6, 13,20,27 6:45-8:45 p.m. — Job Search Skills and Support Group for Hospital and Health Care Workers-a four part series.

Tuesdays April 24 May 1,8,15 6:45-8:45 p.m. — Job Search Skills and Support Group for Retail, Clerical and Office workers-a four part series.

Each of the above workshops will cover skills assessment, resume preparation, networking and interviewing.
Leader: Art Edelstein, career consultant.

April 4 9:15-4 p.m. April 5 9:15-12 repeated May 9 9:15-4 p.m. May 10 9:15-12 — Job Hunting. Two day session focusing on marketing yourself, locating unadvertised jobs, resume preparation and interviewing. *Leader*: Barry Schwartzberg, N.Y. State Department of Labor Job Service.

Wednesday April 11 9:30-11:30 a.m. repeated at 7:00-9:00 p.m. — What Can I Do Anyway? A two hour session designed to help you identify your marketable skills. *Leader*: Phyllis Ochs, career librarian.

Thursdays May 24,31 June 7 9:30-11:30 a.m. — Returning to Work After a Time Out - a three part career/job search workshop for women. Emphasis will be on career selection and marketing yourself during the job hunt. *Leader*: Adrienne Rockwood, career counselor.

LIFE SKILLS WORKSHOPS

Monday March 5 6:00-9:00 p.m. — Time Management and Personal Goal Setting. A workshop designed to help you take control of each day of your life. Pre-registration necessary. Call 382-3500 or register in person at the Central library. *Leader*: John Christman, training specialist.

Saturdays March 10 10 a.m.-12 noon and March 17 10 a.m.-12 noon Attend either or both. — Capturing Life Experiences. A journal writing workshop to help you record the dreams, memories and dialogues of your life. Teens, adults, individuals and families are invited to attend. No pre-registration necessary. Sponsored by the Friends of the Library. *Leader*: Nancy Thornton, training specialist.

FRIDAYS AT NOON

A series of free videocassette and filmstrip programs held in the central library's McChesney Room. No registration required. Attend one or all. Bring a brown bag lunch if you wish.

Friday March 9 12:15-12:45 p.m. — How to Prepare for a Civil Service Exam-Part I. Shown on our large video screen.

Friday March 16 12:15-12:45 p.m. — How to Prepare for a Civil Service Exam-Part II. Taking an oral exam.

Friday March 23 12:15-12:45 p.m. — Career Planning-It's Your Choice. A career planning, decision-making model is presented by two counselors from the University of Akron.

Friday March 30 12:15-12:45 p.m. — Where the Jobs Are. Helpful tips on planning for the future and spotting tomorrow's job trends.

Friday April 6 12:15-12:45 p.m. — Hidden Jobs. 80% of the jobs open are never advertised. Noted author Tom Jackson tells how to find out about them.

Friday April 13 12:15-12:45 p.m. — Job Hunting. Presents techniques and resources for getting a good job.

Friday April 20 12:15-12:45 p.m. — Communication: The Basic Job Skill. Deals with the art of communication (listening, asking questions, body language, telephone skills) as it applies to job success.

ADVANCE YOUR CAREER

SPRING PROGRAM CALENDAR

Educational and Job Information Center
Schenectady County Public Library
Liberty & Clinton Streets
Schenectady, N.Y. 12305
382-3500

FIGURE 7-20: Need Help In Your Job Search? Carnegie Library Of Pittsburgh (PA) And Develop A Winning ResumeWestchester (NY) Library System And Resume Critiquing & Printing Service—Chester County (PA) Library

8 STRATEGIES DESIGNED TO ASSESS THE COMMUNITY, CREATE LINKS, AND MAKE REFERRALS

When planning a job and career center, librarians frequently examine demographic data to identify the educational level or minority populations. A 1990 Gallup study showed that minorities and people with low education levels had more problems getting information about jobs and careers than other people. Planners also look for special need populations such as large numbers of people in the community who have trouble speaking and working in English, a low literacy rate, or a large number of single parents in the community. Most studies show that many single mothers are engaged in an economic struggle.

Linking and referral are essential strategies. They let clientele know that the library does not work in isolation. Librarians alone are not able to meet the needs of career changers and job seekers. However, when working with other agencies, librarians increase their ability to meet needs by strengthening ties to the other resources in the community. Other community resources are particularly valuable in helping people to make job changes, to make decisions about education and training, and to seek support and coping assistance. In many libraries, information and referral (I&R) services have led the way toward staff use of effective methods of referral.

Staff use community linkages to assure appropriate community referrals. An effective approach is to start by reaching the key educational, job and career resource agencies and groups and expand contacts as the need or opportunity arises. Linking will not occur until staff:

1. find out the kind of assistance each agency or group is able to provide (and its limits), and
2. let other agencies and groups in the community know what the library is able to do.

Librarians need to learn about employment and education resources in the community as well as the needs experienced by the job seeker and career changer.

Sometimes library staff will meet with some initial resistance on the part of colleagues from other agencies. It is important to diffuse any feelings of territoriality and to stress cooperation and collaboration.

STRATEGIES DESIGNED TO UNDERSTAND THE COMMUNITY

POSSIBLE OBJECTIVES THAT WILL MAKE THE LIBRARY CENTER FOR COMMUNITY DEMOGRAPHIC DATA

Obtain and Use Demographic Data

When anticipating needs, librarians start with demographics. Demographic data provides information about groups of people. Demographic data can help librarians and others develop services that respond to actual needs. Patterns such as job loss and the resulting need for a job change, career or education choice can be seen more clearly in the context of the demographic and economic indicators in the community.

Census and other economic data can provide indicators. The U.S. Census provides vital community data. It provides important data on the educational level and the kind of labor force that lives in your community. Ethnic and racial make-up, age, income, English language proficiency, and many other characteristics are profiled. A number of agencies and organizations use this data to help them with their work.

U.S. Government Census materials data may show that there are large groups of poorly educated people in a community. This information may trigger action by a variety of groups in the community. Librarians planning a job center in such a community will work closely with existing literacy programs to reach that target population. On the other hand, if there is a large percentage of highly educated people, staff should be prepared for the demands for information about higher education and financial aid as well as business and financial information.

Statistics for the community will show the kind of economic mix which exists in the community (business, manufacturing, farming, sales, service), the numbers of people being laid off and the sectors from which they come, the local economic climate and trends, (such as service jobs replacing manufacturing jobs). These types of changes often mean that there is a skills gap between workers and jobs.

Job and career centers in communities that have suffered from the recession and business closure can anticipate relatively high unemployment and a number of white collar and blue collar individuals who need to write resumes and gain interviewing skills.

General statistical compilations such as the County and City Data Book that reflects the most recent Census can be used to develop librarians' knowledge of trends and patterns in the community. The Bureau of Labor Statistics issues regular data on employment and unemployment trends.

Become a Primary Source for Current Demographic Data

Although it is very important for librarians to assemble community statistics for their own use as well as for businesses and agencies in the community, it may not be necessary for staff to develop their own analysis of the data. In most communities reports have already been compiled by government agencies or non-profit groups concerned with the demographic and economic picture. These reports go beyond statistics and include explanation and interpretation of the data. Sometimes they take a broad community view. Other reports focus on a specific aspect of the problem or on a particular group of people. When the library houses a census data and other demographic data, including copies of agency and group reports, they can be made available to all citizens, including citizen groups who use these data to help their communities, and other community agencies.

Economic and statistical data are increasingly available in the Internet. Staff in many university libraries are already regularly mounting employment and economic development data files on easy-to-use, menu-driven GOPHERS. Public librarians are only just beginning such activities. One fine example of value-added data are the economic profiles developed by M-LINK, an extension arm of the University of Michigan Library. Appendix A: "Source List" and "Community Profile of Alpena" were taken from its Gopher, Go-M-LINK, available on Internet. The Appendix shows the many resources that were used to create this up-to-the minute resource and shows the data for one county in Michigan. This valuable demographic data includes current information about the labor force, principal employers, typical community salaries, the distance to major cities, major modes of transportation, climate, economic indicators such as construction permits, services including utilities, educational and other institutions, including libraries and churches, etc. Several advantages of data in electronic form are: it can be accessed remotely, it can be used by more than one person at the same time, and it is likely to be the most current resource.

Identify and make Available Key Sources of Demographic, Employment, and Economic Development Statistical Reports

Although statistics provide rich data about the community, reports which use statistics and discuss their implications are especially valuable. Rather than relying entirely on the Census or other raw data, identify the kinds of reports which have already been developed to describe the demographic, employment and economic development situation in your own community. Government agencies, universities, and non- profit organizations are the key providers of these valuable reports. Most librarians have some knowledge of the federal government as a provider of statistics. However, not as many are familiar with state and local government sources that develop important statistical reports for local communities.

Key sources of local data at the state government level are state government departments with titles such as the Michigan Department of Commerce, the California Employment Development Department, or the Nebraska Economic Development Department. These statistics are often the best sources for information about small communities which do not have the staff and resources to develop their own. Likewise, regional governmental agencies (such as councils of government (COGS) and regional planning commissions) which may cover two or three counties are excellent sources of demographic and economic data, including interpretations of what this data means.

County and city governments frequently develop valuable reports. Communities where there are universities and colleges, particularly those with urban planning departments, are fortunate. These departments are often sources of helpful reports. At times community non-profit organizations develop reports.

Because each community is different, it is not possible to predict exactly which agencies or groups should be contacted. Three good sources of statistical information developed by various agencies are The Index to Current Urban Documents(ICUD), a national publication which is the source of Figure 8-1, American Statistical Index (ASI) and Statistical Report Index. (SRI) ICUD provides data on medium and large cities, SRI on sources of state statistics, and ASI on sources of federal statistics-all are sources of valuable local data.

By and large, the larger the community, the more sources of statistical reports there will be. In a large city such as Chicago, there will be a number of departments that develop reports which interpret statistical information about the community or about important segments of the community. These reports bring citizens value-added data because it is compiled and is often described in context. Logical agencies to look to for data on small communities

FIGURE 8-1: Typical Titles or Statistical Reports

DEMOGRAPHICS

Prepared by Regional Government:

Southeast Michigan Council of Governments. "Regional Forecast totals [of population, households and employment]."

Prepared by City Government:

Department, Milwaukee, WI. "Summary of general population and housing characteristics."

Planning Department, Albuquerque, NM. "Socio-economic projections."

Department of City Planning, New York City. "Asians in New York City: a demographic summary."

Planning Department, Minneapolis, MN. "State of the city: a statistical portrait of Minneapolis."

Prepared by Non-Profit Organization:

Greater Detroit Chamber of Commerce. "Economic fact book."

Greater Fort Lauderdale Chamber of Commerce. "Broward Country statistical abstract and fact book."

Boston Foundation. Persistent Poverty Project. "In the midst of plenty: a profile of Boston and its poor."

EMPLOYMENT/UNEMPLOYMENT:

Prepared by State Government:

California Employment Development Department. "Annual planning information—San Diego MSA" "Projections of employment by industry and occupation—Los Angeles-Long Beach."

Prepared by Regional Government:

Bay-Lake Regional Planning Commision. "Annual overall economic development program report."

Metropolitan Council of the Twin Cities Area. "Diagnosing the Twin Cities [area] economy."

Prepared by Country Government:

Metropolitan Toronto Planning Department. "Metro facts: key employment areas." Metro facts: population and employment projections."

Prepared by Non-Profit Organizations Chicago Association of Commerce and Industry. "Labor force statistics for metropolitan Chicago."

Prepared by Universities:

University of Michigan, Flint. Project for Urban and Regional Affairs. "Economic impact of G.M. plant closings in FLint."

(continued)

FIGURE 8-1: (continued)

DEMOGRAPHICS

ECONOMIC DEVELOPMENT:

Prepared by Regional Governement:

Wichita/Sedgwick Country Partnership for Growth. "Wichita MSA: the facts at a glance."

Knoxville/Knox Country Metropolitan Planning Commission. "Economic development: an overview."

Prepared by Country Governement:

Country of Los Angeles and Security Pacific Bank. "Entering the 21st Century: the economy of Los Angeles Country and the sixty-mile circle region."

DeKalb Country (GA) Planning Department. "Annual Development Report."

Prepared by City Governement:

Greater Houston Partnership. "Houston economic overview." "Houston facts."

Department of Community Development, Richmond, VA. "Profile '89: a state of the city report."

Community group:

Community Workshop on Economic Development—Chicago, IL.

Department of Community Development, Richmond, VA. "Profile '89: a state of the city report."

include, county planning or economic development agencies or state economic development agencies (with such names as economic development, business development, or commerce). Fewer agencies develop reports for small communities.

For example, the state of Nebraska Department of Economic Development compiles the following economic development data (only) for Nebraska cities and towns (many of which are under 5000 population):

- location relative to centers of commerce;
- population;
- labor statistics such as hourly wages in manufacturing, unemployment figures;

- transportation services which serve the town, including bus, motor freight, distance to nearest interstate, distance to nearest airport, rail access;
- utilities (electricity, sanitation, natural gas, telephone, water);
- tax structure; types of municipal services;
- education facilities;
- recreation facilities;
- housing;
- health facilities;
- climate;
- commercial and other services (such as machine shops, radio/TV/newspapers, churches, etc.), and
- local manufacturing characteristics and industrial sites.

Although it is only a statistical compilation, this Nebraska Community Economic Development Profile provides valuable data for Nebraska's small towns. This kind of information is developed for many other states.

Knowing who is likely to develop and issue demographic reports as well as being able to predict typical titles provides librarians with the knowledge they need to exploit work done by other agencies. Typical titles include: "*Economic Fact Book,*" "*Asians in New York City: A Demographic Summary,*" "*Broward County Statistical Abstract and Fact Book,*" "*Labor Force Statistics for Metropolitan Chicago,*" and "*Entering the 21st Century: The Economy of Los Angeles County and the Sixty-Mile Circle,*" show the wealth of analyzed data which is available for most communities.

Although some of these reports are just statistical tables, many of them interpret the data and draw out the implications of the statistics for the local community. Typical Titles of Statistical Reports, (below) provides a rough idea both of typical titles and their likely creators. Statistics may be found in unlikely places. The briefing papers prepared for local city council members often contain valuable statistical information.

LINKING STRATEGIES

To locate the specific agencies in a community or state, check the local telephone directory under government listings, the library's community information files, and the community United Way Directory. Get additional suggestions from the library director, the reference staff, and your local elected officials. The list of agencies that comes from the search for statistics may result in the library's obtaining new sources of statistics and in ongoing linkages. Librarians often start this linkage process by explaining to the agency that the report will be used first to plan new services, and then made available for other citizens in the community. Librarians often at that time request additional reports as they become available and offer to share other statistical reports that have been identified.

POSSIBLE OBJECTIVES THAT FOSTER LINKING

Identify Community Agencies as the Basis for Referral

Librarians are not alone in developing need-based services. There are other agencies and groups in the community working with the same people who will be coming to the job and career center. Unlike the public library, most do not work with the entire community. Their mission may limit their clientele to certain groupsfor example, the unemployed or low income individuals, Korean-Americans, battered spouses, etc. Together they are meeting a wide variety of needs.

Experienced job and career center staff and national studies say that identifying and working with other agencies in the community is crucial to successful implementation. Linking with other agencies will help avoid duplicating services that already exist. Some of agency staff become part of the job and career center advisory committee. Reaching out to agencies, including their staff on an advisory committee, developing formal networking, and serving on the board of another agency are activities will help librarians develop cooperative relationships with other agencies which will, in turn, develop a broader base of community support for the library.

Typically, job and career information center staff identify:

- the economic and educational resources exist in community;
- the key players in employment and business development, and
- agencies and groups who can help people start new businesses.

Likewise, they identify the education and training programs in the community, determine who they serve, how they communicate with individuals in the community, and their requirements.

To gain background, librarians learn about the nature and impact of such legislation for example, the Job Training Partnership Act (JTPA) and organizations like PIC. They become familiar with the state occupational information system and its computerized educational and financial aid information systems if these exist. This knowledge often is gained in the process of talking with knowledgeable agency staff.

Create Linkages to Appropriate Community Agencies and Groups

Developers of job and career information centers contact a variety of social service agencies, counseling services, economic development, educational, and self-help groups before starting the service. Early on they set up meetings with these groups and develop ways to cooperate.

Well before opening the door of the job and career center, staff should contact social service agencies, counseling services, economic development, educational, and self-help groups. These key agencies and your approach to linking with them will be unique to your community. Chapter 4 of *Serving Job Seekers and Career Changers: A Planning Manual for Public Libraries*, provides a guide to making initial contacts with community agencies. (Durrance, 1993)

Use linkages to raise awareness; long-held perceptions can change. The story below shows how quickly agency staff can come to understand the role and function of the library. It shows how a library manager in a rural community made an important link with a key service agency in her community.

Joan Birnie, director of the Broken Bow Public Library in western Nebraska, periodically attends the meetings of the local Cooperative Extension Board as an observer in order to keep abreast of what this agency that is so important to her rural community, does. Some time after requesting to speak at a meeting to let the board know about the library's new education and career center which had been funded by the W. K. Kellogg foundation, she was allotted 15 minutes at a regular meeting.

Ms. Birnie talked about the new resources which the library had recently obtained. She pointed out that an expensive computer, and interactive career advising software had been made available through the grant. She brought several different types of books from the collection and explained some of the computer software that was available. In addition, she left a stack of promotional materials. As she left she said, "Just bring those things by the library any time. Take a look at them first."

The next morning as the library opened, the extension agents called the library and asked if they could come right over to discuss the library's job and career services. Shortly after, they arrived with the box of resources she had left the night before. The agents were amazed at the resources. They took a personal interest in the library's marketing strategies and spent some time brainstorming with the library director about promotion of the library's job and career information center. Several times during the visit one or the other repeated, "You have such valuable stuff here. You're just going to have to let people know what you've got. It can be so helpful to folks in the county."

With her short presentation, the county agent had gone from a limited understanding of the possibilities of the library as a community resource to ebullience over what he had found. On the phone he apologized for only giving her 15 minutes on the agenda and hoped that she could come back some other time. He said that after they left, the agenda changed to include more discussion of the library's resources and services, and their potential value to the community.

Raising the awareness of community agency staff can make a difference in their perception of the role of the library in the community. Librarians across the country have their own versions of this story. Other versions represent different communities, agencies, and circumstances, but they report similar, very positive responses from agency staff.

Look for Networks among Providers

Before attempting to develop new networks, librarians look for existing linkages among service providers. These, to a number of key providers who will indicate the networks of service providers which presently exist and identify other cooperative efforts, are already underway in your community to link existing resources.

Developers of library job and career information centers develop contacts with agencies and groups that work with the unemployed, displaced homemakers, and others who are in employment or career transition. They also identify and work with people who focus on the economic vitality of the community, such as the Chamber of Commerce, including agencies concerned with economic development, education and job training and some local employers.

Develop an Approach for Making Contact with Appropriate Agencies

Often librarians start the agency identification process with library community information, or information and referral files, or those developed by some other social service agency or group (such as the United Way). In the process of making contacts, they make notes of agencies that are concerned with employment and social services. Serving Job Seekers and Career Changers presents a process and a set of forms that facilitate those contacts. (Durrance, et al., 1993).

The agencies that are to be contacted will depend on the emphasis of the center. Typically, librarians start with agencies concerned with employment. Librarians seeking to emphasize services to business, will contact the Chamber of Commerce, and SCORE. It is more efficient to begin with the agencies that will provide the most information. The local telephone book is an excellent place to get addresses and telephone numbers.

In a number of communities representatives of social service groups like the county job service, the area vocational center, United Way, the Goodwill Center, the community college and other educational institutions, women's support groups, job training adult education programs, community development, and hotline services, meet periodically (often once a month) for the purpose of exchanging information about their services. If the community already has such a social service network, the job of contacting potential key service providers is much easier. Typically informal networks rotate hosts and meet throughout the year at different agencies. There is sometimes a brief formal program; however, a key feature of every meeting is an informal update by each representative on current services and programs. Frequently representatives exchange brochures.

Contacts made at such groups greatly facilitate community analysis and pave the way for librarians to be seen as providing relevant services. Identifying existing agencies avoids needless duplication of effort. A community-centered analysis often introduces librarians to the community in a whole new light. Although libraries are important information resources and librarians are highly skilled providers of information, they are not always thought of as resources in this area unless the message has been sent out by librarians to the community.

The story below illustrates that community analysis designed to identify potential community linkages is very natural and successful process of sharing information.

Months before she opened her new Education, Job and Career Information Center in Chehalis, Washington (population: 6,100), Rivkah Sass, who was then the director of the Chehalis Branch of the Timberland Regional Library, had begun to lay the groundwork in the community. She identified the agencies in her community, and then began to contact them to find out what they were doing and tell them about the service that the library planned to offer. Everywhere Ms. Sass went she found great interest in the idea of the library working in this area. She went to a number of agencies including the Economic Development Council, the local high school, the community college, the county commissioners and the local city council.

When visiting these community agencies, she exchanged information. She explained what the library already had in terms of job and career information and what it was possible to add. She gained information about a number of services in the community that was quite valuable in developing her own job and career information center. She found, for example, that the local high school already used the state occupational information system, but they did not have career assessment software, one of the tools the library was about to purchase. She also learned that the local economic development council was particularly active and included most groups that were active in employment in the area. She was asked to join them.

As Ms. Sass prepared to start her new service, she was at the same time developing a guest list of all appropriate agencies to invite for the new center's grand opening. The local paper scheduled a write up of the event because it brought together an important group of people and because the reporter had been delighted to hear about this innovative library service that was really needed in the community.

Create an Advisory Committee that Includes Representatives of Appropriate Agencies

An advisory committee can speed the pace of development of a library job and career information center. Members will be chosen based on the agencies identified above. Membership will vary from one community to the next. Elect a rotating board.

UNDERSTAND THE VALUE OF LINKING TO THE LIBRARY

A consulting firm that studied the success of job and career centers in four states made ten recommendations for libraries which were just starting these services. The first FIVE recommendations, repeated below, concern reaching out to the community and developing relationships with other agencies. They are:

1. Know your community–for example, identify the types of people who could be best served and what their particular needs are.
2. Identify already existing services to avoid duplication of effort. Take time to connect with other agencies; seek their input.
3. Coordinate services with other efforts in the local community; keep other agencies informed about what the job and career center is doing.
4. Create an advisory committee that includes representatives of appropriate agencies.
5. Develop a base of support within the community by networking with other agencies and community groups.

Networking is essential to providing effective community-centered services like the ones previously mentioned. The steps undertaken to create appropriate links in the community can help assure that this service will succeed. Failure to make links with the agencies which would have been the library's partners in a cooperative venture can doom even a well-funded service.

Libraries that already serve as community information and referral (I & R) centers have a headstart. The I & R experience has shown librarians how to reach out into the community. Community information and referral linkages are the basis for appropriate referrals for your client and they ensure that the librarians do not attempt to work in isolation.

Librarians who work in job and career centers regularly receive notes from agency staff who in the past had completely underestimated or misunderstood the role that the library plays in the community. These two testimonial messages are typical of messages which are regularly received by job and career center staff.

> "My eyes have been opened. The library has become a focal point in this community. The community now thinks

of the library as more than just books . . . it is a place to get real and needed 'life' information."

"Thanks! The library's new job and career information center shows people that the library is not simply a place for obtaining recreational reading material. Our clients have been amazed at your center's ability to help them."

REFERRAL STRATEGIES

POSSIBLE OBJECTIVES FOR DEVELOPING REFERRAL CAPABILITY

Develop Community Information Databases

Community information databases that include community organizations focusing on education, employment, or economic development provide unique information about your community. Directories and databases are especially useful to people who are looking for jobs or planning to go back to school include: educational opportunities in the community and area, financial aid opportunities, and area employers. For example, your library might create a "Community Services Directory" which provides profiles of social agencies in the community or an "Educational Directory" that includes information about providers of education and training in your community. Staff may develop directories or databases of relevant education, job, and economic development community resources or create informational materials which help people use these resources, such as a guide to selecting a child care provider. The following examples show how specialized databases serve an important function.

Community information databases, including databases of statistics and directories of local resources, help librarians show that they can play a viable role in contributing to the economic development of their community. For example, the Nassau County Library staff has shown that libraries that are perceived as sources of vital economic development information can bring key players together to work toward community economic vitality (see Figure 8-2).

Helping people find referral support and coping assistance is no problem for the librarian who has developed community information files. These files are an essential guide to other resources in the community. They can be in database form, in a notebook, or staff may choose to print a directory from the database. This type of directory, *The Survival Guide*, (see Figure 8-3) was developed by the Cuyahoga County Public Library staff. It has information about 61 agencies and institutions which provide some type of employment assistance and 56 key sources of emergency assistance services available to unemployed persons. It is distributed widely through the network of the agencies in the Guide, CCPL branches and regionals, and at "events" such as job fairs. The 1990 edition's first printing of 5000 was gone in a few weeks necessitating an additional printing.

A database of employers or a job notebook that shows the kinds of job opportunities available may also be of assistance.

Refer Clients to Appropriate Community Agencies and Groups

Librarians shine at helping people find information. Importantly, librarians have skills that can identify other professionals and refer library users to special resources. By knowing the agencies in the community, librarians are in a position to make knowledgeable referrals for the people who use the library job and career information center.

There are agencies in the community that specialize in services such as retraining, emergency assistance, literacy, career counseling, or small business development. There are agencies that focus on a certain client group: people on welfare, displaced homemakers, various ethnic groups, refugees, etc. Identify career counselors in the community and develop mechanisms to refer those who need counseling. If the library does not provide career counseling, librarians can provide a valuable service to their clientele by referring them to appropriate career counseling.

Appropriate referral greatly expands the strength of the job and career center. If, for example, there are no career counselors in your library, librarians can identify counselors in the area who are willing to work with your patrons. Find out what fees, if any, they charge and when it is appropriate to refer. Find out if particular people are eligible for their service.

The referral process is one way that libraries get their clientele. Many people who use job and career centers are not regular library users. They have found their way to the center because someone in another agency knew what services were available at the library. This kind of referral is usually the result of a contact made through a community network or personal contacts with agencies.

FIGURE 8-2: Business & Education: Partners For Productivity—Nassau County (NY) Library System

Business and Education
Partners For Productivity

A Long Island Regional Conference

TUESDAY, MARCH 22, 1988
Royce Carlin Hotel
Melville, Long Island, NY

Funded in part by a New York State Education Information Centers grant to Nassau Library System.

BUSINESS & EDUCATION

Our prosperity and quality of life on Long Island depends on a strengthened Regional Partnership between business and education. This conference launches that Partnership. The Nassau and Suffolk County Executives have proclaimed March 22nd as Long Island's First Business & Education Partnership Day.

Come join your colleagues, counterparts, and prospective partners to help forge Long Island's future. This conference will bring together employers from firms of every size, providers of adult learning in colleges, schools, libraries, businesses, government and voluntary organizations, and experts in the development of human resources.

You will benefit from practical workshops based on successful experience. Your horizons will be enlarged by a headline-making keynoter, a mind-expanding luncheon presentation, and a multi-media capstone. New ideas, products and services will be displayed at an exciting Sponsors' Showcase, which will also provide a setting for networking with colleagues. You will discover realistic solutions to problems, and find promising opportunities for the future.

This conference is a "first" nationally, and puts the Long Island Region in the forefront, meeting the challenge to America's competitiveness.

Conference Goals

The goals of this one-day conference are:

- To spark Long Island business and industry to consider new options for attracting, retaining and developing the employees they need.
- To encourage and support those who educate adults to meet today's real needs of employers and employees.

Proclamation

"LONG ISLAND'S FIRST BUSINESS & EDUCATION PARTNERSHIP DAY"

Official Proclamations were presented to members of the Sponsoring Organizations by both
Nassau County Executive
Thomas S. Gulotta
Suffolk County Executive
Patrick G. Halpin
honoring all Long Island Business & Education Partners.

HONORARY CO-CHAIRMEN

The Honorable Thomas S. Gulotta
Nassau County Executive

The Honorable Patrick G. Halpin
Suffolk County Executive

SPONSORS

Advancement for Commerce & Industry
American Society for Training & Development
Education Information Center of Nassau Library System
Educational Opportunity Center SUNY at Farmingdale
Hauppauge Industrial Association
Islip Industrial Development Commission
Long Island Association, Inc.
Long Island Better Business Bureau
Long Island Forum for Technology
Long Island Regional Advisory Council of Higher Education
Nassau Association for Continuing and Community Education
Nassau County Department of Commerce and Industry
Nassau County Library Association
Nassau Library System
110/Action
Personnel Society of Long Island
State Education Department Office of Adult Learning Services
Suffolk Association for Continuing and Community Education
Suffolk Cooperative Library System
Suffolk County Library Association
Suffolk County Private Industry Council
Suffolk County Office of Economic Development
The Urban League
U.S. Small Business Administration

Funded in part by a New York State Education Information Centers grant to Nassau Library System

FIGURE 8-3: The Survival Guide—Cuyahoga County (OH) Public Library

The Survival Guide

1990 Edition

Employment and Emergency Assistance Services

CUYAHOGA COUNTY PUBLIC LIBRARY

InfoPLACE

Career Education and Community Information Services

Cuyahoga County Public Library

EMERGENCY ASSISTANCE AND REFERRAL

85. FIRST CALL FOR HELP
United Way Services
3113 Prospect Avenue
Cleveland, Ohio 44115 391-5800
24-hour information and referral service for questions about agencies in Cuyahoga County which handle health, social welfare, recreational, educational, vocational, supportive, legal or financial problems.

86. COMMUNITY SERVICES DIRECTORY
Directory of social, medical, and legal services available in Cuyahoga County. This is available at all branches of the Cuyahoga County Public Library. Information may be obtained by visiting or calling your nearest branch. Branches are listed on the back of this booklet.

87. PSYCHIATRIC EMERGENCY SERVICES
St. Vincent Charity Hospital
2351 East 22nd Street
Cleveland, Ohio 44115 229-2211
A 24-hour suicide prevention/psychiatric emergency hotline. Provides evaluation and referral for persons in mental health emergencies.

DISCRIMINATION

88. 9 TO 5/NATIONAL ASSOCIATION OF WORKING WOMEN
614 Superior Avenue, N.W.
Cleveland, Ohio 44113 566-9308
Office Survival Hotline 566-5420
Answers questions about equal pay and discrimination.

89. OHIO CIVIL RIGHTS COMMISSION
885 Frank J. Lausche State Office Building
615 West Superior Avenue
Cleveland, Ohio 44113 622-3150
Investigates discrimination due to race, religion, sex, national origin, handicap, age, credit and pregnancy.

90. OHIO WOMEN'S INFORMATION CENTER
State House, Room 19
Columbus, Ohio 43215 1-800-282-3040
Refers people to the appropriate state or federal agency handling discrimination complaints.

Emergency Assistance Services B-5

Skills needed to refer to a wide variety of agencies and resources include a knowledge of the resources in the community and the ability to listen effectively in order to determine the appropriate referral.

Other agencies and other professions can provide assistance to job and career center clientele. Know when to refer a client. It is frustrating for a client to be sent to an agency for a particular service, only to find that they are not eligible. By keeping careful records in the I & R files, staff will be able to make knowledgable referrals. Agencies have different protocols for referral. Staff should find out the most appropriate ways to refer to each agency.

Excellent sources of information about community information and referral techniques include, *Information and Referral: The Journal of the Alliance of Information and Referral Systems, Public Library Information and Referral Service (1978), and Guidelines for Establishing Community Information and Referral Services in Public Libraries 3d ed.*, 1989.

Follow-up and Act as an Advocate, as Appropriate

Maintain contact with clients. Call selected clients back to see if they were able to get the needed service or assistance from the community agency. Think about how staff can ease the way for people in getting help. Be willing to consider calling a community agency on behalf of a client who seems unable to get the needed help, or letting the client make the appointment right on the spot from the library. For guidance on follow-up, advocacy, identification of gaps in service and other information and referral techniques, see the National Standards for Information and Referral, produced by United Way of America and the Alliance of Information and Referral Systems (AIRS).

COLLABORATION STRATEGIES

POSSIBLE COLLABORATION OBJECTIVES

Develop Formal and Informal Network Connections

In many communities formal and informal networks have already been developed. Networks permit representatives of organizations with different programs and approaches to similar problems to meet each other and discuss a common problem and, in the process, develop ways to cooperate. In Marquette, MI, for example, the Peter White Library joined a network called the Combined Employment Service Agency Workers (CESAW) includes representatives from the public and private sector. The group meets once a month to coordinate strategy and resources to deal with Marquette's long-term unemployment problems.

The linking process will vary from one community to another. In some communities, networks such as CESAW which meet regularly are already in place. If they are in place, join them and offer to host a meeting at the library or to prepare background materials on topics of concern. The purposes of these groups are to share expertise, gain new knowledge about the problem or common concern, and to cooperatively develop solutions. If no network exists, consider facilitating the development of one. The library is a good agency to act as facilitator because it is neutral ground and all agencies and organizations are welcome.

Use Linkages to Assist Community Agencies

Networks help members learn the expertise and strengths of cooperative members. Through regular network meetings and individual contacts with community agencies, librarians can show what contributions libraries make to the community. Because libraries are typically excellent sources of information, community agencies need not duplicate these resources. The library has the extensive information on most topics and its staff is skilled in retrieving it, and in identifying and obtaining information from a wide variety of sources. In addition, the library is a place in the community that is available to all people at no charge. Sharing this kind of information with others in the network will help other agencies see the unique library contribution in the community.

Cooperation is greatly enhanced by networking because it overcomes or minimizes potential turf problems. It is important from the very beginning to assure other agencies in the community that the library and its staff are a unique community resource and to show that the library does not seek to compete for their clientele or their funds.

To overcome any initial resistance to library involvement with other agencies, focus on what the staff and the library can do for each agency. Think of ways to assist other agencies. For example:

- Show what the library can do for community agencies.
- Publicize the library's job and career development resources. Often agency funds for materials and resources are limited.

Knowing that materials are available at the library for their clientele can help agencies put their money into programming.

- If the library has public access computer resources and software that can be used by clients of various social services to type resumes and learn computer skills, share that information.
- Develop and share a list of human services agencies in the area.
- Make the library's meeting room available for cooperative ventures.

The testimonials below show what agency staff in several communities say about what they gain from cooperating with the library.

> "My agency is always looking for new resources. I couldn't possibly research all that I need to. The library provides the information we don't have the time and expertise to obtain."
>
> "The library made us more aware of what other agencies have to offer."
>
> "The library's job and career information center cooperates with our program, allowing us to have a more cost effective program and a broader base of resources."

Create Partnerships with Appropriate Agencies

Look for opportunities for cooperative ventures. Work with other agencies on programs of mutual interest. Create partnerships with appropriate agencies with the aim of better responding to the needs of citizens of the community. Cooperation in the '90s has become increasingly necessary. Communities are now developing (and funding) programs which in prior decades were created and financed by the federal government. With fewer dollars available, cooperation becomes a key method of stretching the budgets of community agencies and groups. Cooperative ventures help overcome lack of awareness, avoid duplication of effort, promote more effective services, and develop a base of support for the library.

There is a wide range of opportunity for partnerships in the community. Consider partnerships with groups that serve ethnic or other special populations. Collaborate with the business community and look for their help in serving employment and economic development needs. Below are several examples of partnerships.

- The State Library of Pennsylvania, in cooperation with the Pennsylvania Department of Labor, developed a joint program which resulted in an allocation of $600,000 of Job Training Partnership Act (JTPA) funds intended to assist dislocated workers in 24 public libraries and 10 prison libraries in Pennsylvania.
- The Alliance Public Library and the Alliance Area Family YMCA jointly sponsor an annual "Shadowing Day" for area teens who are matched with adults who work in jobs the teens are interested in.
- A number of California public libraries participate in a program sponsored by the State Library called Partnerships for Change which involves creatively working with a community partner to develop need-based services. The next two examples show how the program fosters partnerships.
- The Pio Pico Branch of the Los Angeles Public Library serves a Korean-American community. Working with representatives of the Korean community, the branch library has developed services designed for this immigrant community. Brochures in Korean describe a various services and workshops.
- Newhope Branch Library in Santa Ana, CA, working with the Vietnamese community has developed literacy programs and programs which introduce life in America. With the help of its partners, the library staff develop announcements in Vietnamese and publicize library programs in Vietnamese language newspapers and other publications, in refugee centers and English as a Second Language classes. The library is a member of the Vietnamese Chamber of Commerce.

The Nassau Library, like a number of libraries that have developed collaborative relationships in their community, has engaged in several recent partnership activities including the following:

- Job Network, a program to connect employers and job seekers, is the outgrowth of the Long Island (NY) Business and Education Partnership. Its several sponsors include a local hotel, bank, a radio station, and several non-profit organizations, including the public library.

FIGURE 8-4: Hints For Working With Other Agencies To Develop A Job Conference

1. Organize a planning committee with the leaders from every sector in the adult education and business communities, including the local American Association for Adults and Continuing Education (AAACE) and the American Society for Training and Development (ASTD) units, the area library systems, job and career centers and Economic Development Centers, major colleges and universities, and commerce, industrial, and business development groups.
2. Find the practical, effective efforts currently afoot to make maximum use of workers and managers in your region exemplary and pilot programs from which others could benefit immediately if they knew about them.
3. Get your top local governmental officials to proclaim a "Business and Education Partnership Day."
4. Generate maximum visibility in the local press via speeches, stories, and site-visits by members of the planning committee.
5. Plan a dazzling one-day conference on the now-official and eagerly-awaited special day.
6. Obtain support from local businesses as exhibitors in a "Sponsor's Showcase."
7. Recruit the leading TV business reporter in your area as a "name" keynoter (likely available without cost).
8. Design on-target, practical work-shops on topics like revitalizing the work-ethic; employing the disadvantaged handicapped, exoffenders, and displaced homemakers; addressing the problem and opportunity of new immigrants; and meeting new needs in the workplace (child care, flex-time, etc.).
9. Draw an SRO (Standing Room Only) crowd, spark a story in the next day's paper, and stir participants to volunteer to carry the work forward.
10. Climax the conference by having the several hundred conferees adopt a "Declaration" affirming their commitment to strengthening the partnership between business and education, and providing a mandate for follow-up projects.

(These pointers were used in a conference developed by Dorothy Puryear of the Nassau Library System, Long Island, NY.)

- The Nassau County Youth Board, of which the public library is a partner, sponsors JOB LINK, a computerized job listing service for youth.
- Partnerships for Productivity, made up of the library, the region's educators, and business and industry leaders, sponsored a regional economic development conference, Business and Education Partnership Day.

As seen from the examples, above partnerships are a natural outgrowth of shared interest in serving the citizens of the community. Some partnerships are excellent vehicles for raising the awareness of citizens in the community about the activities of all participating partners. The steps taken to develop a highly successful conference sponsored by Nassau Library and other partners. These suggestions can work for any kind of public event such as an open house or job fair, see Figure 8-4.

RESOURCES

Durrance, Joan C. *Serving Job Seekers and Career Changers: A Planning Manual for Pubic Libraries.* Chicago: Public Library Association, American Library Association, 1993.

Jones, Clara Stanton, ed. *Public Library Information and Referral Service.* Syracuse, NY: Gaylord Professional Publications, 1978.

Public Library Association. Community Information Section. *Guidelines for Establishing Community Information and Referral Services in Public Libraries: Including a Selective Guide to the Literature of Community Information and Referral.* 3d ed. Chicago: American Library Association, Public Library Association, 1989.

United Way of America, and Alliance of Information and Referral Systems (AIRS). *National Standards for Information and Referral.* Alexandria, VA: United Way of America, 1983.

Alliance of Information and Referral Systems. Comprehensive Bibliography of the Literature of Information and Referral. The Journal of the Alliance of Information and Referral Systems, Volume 14, March 14, March 1993 [special issue].

9 PUTTING IT ALL TOGETHER

This guide started with a discussion of the real need people have for assistance in selecting, changing, or getting a job. Chapter 1 identified the reasons that public librarians become involved in helping people who are changing jobs, exploring a career, or starting a business of their own.

Chapter 2 profiled specific libraries across the nation from small towns to big cities which have undertaken the challenge of responding to the job seeker.

Chapter 3 introduced a number of needs that can be met by public library staff who learn more about the needs and the people who are experience them.

Chapters 4-8 identified specific strategies that have been used successfully to respond to the needs of job seekers and people who are choosing and changing careers. This chapter brings all of the needs and strategies together, first by showing how strategies should directly respond to needs, and then by profiling three experienced library staff members, two librarians and one counselor; and finally, by showing how these services build on typical library services and how they diverge from them.

NEEDS

The Need For Knowledge/Self-Knowledge

Self-Assessment

Information to Increase Personal Knowledge

A number of needs associated with job seeking and changing careers were grouped, for convenience, into three families of need. The first—the need for knowledge or self-knowledge—is the most obvious for librarians although, interestingly, not for those who are experiencing job or career transition. Although people think in terms of solving a problem, librarians think in terms of knowledge and information. Many people need to gain an understanding of themselves—their skills, knowledge, abilities, and limitations before they are able to get the information needed to solve (or explore) a problem.

Decisions To Be Made/Problems To Solve—The Need To:

Make Decision

Develop Resume Writing and Interviewing Skills

Obtain Basic or Remedial Skills

Find Support and Coping Assistance

The second need grouping includes a range of problems encountered by adults who may be facing a major transition in their lives—such as a lay-off, divorce, the decision to launch a new business, or change careers. These people are attempting to make a series of decisions and in the process encounter a series of hurdles to overcome (or problems to solve). In the process, they may also need to find support (often in the form of encouraging words).

Actions To Prepare For—Such as:

Starting a Business

Preparing for a Job Change:

Conducting a Job Search

Getting More Education or Training

The final category consists of a variety of actions which require some sort of preparation. Often the preparation involves needing to learn a process, an approach, or undertaking a course of study. The emphasis in preparing a client for an action is to facilitate the decision-making process, not to make the decison.

Note that here as in all of the needs discussed in this book, the focus is on individuals and the unique needs that bring them to the library. To help citizens meet these needs, librarians and career counselors have developed strategies aimed at building services around needs.

STRATEGIES

Meeting Community Needs with Job & Career Services has identified five families of strategies—those designed to do the following:

1. raise awareness and increase access;
2. increase access to information;
3. foster problem-centered diagnosis and intervention;
4. provide instruction and instructional materials, and
5. bring the library closer to the community and include assessment, creating linkages, and making referrals.

Each family of strategies is made up of one or more groups of objectives. They show the direction in which the service is heading. Each group includes several possible objectives that can be used to carry out the larger strategy or goal area. The objectives included in this guide are meant to be illustrative rather than prescriptive. Service developers can use them as examples. Objectives and the activities used to carry them out provide the specific indicators of success.

This guide has been developed around model objectives which were developed from those which shape many job and career centers in public libraries. Because *Meeting Community Needs with Job & Career Services* has incorporated specific objectives for each of the five strategy families, it can be used as a workbook for selecting program objectives. The section below reviews the five strategy families.

Strategies to Raise Awareness and Increase Access

The first family of strategies are designed to raise awareness about and increase the visibility of need-based services such as job centers. Within this family there are four major groupings of objectives—those which:

1. raise awareness,
2. take the service to the people (outreach), and
3. increase the visibility and accessibility of the resources in the library.

Chapter 4 includes nearly twenty-five objectives that can be used to make these strategies work. Planners of these services might choose to increase visibility and increase access to information by using some or all of these objectives, and by developing objectives which reflect local needs as well. The text that accompanies each of the objectives provides background for understanding and implementing it.

Strategies Designed to Increase Access to Information

This group of two dozen strategies are designed to help staff:

1. send welcoming signals to people who actually come into libraries for assistance;
2. conduct reference interviews with the aim of being able both to diagnose and provide appropriate reference intervention, and

3. advise about resources and information. These strategies include twenty-four diverse objectives whose aim is to help librarians focus on increasing access to information.

Strategies which Promote Self Assessment, Problem-Centered Diagnosis and Intervention

There are two kinds of problem-centered objectives. The first focuses on promoting self-assessment and need diagnosis; objectives that focus on finding out more about the need behind the question which has been asked are included here. These strategies include developing listening skills, building trust, and providing the tools necessary for this process. The second includes strategies which focus on determining appropriate approaches to work with the client on the problem, for example, intervention. They include:

1. providing needed information,
2. giving advice, and
3. providing support and reassurance.

This family of eleven strategies introduces approaches that are not widely used by librarians. Therefore, it is important that activities be undertaken to carry out these strategies. New approaches like these require practice. Evaluation of these objectives should focus at first on the extent to which training has been made available to staff. Staff members should use the staff development approaches suggested in Ross and Dewdney to develop (and evaluate) listening and questioning skills.

Strategies to Provide Instruction and Instructional Materials

Instruction plays a key role in the success of job and career information centers. These approaches (along with personal assistance strategies) are used to help users who need and get extra assistance. As a result, librarians and other career center staff create instructional materials that explain library services, recommend specific materials, explain how a software program works, focus on resume writing, or present financial aid information. Likewise, workshops and programs on interviewing, resume writing, the career decision process etc., are developed by career center staff.

Strategies Designed to Assess the Community, Create Links, and Make Referrals

Finally, there is a large group of objectives that focus on linkages to the community. This family of strategies helps librarians not only assess the community, but make the library the center for community demographic data. There are also objectives which foster linking with other agencies and community institutions, and which foster referral and collaboration among providers. Job and career centers are community and need-based services. They must be developed in conjunction with other institutions.

A key to "putting it all together" is to make sure that the families of strategies chosen and the objectives which carry them out directly flow from the needs identified in the community. Durrance et al: *Serving Job Seekers and Career Changers: A Planning Manual for Public Libraries* provides a method for envisioning the services and developing specific objectives which will keep the program on target. (pp. 33-58).

Meeting Community Needs with Job & Career Services has provided a full range of objectives that can be used to shape public library job and career center services. Develop a series of matrices which match the needs identified with the strategies and objectives that are being used in the center. The figures below can be used as guides. Figures like these will help to assure that services are need-based and that appropriate objectives have been selected. Each matrix you develop should be arranged by the stragegy group and include the specific objectives for that group. Across the top are the need groupings. Along the left margin are the strategies designed to respond to the needs. This approach will assure that the strategies, objectives, and activities chosen reflect the needs identified in the community.

The following discussion of approaches taken by job and career center staff—librarians and a career counselor—show the similarities and differences in practice by professionals who head job and career information centers in public libraries. The concluding section of this chapter looks at the changes that can result from developing services such as these.

FIGURE 9-1: Strategies Which Raise Awareness And Increase Access

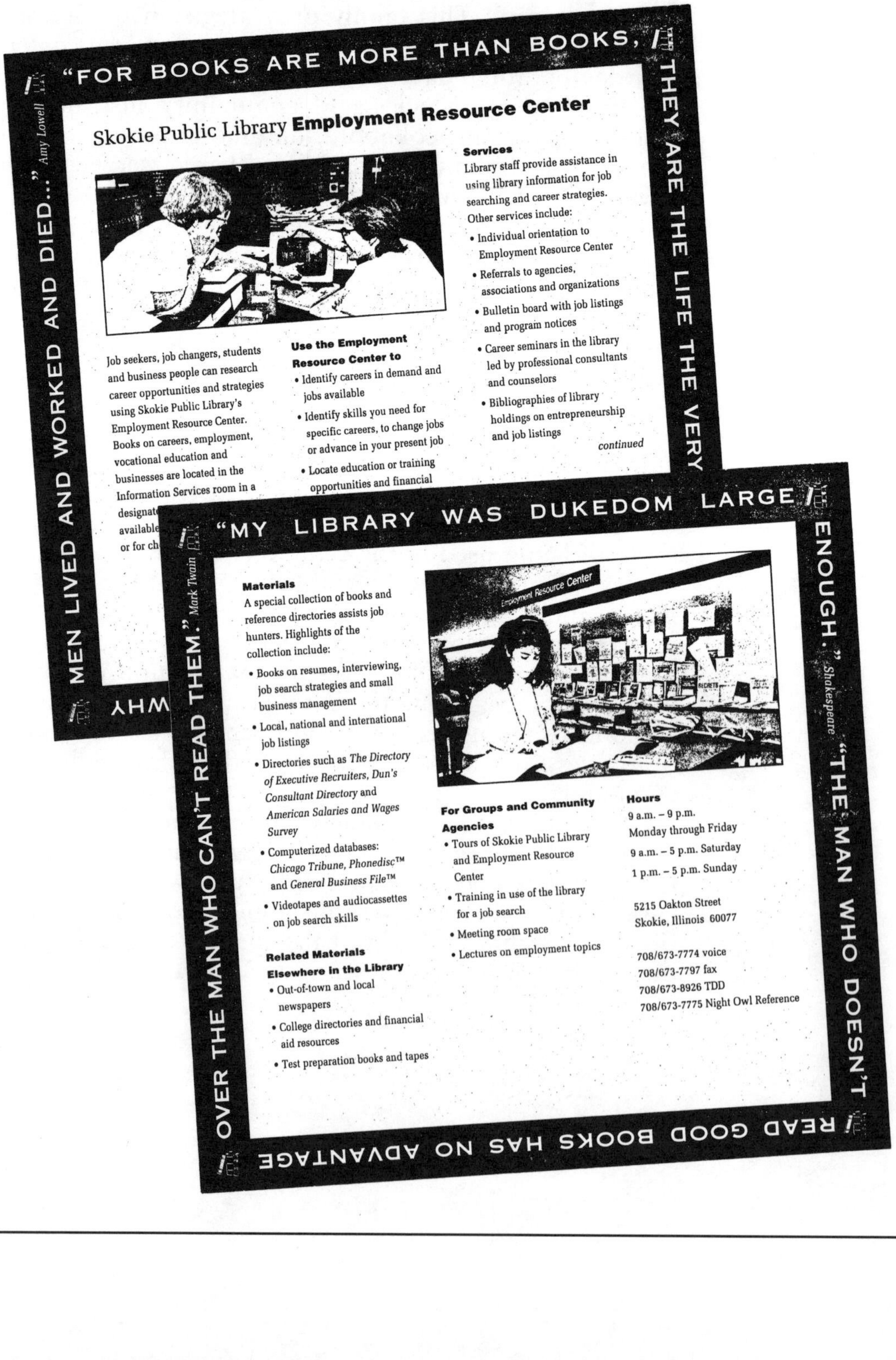

FIGURE 9-2: Strategies Which Promote Self Assessment, Problem-Centered Diagnosis And Intervention

Find out what the client needs by focusing on the problem behind the question asked.

Develop listening skills to aid in diagnosis.

Build trust.

Develop excellent interviewing skills as an aid to diagnosis.

Develop method to continued diagnosis over time.

Help the client with self-assessment.

Purchase self-assessment tools.

Develop an understanding of the use of interactive career assessment software.

Use advice as appropriate.

Provide appropriate career counseling assistance.

Figure 9-3: Strategies Designed To Assess The Community, Create Links, And Make Referrals

Obtain and use demographic data.

Become a primary source for current demographic data.

Identify and make available key sources of demographic, employment, and economic development statistical reports.

Identify community agencies as the basis for referral.

Create linkages to appropriate community agencies and groups.

Use linkages to raise awareness.

Look for networks among providers.

Develop an approach for making contact with appropriate agencies.

Create an advisory committee which includes representatives of appropriate agencies.

Develop community information databases.

Refer clients to appropriate community agencies and groups.

Follow-up and act as an advocate as appropriate.

Use linkages to assist community agencies.

Create partnerships with appropriate agencies.

THREE PROFESSIONAL PROFILES

ANITA JOHANSEN: CAREER COUNSELOR, EVERETT, WA PUBLIC LIBRARY

Anita Johansen has worked from 1989 as the career advisor at the Everett (Washington) Public Library Career Center succeeding another counselor. During that time she completed a degree in human services at a local college. Over the years Anita has worked closely with Ruth Nelson, an MLS librarian and founder of the Everett Public Library's job and career center. Her approach to providing job and career center services is seen in a number of ways. The message on the Center's answering machine, explains her approach.

Sending a Clear Opening Message

> "You have reached the Career Information Center at the Everett Public Library. I am currently helping someone. If you want an individual appointment with the career advisor, Anita Johansen will call you back. If you have other questions that the reference librarians can help you with, please call (206) 259-8896. Thank you for calling."

Commenting on the message, Anita notes, "The people who have come in here are the most important people to help. They have made the effort. I am always available by appointment and the reference librarians are able to answer general reference questions and provide information."

Setting Up the Environment

In planning the Career Center desk arrangement, she has sought to encourage interaction and foster the initial contact with the person who needs assistance. During the time that Anita has been the career advisor, the career center has moved twice due to a major library renovation. In all locations she has sought to create an environment that will permit relatively uninterrupted interviews with her clientele. As part of the renovation, she had a partial wall built to set off her desk. In interviews she and a client sit facing each other at a small desk.

One-On-One Interactions—Advising by Appointment, Assessment, and Options

Anita meets on a one-onone basis with people to prepare them to use the career advising software and later to discuss the printouts. She assists in the assessment process, advising on options and approaches, and skill-building. Appointments serve as an organizing mechanism in her practice. Some appointments are with DISCOVER, an interactive career assessment program, and other assessment software; others (such as follow up appointments to discuss print-outs) are directly with Anita Johansen. She schedules clients for the purpose of discussing the job search process or to focus on a client's resume. She will schedule a 20-30 minute appointment to discuss the print-out which results from a session with DISCOVER or other career assessment software.

> "I like appointments. I feel like I have an on-going relationship with the client. I can help better through an ongoing relationship. They need to get their real needs outlined. Also when I make appointments I have control over the numbers of people who see me."

Walk-Ins

Not all interactions are by appointment. Anita talks with walk-ins for 15 minutes or so to introduce new people to the services. "This is an open setting. I don't want to put people off initially. For sessions involving skill building I ask them to make appointments."

Working with People

Anita wants to help people focus. She may meet one person over six to ten short visits or she may schedule one to three longer visits. She notes that people often check in periodically as they are proceeding with their job search. They come to compare information with her and talk over options.

Relationships with Reference Librarians

Anita has developed a positive relationship with the reference librarians who respond to job, career, and education reference questions when she is unavailable for consultation. They answer job and career questions and locate needed materials they may get people started on job and career center career software. She says that librarians appreciate what she does, understand the intensive nature of the work with clients, and have testified before the Library Board about the value of this special service, saying essentially, "The job and career center with a career advisor meets a real need. Without a career advisor we'd have just a collection."

Networking, Referral, and Community Connections

Everett Public Library's career advisor maintains a close relationship with the state Job Service Center. The local office uses the job and career center resource materials available with their clientele and refers clients to the job and career center. A staff member from the Washington State Job Service recently said, "I never let a day go by without talking about you guys at the Career Center."

Workshops and Teaching

Each fall Anita Johansen does a series of workshops at the library. Workshop topics include: "Resume Writing," "Interviewing," "Federal Job Application Process," and "Getting To Know Yourself;" she also holds a one session program introducing the career change process. Last year she added an eight-week "Career Changer" brown bag series at lunch time.

Anita maintains a close interaction with the Everett Community College; each quarter she lectures to selected classes on materials of value to people choosing a career, the services of the Career Center. She conducts a separate resume writing class. A workshop on career choice was presented recently at Western Washington University.

Evaluating Work with Clientele

Anita has devised various ways to evaluate her work with career center clientele. She keeps a log book of activities and questions and keeps track of walk-ins, telephone calls, and appointments. Feature articles in local newspapers about the career center are kept. As for impact on specific clientele, often people let her know how they have been helped. She periodically does formal evaluations, but says, candidly, "I don't always know. I can't follow that as much as would like. Once the problem is solved, they don't come back any more."

Recognizing Service Value

The career center has helped the library become more visible in Northwest Washington and has developed relationships between the library and other agencies. The referral process has fostered a two-way source of interaction with a variety of community agencies. Anita Johansen serves on several advisory committees and boards of directors. She is chair-elect of the executive committee of the Washington Occupational Information System (WOIS).

VERA GREEN: LIBRARIAN, HEAD, WORKPLACE, CARNEGIE LIBRARY OF PITTSBURGH, PA

Vera Green is a seasoned job and career center librarian. She has many years of experience as a public service librarian and nearly a decade as head of the center at the Carnegie Library of Pittsburgh. We asked her to draw on her background and practice to offer a few tips on working with people who come to the job and career center. These comments are in Vera's own words.

Focus on People

"Being a job and career center librarian is at the same time patron-intensive and very rewarding. I feel that my work really makes a difference in a person's life. I know because people write glowing letters to the main office praising what we in the job and career center have done for them. It is very rewarding to have someone you've worked with for a while come in to say, 'Thanks. You really helped! I got the job!'"

"Librarians who work in a career center need to have a real desire to help people. That's not enough, though. They need to also develop good listening and interviewing skills and try different approaches as they are needed. It's also very important to really know the library's resources and those of the community."

Welcoming Strategies

"Greet the people who come into the center right away. Don't wait for them to wander around. Many people who come to the center are not regular library users and they feel uncomfortable at first. How you approach them depends in part on their responses to you. However, they will open up to you if they feel that you are listening to them. Listen for the kind of opening you should use."

Finding Out about the Need

"I try to find out more about what somebody needs. I ask a lot of questions. Open questions work best. They help you find out what somebody really needs. They also give the feeling that you are really listening to your patrons and that helps them talk."

Explaining Resources and Services

"I often volunteer a lot of information about what we do at WORKPLACE. People are surprised we have so much. I tell them about the different kinds of resources we have at WORKPLACE, about our computer programs, our job clubs, the special files we have on careers, the financial aid information, and the fact that we work with people on a oneDtoDone basis."

Seeing People as Individuals

"I work with people on an individual basis, advising them as they try to sort out what they are looking for. I usually ask return users how things have progressed since we talked last. People like that. Sometimes, they need support and reassurance. For example, I usually tell them that in this kind of job market, you just can't take rejection personally."

Choosing the Right Strategy

"Most of the time the Center is open we have at least half a dozen people in here at the same time working on different things. Often people help each other. We even have job clubs so that people can talk with each other and exchange strategies. It is the job of the WORKPLACE librarian to keep track of all that's going on with our various patrons who might be using the computer to get financial aid information, doing a self-assessment on the computer, researching a career, typing a resume on our typewriter, or talking over job-seeking strategies with another patron. I often go from one patron to the next checking on their progress and talking with them about what they are doing."

Recognizing Service Value

"Frequently people will call me on the phone or come up to me at the Center and tell me of their successes. It is very rewarding to have someone you've worked with for a while come in to say, 'Thanks. You really helped. I got the job!'"

"This is a wonderful job and the administrators appreciate what we do. My boss pointed out in a meeting recently how valuable WORKPLACE is as a library service. He said that he gets more mail and comments about WORKPLACE than any other service in the library."

STEVE OSERMAN: REFERENCE LIBRARIAN, EMPLOYMENT RESOURCE CENTER, SKOKIE PUBLIC LIBRARY, IL

The following profile of Steve Oserman was developed from interviews and from an article in Public Libraries. (RA: cite)

Networking

Networking is crucial to the development of an effective job and career center. Skokie Public Library's Steve Oserman has developed strong networking skills. He says:

"For the past seven years I have been on a networking odyssey. In 1987 when I first converted a conference room near the Skokie Public Library (IL) reference desk into the Employment Resource Center on a one day a week basis, I never imagined where this project might lead. Because my reputation in the community was already well established through years of reference service and a wide range of business and psychology programs, the transition to the new role that I was about to assume progressed rapidly. Publicity for the new Center grew out of articles that appeared in local newspapers as well as networking visits to job fairs, social service agencies, junior colleges, technical schools, the Private Industry Council, and the Illinois State Employment Service job finders groups. The initial response was both supportive and enthusiastic. Some agencies were interested in bringing groups of job seekers to the library on a regular basis. As many as fifty people visited the Center in a single day."

Increasing Visibility

Steve Oserman and Skokie Public Library Director Carolyn Anthony see the value of increasing the visibility of these services. They understand that the general public is less aware of the specialized services which public libraries provide. Thus, when the library was renovated recently the library director and renovation planners consulted with Steve about the needs of the Employment Resource Center. They decided to place the Center near the Information Services Desk.

As a result, a large bulletin board became a center focal-point. It is filled with job listings and notices of instructional workshops. Steve also notes that the visibility of the center has increased by adding signs placed outside of the meeting room and at the check-out desk. To add to the visibility of the center, materials such as books, video and audio cassettes, newspapers and magazines with job listings and career-related information are prominantly displayed.

In addition, job search bibliographies, and job listing handouts have been developed. These can be given away at workshops and job fairs and other community events. They, and other publicity which appears regularly in local newspapers, greatly increase the visibility of the job and career center.

Another excellent way of increasing visibility has been holding programs and workshops and bringing in extra chairs so that a larger number of job hunters can simultaneously use the materials and exchange ideas.

Responding to Needs with Workshops

Community contacts have been invaluable in developing workshops for the Employment Resource Center clientele. Steve has obtained the services of local counselors, psychologists, and authors as speakers at no charge for the Library's free career seminars. Steve notes that "contacts had been made through job fairs, and other speakers were willing to reciprocate for presentations or library tours that I had given to their clients. Guest speakers agreed to speak free of charge since there were no available grants or budget allocations. Most noteworthy of our first group of speakers was Marilyn Moats Kennedy, a local career counselor with a national reputation as editor and author of best selling job search books. Marilyn's program was inspiring to all of the 210 people who filled our auditorium. Total attendance for the five-part series was over 500!"

Raising Awareness and Making Contacts for the Center

Steve has actively promoted the Skokie Public Library's Employment Resource Center within the community through his agency contacts. Recently the Center's Study Committee worked with him to develop a new brochure which describes the work of the Center. The brochure describes the services of the center (and the library). It is an excellent vehicle to raise the awareness of people who have not used the library. The brochure has become part of the general library information handout. Steve notes that fhe Skokie Chamber of Commerce has requested the brochure as an insert in their monthly newsletter. "We hope that this will bring new job listings for our bulletin board and enhance local visibility for the Employment Resource Center."

Steve is aware of opportunities to promote the needed services of the Employment Resource Center. Unemployment in the midwest has remained high and this Center has worked with numerous people who have been caught in the economic down-turns. He alerts the local media of the services of the center. Steve notes that an interview in the Chicago Tribune led to an Associated Press interview that appeared in newspapers throughout the country. As the result of the AP story, CNN called and asked for an interview (which occurred, coincidentally, during the 1992 presidential campaign). A CNN crew came to film the center on the day that Bill Clinton was to be in town.

Steve notes with delight that "Clinton [did not arrive in time for] the CNN interview," so CNN decided to spend more time than originally planned filming at the Skokie Public Library. When patrons and staff saw the CNN trucks arriving in the parking lot they thought that a presidential candidate might be making an appearance here. I will never forget the shock and disbelief when I told a library staff member that CNN was here to see the Employment Resource Center and film me in action with the unemployed. My colleague's words were something like 'you must be kidding.' The CNN spot resulted in hundreds of phone calls (20 in one hour) and patron visits following the weekend of features on hourly telecasts. One man came all the way from Virginia to show me his resume. A library student from New Jersey called immediately after the first broadcast (March 13, 1992) wanting to know how to become a "career" librarian. Phone calls came from as far away as California, Hawaii, Texas, and Florida. Many of the calls came from employers who were looking for workers. People continue to come in as a result of having seen the CNN interview last year.

Although most librarians will not be interviewed on CNN, Steve's experience shows that when opportunity knocks, librarians should take the opportunity to raise the awareness of citizens to the kind of services that librarians perform in their communities.

The stories above demonstrate how wide ranging the approaches are taken by job and career center staff. While staff differ in their approaches, they do share a common need-centered approach.

TYPICAL DIFFERENCES BETWEEN JOB AND CAREER CENTER STAFF AND OTHER PUBLIC SERVICE STAFF

Although most librarians are generalists and answer questions on a wide variety of topics, job and career center staff members are more likely to be specialists who focus on the needs associated with changing jobs or careers and getting more education. Although most reference interactions in libraries take place while both the librarian and the "patron" are standing, job and career center staff have changed the environment in which their client contacts occur, creating a place where both can be seated to discuss the situation and the need.

Many job and career center staff use interactive career assessment software (such as DISCOVER and SIGI Plus), to help their clients learn more about themselves and their need; most reference librarians focus on the question rather than the need behind the question. There is a major difference in the nature of the interaction; when the typical reference interaction is less than three minutes, job and career center client interactions may last an hour.

There are differences in the primary referent group, (while most reference librarians relate primarily to other librarians, job and career staff focus on others in the community who are working to solve employment and economic development problems, build networks in the community, and draw on the expertise of agency staff and groups in the community).

Librarians are accustomed to calling all people who use libraries "patrons." The term "patron" as commonly used by librarians does not distinguish between library use and the helping relationship implied by the term "client." Librarians tend not to know the names of the people they work with, and people who use these kinds of services and who return for several visits are likely to become clients and to become known by name to the staff. To keep track of people who come back over a period of time, a few job and career center staff (especially trained counselors) have developed confidential records which record actions and progress. A few notes about the client's background, situation, goals, and use of job and career center resources and progress greatly facilitate staff memory of the kinds of assistance which has been given; these notes serve to inform future action. This is a new approach for librarianship and is not yet widely known or accepted.

THE CLIENT-PROFESSIONAL RELATIONSHIP

In the process of obtaining assistance from staff, a client may make several visits to the job and career center. Depending on the nature of the services offered, a client might come to do one or several of the following kinds of activities which result from the strategies discussed in Chapters 4-8. A client may do the following:

- use career assessment software,
- work with staff to discuss resulting computer printouts,
- be referred to a career counselor on contract with the library,
- be referred to another community agency for additional assistance,
- attend a workshop on a job-related topic such as writing a resume, or
- participate in a job club to discuss common concerns with others who share their situation.

In the course of developing an ongoing relationship, a sense of trust is displayed by the client. After trust is developed, Career Center staff may learn intimate details of a person's life such as a the effects of a job loss, a marital break-up, or personal illiteracy. There are occasional tears and expressions of anger. Staff have found that conversations which reveal personal concerns may come as a result of discussing the nature of the problem or situation that brought them to the Center.

The typical reference desk with its two to three minute interactions is not conducive to a serious discussion and therefore does not foster the kinds of interactions that involve confidential personal information. Some staff have altered library space to facilitate uninterrupted, or at least extended, discussion. This may mean moving to a quite corner of the reference room, or it may involve making basic changes in the job and career center area to accommodate a private desk and chair or a separate office.

CHANGES IN THE ENVIRONMENT

Job and career centers are located in a variety of environments. They may be at a separate desk in a main reference area, in a small room off the reference area, or in a more remote location. In some cases there is no separate location. Some job and career center staff have an office where, at times, they can bring clients. Others have re-arranged the space to permit more private interactions.

Given the kinds of interactions that occur at Career Centers, staff have made changes in the environment which facilitate their occurrence. In contrast to those at regular reference departments, interactions often occur when both the staff member and the client are seated. This may mean setting up a small desk with a chair for the client located to one side—or in the absence of this, walking to a table nearby when there is a need for a discussion. The general reference desk with its openness and its public nature, may impede the kinds of ongoing discussions that occur in these centers.

Workshops require space which is often borrowed. Staff like to be close to the meeting room so that it can be used for periodic workshops. A back room (staff room or cataloging area) can be commandeered from time to time.

DEVELOPING NEW APPROACHES

Job and career center practitioners, often unconsciously, are developing sets of protocols and mechanisms to respond to needs and facilitate problem solving. At most centers there is a certain amount of on-going interaction. In these cases often a client-professional relationship based on trust develops. The length of time in each interaction varies with the type of interaction, but generally exceeds the average reference interaction. Interactions may last as long as an hour and are often by appointment.

The most common type of interaction in most reference departments consists of people who ask questions on the spot without an appointment. These kinds of questions also come to staff of job and career centers, and are often handled when asked. However, often the librarian will determine that an appointment should be made to provide more in-depth assistance. When that occurs, clients may be provided with information or resources on the topic needed on the spot and scheduled for an appointment.

Appointments

Appointment practice varies from one site to another. Many practitioners arrange appointments for one or more of the following:

- Needs assessment (diagnosis);
- Career advising;
- Computer time for such interactive programs as DISCOVER and SIGI Plus and the use of state occupational information systems-OIS;
- To review and/or revise resumes;
- To discuss job strategies, and
- Career counseling, either with library staff or contract or part-time counselors).

Name Identification and Professional Memory

If a person is to be served at a later date or if an appointment is to be made the staff member must obtain the client's name. It is normal for Career Center staff and their clientele to know each other's names. Name identification may help build trust between a staff member and a potential client. With appointments and referrals, patrons are more likely to become clients who interact with the staff member on a repeat basis. Staff know the names of many clients (and vice versa). Staff often identify themselves to people who enter the job and career center. They answer the telephone identifying the center and giving their own names.

Staff sometimes develop ways to remember clients on return visits. Some job and career center staff make notes on cards or in folders on selected repeat clientele to make it easier to remember why the person has come to the center. Notes are likely to be taken after the interview is over; staff feel that note-taking makes the client feel uncomfortable.

CONCLUSION

In conclusion, these services build successfully on the kinds of people-centered services developed by many librarians in libraries across the nation. These services add value to the information provided by librarians because they focus on the need, on helping people get and use information, and on providing extra help to make sure that people will be able to take full advantage of the wealth of information that is available at the public library. The addition of new services such as interactive computer programs brings to users of libraries the power of information technology. Job and career center library staff have developed a wide range of strategies designed to help individuals get the information they need. The result has been services that enhance the role of the library in the community, make people realize the role of librarians in their communities, and which change lives.

The final chapter of this book focuses on appropriate ways to evaluate these unique and valuable services. These services deserve and demand more appropriate approaches to evaluation. Proper evaluation of these services will provide the tools which show the true value of the public library in the community. Methods used in the past (counting shelf space, square footage, the numbers of books purchased, as well as output measures—circulation, reference questions answered, in library materials use, program attendance, etc.) do not serve libraries well. They are not indicators of the real value of the public library. The final chapter in this book proposes a series of effective evaluation methods and indicators of use and value.

RESOURCES

Interviews with:

Ross, Catherine Sheldrick, and Patricia Dewdney. Communicating Professionally: *A How-To-Do-It Manual for Library Applications*. Neal-Schuman Publishers, Inc., New York. 1989.

Durrance, Joan C., et. al., *Serving Job Seekers and Career Changers: A Planning Manual for Public Libraries*. American Library Association, Chicago. 1993.

Oserman, Steve. "Setting Up a Job Search Service." *Public Libraries* (Oct.-Nov. 1993): 347-348.

10 EVALUATING JOB AND CAREER INFORMATION CENTERS

In most communities, budgets are so tight that publicly funded agencies are operating under more scrutiny than ever before. Libraries are no exception to this rule. People love public libraries, but increasingly managers are asked to demonstrate their value. Effective evaluation is crucial in an era of accountability. Yet evaluation is often set aside to be undertaken at a more convenient time by staff eager to develop services. Evaluation is essential to need-based service development and can be a tool to help librarians determine how effectively they reach those who will most benefit from the service.

This guide has the advantage of being built on the experience of scores of job and career centers started with money from national or community foundations or the federal government. Services which start this way almost always build in a strong evaluation component. Most funders want to know how their money helped and what difference the services they paid for made in the community. They want to know how the services helped individuals and, collectively, the community. These plans always include asking people who use these services how they were used and how valuable they proved to be. A need-centered approach to evaluations should be the cornerstone to evaluating job and career centers. It shows how people use the services and how they benefit from them. This approach encourages the collection of the kinds of stories and testimonials seen throughout this guide—from real people whose lives have been influenced by coming to the library for assistance.

Evaluation is the key to making need-based programs work effectively. It may also be the key to the program's longevity. Library directors often say that they get more positive feedback from their job and career information centers than any other service offered by the library. Often that feedback is the result of an evaluation plan that has included asking the clientele how they were helped.

BASED ON EVALUATION

PROGRAM STRATEGIES, GOALS, AND OBJECTIVES

The framework for service development, identifying and developing families of strategies, doubles as the basis for evaluation. The strategy families discussed throughout this book will shape the program.

FIGURE 10-1: Letter From Carolyn Anthony Agency—Skokie (IL) Public Library

Village of Skokie

OFFICE OF HUMAN SERVICES
5120 Galitz St. • Skokie, Ill 60077 • 673-0500
Fax 673-0525

October 22, 1993

Mrs. Carolyn Anthony
Director, Skokie Public Library
5215 Oakton Street
Skokie, IL 60077

Dear Carolyn,

Please accept my heartfelt thanks for allowing Steve Oserman to co-facilitate the Unemployment Support Group that recently ended. Steve's compassion and expertise in the field are invaluable gifts that benefited both the members of the group and myself. It is exciting to participate with the Library in this new venture, which, judging by the number of people who responded, and feedback we received, was a success.

Thank you for your support in this endeavor.

Sincerely,

Nan O'Connor

Nan G. O'Connor, MSW
Skokie Office of Human Services

NGO:rh

They are, therefore, the basis for program evaluation. Figures 1-3 in Chapter 9 can provide an excellent beginning for evaluation. Job and career center staff should make a list of all the objectives selected, as well as the strategies that will be used to carry them out.

A three column table such as the one below which includes the strategy area, specific objectives within that area, activities which will be undertaken to carry out the objective, and, finally, indicators of progress and success, can be used to evaluate the overall program.

Indicators of progress and success will grow from the objective. Discuss them with the advisory committee. Decide which evidence that the objective is being fulfilled with will be accepted. For example, if library staff seek to become a primary source of current demographic data, listing the data which has been collected steps that have been taken to inform agency staff will measure progress toward the attainment of that objective.

In order to evaluate the objective, service developers will need to discuss strategies to carry out the objective, and then regularly monitor the objective to see if they are actually carrying it out. Service developers who want, for example, to "Develop a clear, understandable message" might choose to develop a clear, concise mission statement for the service. They may examine the promotional materials which appear in this guide for suggestions. They may also decide to develop a brochure that explains the service in clear terms.

A number of other activities can be taken to continue working toward this objective. This and other objectives will set the tone for the service. Periodic sessions when staff meet can include discussion of activities which have been undertaken and those which should be tried in order to define the message and get it out. During these sessions staff should develop methods of determining, for example, how people find out about the program and how they use it. Surveys can help staff understand how effectively they have raised awareness and made information accessible.

Objectives here as for most of the other strategies are not stultifyingly measurable such as those simplistic objectives ("The librarian will be able to thread a microfilm reader in 30 seconds") that gave measurement a bad name. They are beacons. Guides. When activities are undertaken to carry them out, the activities can be indicators of the success of the objective. Library staff, for example, who choose to "Show approachability" can practice with a partner who critiques the approaches they use. Staff who decide to "Develop skills in the effective use of open and neutral questions" can likewise work with a partner who will observe and critique the approaches used. Look for indicators of program success such as comments from new users.

Strategies chosen to develop job and career centers may stretch librarianship into the development of new approaches to practice. That is the case with the instruction strategies and those which focus on problems. Ross and Dewdney recommend staff development programs that can be used to improve staff performance in this area and in reference interactions. A number of librarians have worked with counselors to develop a counseling component. If such a program is developed, staff should determine how well it works. If career assessment software packages have been purchased, staff should want to know if people are able to use them effectively.

Evaluating specific workshops and outreach activities will require examining these events separately to determine if they are meeting the objectives that have been developed for them. An examination of such elements as workshops, job fairs, marketing, and publicity can fine-tune these program elements. Workshop objectives should be developed in such a way that they can be used to evaluate the effectiveness of the workshop. These evaluation sheets should not exceed a page or two.

Make sure to evaluate the collaborative aspects of the program. It is the community and collaborative nature of these services which sets them apart.

DEVELOPING INDICATORS OF USE

Statistics for Need-Based Services

Evaluation is often confused with measurement. Most library managers focus only on how many and how much. This service is markedly different from other, more traditional—and much more accepted—services. Although reference staff are handling twenty or thirty two minute reference transactions, job center staff may be using the strategies described in earlier chapters of this book and working with only one to three individuals.

A well designed evaluation will help staff determine if the service is worth the time, money, and effort being put into it. It will show if the library can justify putting money and resources into an innovative service which meets the needs of only a segment of the population—those who are on the job market or who need more education or training (admittedly this is a large segment in most communities). The approaches and measures chosen will be crucial in finding this out.

Need-based services such as job and career centers must be examined by approaches that go beyond the measures of efficiency and effectiveness presented in Output Measures for Public Libraries. OMFPL presents basic ways to count circulation, materials use and access, and reference transactions, and provides basic data on general library use and program attendance.

PLA's output measures are too general to provide the kind of help needed to gauge the effectiveness of need-based services. Because interactions at career centers are longer and more involved than most reference interactions, using the OMFPL reference measures will result in low counts of reference interactions. The fact that referrals are excluded by definition from OMFPL reference figures further depresses overall counts which will already be low because more time is spent on average with each user. More importantly output measures as presented in OMFPL will not provide a valid measure of this need-based service.

A word of caution: DO NOT compute PER CAPITA output measures on circulation, in-library visits, in-library materials use, or reference questions. Although the entire population of an area may be an appropriate figure on which to base output measures for all library services, a more appropriate figure for these services would be the total number of unemployed. Overall, however, a more effective way of determining value is to examine the impact of the service on specific users, an approach that will be discussed later in this chapter.

Job and career center staff should, of course, keep statistics required by the library, but measurement is only one evaluation tool and those who limit themselves to the numbers are at a distinct disadvantage. The need-centered evaluation will attempt to look at quality as well as quantity. Collect data which are appropriate for the service.

Two kinds of statistics are appropriate—those which are part of the periodic statistical collection done in general in the library and those which result from surveys of center clientele. Keep track of individuals who come to use the center, as well as agencies and groups who come for workshops. Keep statistics on numbers of workshop attendance, as well as outreach activities. Statistics should also be kept on software and other computer use as well as on appointments made. Statistics alone will not show the true value of job and career information services, but can provide a profile of the use of the library.

Statistics which Reflect Use

Although the numbers of people who use job and career centers are not the best measure of the service, statistics should be kept on the program as an indicator of use.

What Kinds of Statistics to Collect the number of people who use the roomin-house use of materials reference questions answered by phone and in person advising and/or counseling sessions use of software program and workshop attendance outreach activities agency use of the job and career center; (visits, referrals, etc.) circulation of education and career materials (if possible).

Statistics can be included in a period (monthly or quarterly) report to the director and shared with other agencies and library staff. Statistics kept over time will indicate peak and slow times. They can serve as the basis for deploying staff. Statistics can be used to compare use of time and plan changes in the program.

Collecting Use Statistics

OMFPL includes methods for collecting data on in-library use and program attendance which can be readily adapted to the job and career center. Refer to that manual for techniques for collecting data. OMFPL suggests the use of sampling, rather than daily counts. Data collection and analysis are carefully explained.

SURVEYS TO DETERMINE USE

Surveys of users can help staff determine the extent to which the strategies they have selected are successful. Surveys will help determine if the service is reaching its target audience, how they found out about the service, and how they use it. Surveys should be kept simple. The survey elements in Figure 10-2 illustrate the kinds of questions which reveal that the service is meeting the needs of its clientele. The survey includes the following kinds of data:

How people found out about the service: Library services are not widely understood by people in the community. Job and career center staff who try to reach both library users and non-users, should be concerned about how people found out about your services. An approach which works quite well in many job and career centers is simply to ask, "How did you find out about our services?" Try to increase use by those who are not library users.

Patterns of library use: Evaluation studies have shown that many people who seek help in job and career centers are not regular library users. They are often less well educated than the typical library user and therefore may need extra help using library services. In addition, some need additional assistance because of poor literacy skills. An evaluation which reveals new library users should be translated into the need to develop services and materials which respond to the need.

FIGURE 10-2: How People Found Out About Your Service

How did you first find out about the library's Education, Job, and Career Center?

a. __Library staff member in library
b. __Library staff member talk or visit (outside the library)
c. __Friend or relative
d. __On the job
e. __Teacher/instructor
f. __Agency or group in the community
g. __Radio/TV/newspaper
h. __Sign, brochure, or other information in the library
i. __Poster or flyer (not in the library)

Demographic data: A demographic profile, including educational level, employment status, and ethnic group will indicate the extent to which this service is reaching those in the community who need it most. If the profile of the user of the job and career center is the same as the typical library user, staff may need to strengthen the outreach program.

Use-data based on services offered by the job center—develop questions which can help staff determine how the actual materials, workshops, computer programs, services, etc. are being used. The questions in the accompanying questionnaire can be used as guides, but should only be used if they reflect the local situation. Be sure to make the distinction between the self-service aspects of the job center and the assistance provided by staff.

Determining Benefits: Include open ended questions. Open ended questions help determine patterns and are frequently the source of valuable testimonials. Librarians often use the responses to open ended questions to get a picture of the service from the perspective of

FIGURE 10-3: Library Use

How often did you use this library before you came to the Education, Job, and Career Center?

a. __ Seldom or never

b __ A few times a year

c. __ Once or twice a month

d. __ About once a week

e. __ More than once a week

FIGURE 10-4: Demographics

What is your sex?

a.__ Male

b.__ Female

What is your age?

a. ___under 18

b.___18-24

c.___25-34

d.___35-44

e.___45-54

f.___55-64

g.___65-74

h.___75 and over

(continued)

FIGURE 10-4: Demographics (continued)

What is your race or ethnic group?

a.___Asian American

b.___Black

c.___Hispanic

d.___Native American

e.___White

f.___Other

What is your highest level of education?

a.___Less than high school

b.___Some high school

c.___High school graduate or equivalent (GED)

d.___Some college

e.___College graduate

f.___Graduate school

g.___Other (please describe)

How often did you use this library before you came to the Education, Job, and Career Center?

a. __ Seldom or never

b __ A few times a year

c. __ Once or twice a month

d. __ About once a week

e. __ More than once a week

their clientele. Although checklists and scaled answers are easy to code and analyze, they cannot convey the excitement and gratitude which may be generated by a question such as, "How did we help?"

Ask about the kind of help they received from the perspective of the need. Include a question which seeks to determine if coming to

FIGURE 10-5: Remployment

Which of these best describes you now? (Check all that apply.)

a.___Employed full time

b.___Employed part time

c.___Unemployed; between jobs

d.___Retired

e.___New to job market

f.___Full-time homemaker

g.___Student full time

h.___Student part time

j.___Other(please describe)

If you have been employed but are unemployed now, how long ago did your last job end?

a.___0-2 months

b.___3-6 months

c.___more than 6 months

the job center contributed to getting a job or taking some kind of action (going back to school, etc.). This kind of information is far more valuable to funders and others who are assessing the service than statistics on the number of employment books that circulated.

There is no need to ask all the questions at one time. Focus. Keep the survey instrument short and easy to use. Use a guide to developing surveys to guide in designing questions. (Babbie; Line; Dillman) Test any survey before it is used. Think of how the responses will be analyzed as the questionnaire is developed. Leave space for user comments on all surveys. Comments in a patron's own words add to librarians' knowledge of how the job and career center is used. Be sure to distinguish between self-service and staff-assisted service.

Pick a sample period to distribute the survey to all who use the center. Make sure to include patrons you reach through any outreach services.

FIGURE 10-6: Service Use

Which services below have you used at the Education, Job, and Career Center? (Check all that apply.)

(a) very helpful (b)somewhat helpful (c)not at all helpful

__ Finding information that helped

__ Solving a problem or planning

__ Using the computer

__ Workshop or group discussion

__ Finding out more about library materials

and services

__ Referral to another agency or group in the community

__ Other(please describe)

FIGURE 10-7: Help Received

When you were at the Job and Career Center did you get help with any of the following? (Check all that apply.)

For each kind of help you received, please check how valuable it was to you.

(a)very valuable (b)somewhat valuable (c) not at all valuable

___*A job change or a job search

___*Education or training decisions

___*Starting or expanding a business

___*Thinking about my interests and abilities

___*Resume writing or job interviewing

___*Reading, writing, or math

___*Support or encouragement

FIGURE 10-8: Use of Resources

Which of the things below have you used at the Education, Job, and Career Center? (Check all that apply.)

For each thing you used, please check how helpful it was to you.

(a)very valuable (b)somewhat valuable (c) not at all valuable

__*Computer

__*Classified ads in newspapers

__*Books and pamphlets

__*Typewriter

__*Videotapes

__*Other (please describe)

FIGURE 10-9: Outcomes

What, if anything, were the results of using the Job and Career Center? (Check all that apply.)

a.__I found out some new information.

b.__I became more aware of my interests and abilities.

c.__I found out that I was right about what I was thinking.

d. __I received the support to do something about my situation.

e. __I became clearer about my goals.

f. __I found a job.

g. __I began to feel better about what I am doing.

h. __I enrolled in a high school equivalency program.

i. __I enrolled in college.

j. __I enrolled in a skill training or adult education program.

k. __I obtained a library card.

j. __Other(please describe)

FIGURE 10-10: Overall Response

In general, how well did the Job and Career Center help you meet your needs?

a. __Very well

b. __Quite well

c. __Somewhat well

d. __Not too well

e. __Not at all well

Be sensitive to possible literacy problems. Not all of the users of the job and career center will be able to fill out a questionnaire because of poor literacy skills. You may easily obtain the information by asking. If any of your clientele will have difficulty filling out a written questionnaire, help them by going over the questionnaire with them.

TESTIMONIALS AND STORIES AS INDICATORS OF IMPACT

Most librarians have never tried to find out how what they do impacts the lives of people. Although surveys can provide some data on impact, most cannot be structured to collect stories that reflect real impact. One of the most effective methods to determine impact is to collect testimonials and anecdotes in the client's own words. The stories and vignettes which appear throughout this manual were contributed by librarians and job and career center staff from all over the country based on their own experience working with people.

Obtaining Testimonials

Although many testimonials and stories come unsolicited, they may also be obtained through the use of follow-up phone calls or post cards. Most information can be gained about need-based use of

FIGURE 10-11: Interview Guide

How did we help? ______________________________

____

____

____

What do you think are the strengths of the Job and Career Center? ______________________________

____

____

____

What suggestions do you have for additions or changes at the Job and Career Center?______

____

____

____

your services by collecting anecdotes, vignettes, and testimonials from those worked with over a period of time, people who have worked with your staff on career counseling, or who have attended workshops on resume writing, career decision making, etc. Often those who have received such assistance will stop by and tell librarians of the successes that have followed. They will say, "I got the job! I feel so much more able to start thinking about a new career." When people spontaneously tell you of their successes, include them in your file of stories.

The Follow-up Interview as an Indicator of Impact

Set aside time each month to make follow-up calls to some of the individuals who scheduled appointments with you or with whom you worked closely. These calls should be made at the convenience of the client and should be kept short. Calls can be scheduled in advance. If the call has not been scheduled in advance be sure to ask if it is OK to hold a short conversation at the time of the call. If not, schedule a return call.

The opening comments on this type of follow-up should transmit to the individual the purpose of the call as well as the fact that all information is confidential. The purpose of the call, of course, is to find out if (and how) the staff and resources have been helpful in the client's current endeavor (job search, career change, whatever). It will be helpful to know what successes the individual has had. Ask what the staff might do to provide more effective services. Wish the person success and extend an invitation to visit again. Immediately after completing the call, make extensive notes on what was said. When writing up any anecdote, be sure that you maintain the confidentiality pledge.

COLLECTING IMPACT DATA

COLLECTING DATA ON IMPACT

Keep a file of testimonial letters. Jot down all spontaneous testimonials. Make sure they reflect how that person used the service and benefited from bringing their need to the library. Be specific. Use the stories in this manual as guides.

In collecting the stories, take care not to violate the client privacy. Do not reveal names or information which can be used to identify a particular individual, unless they ask to have their name included. First names are not likely to reveal an identity and will serve as a way of personalizing the stories.

Staff who have kept records of the people who have made appointments to see you, or who have scheduled times to use your career software will be able to use these names and telephone numbers to follow up to find out if the service was helpful to them. If in the follow-up conversation a client indicates that a staff member showed insensitivity during a visit, use that feedback to remind or instruct staff to be sensitive to their clientele.

A simple record may be kept of each person who has made an appointment. Include the client's name, address, telephone number and a brief record of the kinds of assistance provided (career assessment, resume writing assistance, etc.). Remember even simple records should be kept confidential. Assure your clients of the confidentiality of career center records.

Try to reach a specific number of people, say a minimum of three per month. A follow-up call will serve a several evaluative purposes at the same time. It will help staff find out how well they doing and what might be done more effectively, and it will provide valuable anecdotal material.

Keep the interview brief. If you are calling someone that you worked with last month, ask questions based on the kind of help that that person came for.

Indicators of Impact on the Community

Looking at your stories and testimonials in the aggregate will give you an indication of the kind of impact that you are making in the community. Another way of gauging the impact of your service is to obtain feedback from the agencies you work with. Talk with other service providers. This is an informal evaluation, but it will give you some idea of the library's influence.

DATA ANALYSIS AND REPORTING

This chapter has presented three different kinds of data: statistics which result from counts of people who use various aspects of your service, statistics and comments which are the result of having people fill out questionnaires in the library, and letters, stories and anecdotes which are obtained spontaneously and as the result of follow- up evaluation of the service.

Although a calculator will do a basic job of helping you keep track of your numbers, a simple statistical package for a microcomputer will permit you to analyze your statistics and compare one month to another. A statistical package will help you see the relationships among the different elements you have been examining.

A statistical software package that is easy to use and reasonably priced is ABC available from Inter-University Consortium for Political and Social Research, P.O. Box 1248, Ann Arbor, MI 48106. See the end of this chapter for a review article of comprehensive statistical software packages.

Graphics will add to the power of your evaluation presentation. Many libraries now have computers which include both statistical analysis and graphics software. Graphics are particularly useful in presenting data over time (such as number of visits, number of individuals who used career advising software or who attended workshops compared by month with last year).

EVALUATION AS A REPORTING TOOL

There are several distinct audiences for the evaluation. The key audiences for an evaluation are the staff who run the service and managers and decision makers such as library trustees.

Job and career center staff: It is essential for service staff to know if they are fulfilling the objectives which drive the service. Staff need to know who they are reaching and how effectively their primary clientele is being served. Job and career service staff are the primary audience for an evaluation. They need all of the data and the stories.

Library management and those who make the funding decisions: Job and career center staff often make frequent (monthly or quarterly) reports to the director. Since these services are staff-intensive, it is particularly important for directors be given indicators of the impact of the services. Periodic reports to directors often include stories of how people were helped as well as copies of testimonial letters from agencies (thanking staff for work done on behalf of their clients), copies of letters and other testimonials from gratified users. Library Board members (who have control of the purse strings) also like to hear stories about how people in the community have been helped by these services.

Other library staff: It is crucial to inform other library staff of the work of the job and career center. Approaches used by job and career center staff are quite different from most public library services. Staff need to be aware of the goals, objectives, and progress of the career center. Sharing the evaluation is an effective way of bringing these staff into the loop. Evaluation-based reports will provide staff with the information they need to make effective referrals to the job center.

Community agency representatives: Agencies and non-profit groups who work closely with job and career center staff will benefit from learning about how the service is used and who uses it. They need highlights only, but will benefit from anecdotal information and testimonials. Evaluation-based reports (and regular two-way communication) facilitate appropriate referrals.

Local Media: Testimonials and Examples of Impact of Service

Potential users need to know of the success stories of others.

Reports to the library director, board, and/or funders need not be lengthy. They should, however, be on target, attractive, and send your message clearly. As the service is developing, make these reports fairly often. Monthly or quarterly career center reports are not uncommon.

What should be included in your formal reports depends entirely on what you are doing and on the emphasis of the service. You may wish to include the following:

- A brief statistical summary that might include: statistics on first time users, total users, program attendance, reference questions, in library use, and circulation of job, education, and career materials if it is possible to break them down;
- A summary of how well the job and career center is carrying out its goals and objectives;
- A summary of impact of job and career center on selected users: (stories collected as the result of follow-up calls);
- Copies of letters received; testimonials collected during the reporting period, and
- Indicators of impact of program on community or library (can be seen from patterns in anecdotal material; can also be obtained from agencies that the job and career center works with).

Remember that you don't need to wait until the quarter has ended to inform your director of some feedback that you receive. Share a story. Invite the director to stop by while you are holding a workshop. Reporting can be done in a number of ways.

When your center is heavily used, you may be tempted to say that you just don't have the time to write into a report. It is appropriate to repeat here that directors really appreciate and use these special reports. Your director will likely share your findings with the board, with city council, and with other agency heads in the community.

Evaluating your services and reporting on this evaluation is an excellent way to keep you service on target and growing.

RESOURCES

Babbie, Earl R. *Survey Research Methods.* 2d ed. Belmont, CA, Wadsworth Pub. Co., 1990.

Fridlund, Alan J. "*Number-Crunching Statistics Software.*" Infoworld (February 26, 1990): 59-69.

Line, Maurice B. *Library Surveys: An Introduction to the Use, Planning, Procedure, and Presentation of Surveys.* London, C. Bingley, 1982.

Van House, Nancy A. et al. *Output Measures for Public Libraries: A Manual of Standardized Procedures.* Chicago: American Library Association, 1987.

APPENDIX A

A Sample County Economic Profile

Local communities can be described in many ways. Among the most valuable descriptions of a community for a job seeker or an entrepreneur is one which provides information about the employment and education picture, including major employers, educational institutions, and major economic and demographic information. The Alpena County Economic Profile, below, is part of the Michigan Department of Commerce County Economic Profile Series. This Economic Profile brings together data from a wide range of resources. This economic sketch was prepared by the Industrial Development Division (IDD) of The University of Michigan.

This table was taken (with permission) from the statistical section of the M-Link Gopher, an Internet resource provided by the University of Michigan Library. A list of the sources and an explanation appears at the end of the table. The source list is valuable as a guide for those who seek to bring together economic data for their communities. Specific sources will vary from one state to the next, but the types of resources will be similar.

COMMUNITY PROFILE FOR ALPENA COUNTY, MICHIGAN
May 17, 1993

LOCATION SERVICES
Target Alpena 2000
P.O. Box 65
Alpena, MI 49707

Contact:	Kenneth Kolasa
Phone:	517/354-2666
FAX:	517/356-3999

County Seat: Alpena

POPULATION	
1970 Census	30708
1980 Census	32315
1990 Census	30605
Median Age (as of 1990)	35.3 years
LABOR FORCE (1992 average)	
Total Labor Force	14,025
Employed	12,150
Total Unemployment	1,875
Unemployment Rate	13.4%
3-Year Average	12.1%

PRINCIPAL ECONOMIC BASE EMPLOYERS

Firm	*Employees*	*Product/Service*
Alpena General Hospital, Alpena	605	Regional medical care facility
Besser, Alpena	450	Concrete block making machines
Abitibi-Price, Alpena	415	Hardboard mfg.
LaFarge, Alpena	317	Cement
NEMROC, Alpena	221	Wood pallets, lumber, stoves
Fletcher Paper, Alpena	220	Paper
Thunder Bay Mfg., Alpena	111	Machine shop; iron foundry
Phelps Collins ANG	100	Military
D. G. Trim Products, Alpena	85	Automotive carpeting
Alpena News Publishing, Alpena	75	Public newspaper; publishing
Alpena Power	60	Power
Baker Enterprises, Alpena	60	Parts and machining
Panel Processing, Alpena	55	Hardboard
Phillips, J.D., Alpena	42	Machine tool design
Omni Metalcraft, Alpena	40	Material handling equipment
Ossineke Industries, Ossineke	40	Gun drill mfg.
Eagle Engineering & Supply, Alpena	39	Electrical control panels
Alpena Mfg., Alpena	22	Screw machine, job shop
Benjey, W.G., Alpena	19	Custom machine design
Magnaloy Coupling, Alpena	16	Flexible coupling
Fiber Char, Alpena	13	Custom wood fabrication
Dedoes Indus., Ossineke	12	Turf aerotor mfg.
Loujon, Alpena	10	Hydraulic cylinders

EARNING LEVELS

Classification	Average Hourly Rate Minimum	Maximum
Assembler - Light	$4.87	$7.80
Clerk	$4.75	$5.53
General Laborer	$4.75	$7.80
Machine Operator	$5.84	$10.39
Maintenance Mechanic	$6.75	$12.87
Maintenance, Building	$4.75	$8.49
Millwright	$6.11	$10.98
Receptionist	$4.75	$5.84
Secretary	$4.75	$6.49
Welder	$5.84	$12.24

Source: Based on Consumers Power community survey, adjusted for inflation to 1991 using Consumer Price Index.

DISTANCE TO:

	Miles	Kilometers
Chicago	450	724
Cleveland	460	740
Detroit	230	370
Indianapolis	510	820
Lansing	210	337
Toronto	400	643

TRANSPORTATION

Main Highways:	M-32, M-65, US-23
Bus Lines:	Indian Trails, City of Alpena, Dial-a-Ride
Truck Lines:	2
Rail Lines:	Detroit & Mackinac
Ports:	Deep water port facility via LaFarge Corp.
Airports:	Alpena County Regional
Airlines:	Great Lakes Air, Northwest

CLIMATE
As reported by weather station at Alpena.

January Average Minimum:	13 F./-11 C. Average Maximum: 27 F./ -3 C.
July Average Minimum:	58 F./ 14 C. Average Maximum: 77 F./ 25 C.
Growing Season:	156 days
Days below 0 F or -18 C:	11 Average Annual Rainfall: 28 in./ 71 cm.
Days above 90 F or 32 C:	4 Average Annual Snowfall: 67 in./170 cm.

INDUSTRIAL SITES
(As of January 1993)

Community	Sites	Acres	Hectares	Industrial Parks
Alpena	3	801	324	1
Alpena Twp.	11	81	33	2
COUNTY TOTAL	14	882	357	3

Zero acres indicates less than half an acre or no information available.

CONSTRUCTION PERMITS

	Residential		Industrial		Office		Mercantile	
	Units	Value	Units	Value	Units	Value	Units	Value
1991:	79	$4.	1	$0.22	8	$1.37		
3-Year Average:	72	$4.32	0	$0.01	1	$0.20	6	$1.01

Values are reported in millions of dollars. A three-year average value of one may indicate no construction activity in one or more of the last three years.

NEW INCORPORATIONS

Incorporations in 1992:	47	State Median:	68
Incorporation Rate:	154	State Median:	183

Incorporation Rate = incorporations per 100,000 population.

PROPERTY TAX BASE
(As of 1992)

Agricultural	Residential	Industrial	Commercial	Other
11%	59%	3%	13%	15%

County Total State Equalized Value:	$385,058,039.00
County Average Tax Millage Rate (in 1991):	52.13

UTILITIES

	Electric	Gas	Telephone*
Alpena	Local	MichCon	GTE, D

* D=digital switching; EA=equal access to interexchange carriers; see Source List note.

WATER

	Source	Gallons Capacity	Liters Use Capacity	Use	Pressure (lbs./sq.in.)
Alpena	Lake	52	35	197	132

Capacity and maximum use in hundreds of thousands of gallons/liters per day.

SEWER

	Type	Gallons Capacity	Liters Load	Capacity	Load
Alpena	Secondary	55	30	208	114

Capacity and present load in hundreds of thousands of gallons/liters per day.

MUNICIPAL SERVICES

Community	1990 Phone Number	Master Population	Public Zoning	Library Plan	(Volumes)
Alpena	517-354-2196	11354	yes	yes	51,425

Community	------- Fire Department -------- Class.	FT Paid	Police PT/Volunt.	(Full-Time)	Solid Waste
Alpena	6	22	22	17	Independent

County Sheriff Officers: 15 Licensed Landfills in County: 0

communities in parenthesis):

Alpena Twp. (9602), Bolton, Cathro, Green Twp. (1095), Herron, Hubbard Lake, Lachine, Leer, Long Rapids Twp. (1021), Maple Ridge Twp. (1514), Ossineke Twp. (1652), Sanborn Twp. (2196), Spratt, Wellington Twp. (269), Wilson Twp. (1902)

EDUCATIONAL FACILITIES (1992-1993)

Community	School District	K-12 Students	Instruc. Staff	High Schools
Alpena	Alpena Public	5609	222	1

COLLEGES AND UNIVERSITIES
(As of Fall 1991)

Name and Location	Enrollment
Alpena Community College, Alpena	2442

MEDICAL FACILITIES
Hospitals in County: 1 Total Beds: 176
Nearest Large Medical Center: Alpena
Extended Care Facilities: 2 Total Beds: 153
Physicians (MDs and DOs) in County: 58

HOUSING AND CHURCHES
(Housing as of 1990)

Owner occupied: 9251 (78.1%) Median Home Value: $41,600.00
Renter occupied: 2587 (21.9%) Median Contract Rent: $245.00
Churches: Catholic: 7 Protestant: 32
Synagogues: 1

RECREATION, ATTRACTIONS, AND EVENTS
Thunder Bay Underwater Preserve; Thunder Bay and inland lake game fishing, boating; downhill & cross country skiing, golfing, hiking, snowmobiling, hunting. Jesse Besser Museum/Planetarium, Island Park and Alpena Wildlife Sanctuary; Thunder Bay Live Theatre; Dinosaur Gardens Prehistorical Zoo; Alpena Civic Theater; Besser Natural Area; Cripps Fruit Farm; Canoe Races; industrial plant tours. Winter Carnival (February); July events: Riverfest, Fourth of July Chicken Bar-B-Que & Strawberry Dessert, Brown Trout Festival, Art on the Bay, Ramblin' Rods; August events: Antique Tractor & Steam Engine Show, Alpena County Fair; Fall Air Color Tours.

COMMERCIAL SERVICES
(As of 1989)

General Building Contractors	18
Metalworking Machinery	4
Commercial Printing	5
Advertising	1
Personnel Supply Services	2
Computer and Data Processing Services	2
Legal Services	11
Accounting, Auditing and Bookkeeping	11
Retail Establishments	252
Wholesale Establishments	67
Hotel/Motel Rooms (as of 1990):	493
Television Channels:	12, with cable
Radio Stations:	3
Newspapers:	Alpena News, Ad-vertiser

FINANCIAL INSTITUTIONS
(As of 1993)

	Main Office	Offices in County
Farmers and Merchants State Bank of Hale	Hale	2
First Federal Savings & Loan Assoc. of	Alpena	2
First of America Bank-Northern Michigan	Traverse City	5
Great Lakes Bancorp, A Federal Savings	Ann Arbor	1
NBD Bank, N	Detroit	4

EMPLOYMENT AND EARNINGS BY INDUSTRY

	Employment		Earnings ($ millions)			
	1985	1990	1985	1990		
Total Employment			13073	15063		
Total Income			$334.95	$450.23		
Earnings by Place of Work			$221.67	$303.40		
Components by Type:						
Wage and Salary	10588		12318		$178.07	$238.06
Proprietors	2485		2745		$25.91	$41.79
Farm	489		424		$0.76	$3.10
Nonfarm	1996		2321		$25.16	$38.69

Components by Industry:

Farm	596	510	$1.39	$3.85
Nonfarm	12477	14553	$220.28	$299.54
Private	9990	11761	$176.04	$237.64
Agric./For./Fish.	88	97	$1.05	$1.06
Mining	72	26	$2.52	$0.51
Construction	462	805	$9.31	$19.35
Manufacturing	2347	2463	$73.34	$85.37
Non-Durable Goods	—	—	$8.29	$11.99
Durable Goods	—	—	$65.05	$73.38
Transp. & Utilities	705	783	$18.75	$26.57
Wholesale Trade	510	672	$10.15	$16.41
Retail Trade	2339	2646	$20.92	$28.14
Fin./Ins./Real Est.	757	774	$7.04	$8.31
Services	2710	3495	$32.96	$51.91
Government	2487	2792	$44.24	$61.90
Federal	95	130	$2.33	$3.58
Military, Civilian	75	72	$0.46	$0.50
State and Local	2317	2590	$41.45	$57.82
Earnings by Place of Residence			$197.34	$267.08

Zero values indicate confidential information or fewer than 10 employees or less than $50,000.

Per Capita Income: 1985 $11,070.0 1990: $14,691.00

County Economic Profiles are prepared for the Michigan Department of Commerce (phone: 517/373-9808) by the Industrial Development Division, Office of Technology Transfer (OTT/IDD), The University of Michigan (phone: 313/764-5260).

Permission is hereby granted to reprint the information.

Source List of Data for Michigan Community Economic Profiles

Location Services

Local Development Offices and Local Development Services, Michigan Department of Commerce, Lansing, Michigan 48909 (phone: 517-373-9642).

Population

The 1970, 1980, and 1990 population, and median age are from the decennial U.S. Census of Population.

Labor Force

"Area Labor Statistics (1990 Annual Average)", Bureau of Research and Statistics, Michigan Employment Security Commission (phone: 313-876-5427).

Principal Economic Base Employers

Local Development Offices; regional planning agencies; the Harris Michigan Industrial Directory, published by the Harris Publishing Company; the Michigan Manufacturers Directory, published by Pick Publications, Inc.

Earning Levels

Michigan Business Retention and Expansion Program, a series of studies conducted by the Economic Development Department of Michigan Bell Telephone Co.; the Economic Development Department of Consumers Power Co.; and wage rate surveys conducted by local development offices.

Transportation

Data for major highways and rail lines are from the Official Transportation Maps published by the Michigan State Transportation Commission. Data for bus lines, airports, and airlines are from the Michigan Public Transportation Directory, also published by the Michigan State Transportation Commission, and from local development offices. Data for ports are supplied by local development offices and Regional Planning Agencies.

Climate

Climatological Summary, National Climate Data Center, National Oceanic and Atmospheric Administration.

Industrial Sites

Michigan Site Network (MSN), a statewide database of vacant industrial land, buildings and industrial parks, operated by the Southeastern Michigan Council of Governments. The sources of data for the MSN are local development offices and the Location Services Division, Manufacturing Services Bureau, Michigan Department of Commerce.

Construction Permits

Building Permits Branch, Construction Services Division, U.S. Bureau of the Census.

New Incorporations

New Incorporations in Michigan, Business Research Office, Michigan Department of Commerce (phone: 517-373-4600).

Property Tax Base

Assessed Valuation, State Equalized Valuation, Assessment Level, and S.E.V. Multiplier for Separately Equalized Classifications, and Ad Valorem Property Tax Levy Report, Michigan State Tax Commission, Michigan Department of Treasury (phone: 517-373-0500).

Utilities

Utility Area Service Maps, Michigan Public Service Commission (phone: 517-334-6399), and service maps of the state's public utilities. Telecommunications services listed for GTE and Michigan Bell are available as of November 1991 (digital switching and equal access to interexchange carriers); due to ongoing network modifications, services may vary by specific site location.

Water and Sewer

Water Production Capacity of Water Supplies, published by the Michigan Health Department (phone: 517-335-8000), and from local development and Regional Planning Offices.

Municipal Services

Community phone numbers from the Directory of the Michigan Municipal League. Data for population from the decennial U.S. Census of Population, U.S. Bureau of the Census. Data for zoning ordinance, master plan, and solid waste provided by local development offices and Regional Planning Agencies. Data for public libraries from the Michigan Public Library Directory and Michigan Public Library Statistics, published by the State Library of Michigan (phone: 517-373-1593). Data for fire personnel from the Michigan Fire Services Directory, Michigan State Fire Marshal, Michigan State Police (phone: 517-322-1924). Data for police and sheriff personnel from Number of Full Time Law Enforcement Employees from the Uniform Crime Reporting Section, Michigan State Police (phone: 517-322-5531). Licensed landfill data provided by the Waste Management Division, Michigan Department of Natural Resources (phone: 517-335-4034).

Other Communities in County

Local Unit Computerized Information database (MDOC), and highway map.

Educational Facilities

Office of Information and Research, Bureau of Planning and School Management, Michigan Department of Education (phone: 517-373-3909).

Colleges and Universities

Higher Education Management Services, Michigan Department of Education (phone: 517-373-3820).

Medical Facilities

Bureau of Health Facilities, Michigan Department of Public Health (phone: 517-335-8500), and local development offices.

Housing and Churches

Housing data are from the 1990 Census of Housing, General Housing Characteristics: Michigan, U.S. Bureau of the Census. Church data are from Churches and Church Membership, National Council of Churches (1980). Synagogues are from Jewish Community Council, Royal Oak, Michigan (phone: 313-962-1880).

Recreation, Attractions, and Events

Local development offices and Michigan Travel Planners, Michigan Travel Bureau, Michigan Department of Commerce (phone: 517-373-0670).

Commercial Services

County Business Patterns, published by the U.S. Bureau of the Census. Data for newspapers, television and radio stations supplied by the local development offices and Regional Planning Agencies. Data for hotel rooms from the Michigan Guide to Hotels & Motels, Michigan Travel Bureau, Michigan Department of Commerce (phone: 517-373-0670).

Financial Institutions

Directory of the Michigan Bankers Association, and local development offices.

Employment and Earnings by Industry

Regional Economic Information System, Bureau of Economic Analysis, U.S. Department of Commerce.

SELECTED JOB AND CAREER SERVICES IN PUBLIC LIBRARIES

Arranged alphabetically by region and state.

EAST

DC

District of Columbia Public Library
Martin Luther King Memorial Library
Job Information Center
901 G Street NW
Washington, DC 20001

MARYLAND

Enoch Pratt Free Library
Job/Career Information Center
400 Cathedral Street
Baltimore, MD 21201

NEW JERSEY

Camden County Library
Job/Career Information Center
203 Laurel Road
Voorhees, NJ 08043

NEW YORK

Brooklyn Public Library
Education/Job Information Center
Grand Army Plaza
Brooklyn, NY 11238

Buffalo and Erie County Public Library
Lifelong Learning Center
Lafayette Square
Buffalo, NY 14203-1887
Bethlehem Public Library
Career Resource Center
451 Delaware Avenue
Delmar, NY 12054

Westchester Library System
8 Westchester Plaza
Elmsford, NY 10523

Freeport Memorial Library
Merrick Road and South Ocean Avenue
Freeport, NY 11520

Crandall Library
Job Information Center
City Park
Glen Falls, NY 12801

Gloversville Free Library
Education/Job Information Center
58 East Fulton Street
Gloversville, NY 12078

Hempstead Public Library
Job/Education Information Center
115 Nichols Court
Hempstead, NY 11550

Hudson Area Library
Education/Job Information Center
400 State Street
Hudson, NY 12534

Kingston Area Library
Education/Job Information Center
55 Franklin Street
Kingston, NY 12401

Long Beach Public Library
111 West Park Avenue
Long Beach, NY 11561

Mahopac Library
121 East Lake Boulevard
Mahopac, NY 10541

Manhasset Public Library
Career Counseling Service
30 Onderdonk Avenue
Manhasset, NY 11030

New York Public Library
Branch Services
455 Fifth Avenue
New York, NY 10016-0122

Ossining Public Library
Education/Job Information Center
53 Croton Avenue
Ossining, NY 10510

Clinton-Essex-Franklin Library System
Job/Education Information Center
17 Oak Street
Plattsburgh, NY 12901

Riverhead Free Library
Job Information Center
330 Court Street
Riverhead, NY 11901

Rochester Public Library
Education/Job Information Center
115 South Avenue
Rochester, NY 14604

Schenectady County Public Library
Education/Job Information Center
99 Clinton Street
Schenectady, NY 12305

Nassau Library System
900 Jerusalem Avenue
Uniondale, NY 11553

West Islip Public Library
Job Information Center
3 Higbie Lane
West Islip, NY 11795

White Plains Public Library
Job Information Center
100 Martine Avenue
White Plains, NY 10605

PENNSYLVANIA

B.F. Jones Memorial Library
663 Franklin Avenue
Aliquippa, PA 15001

Chester County Library
400 Exton Square Parkway
Exton, PA 19341

Lancaster County Library
125 North Duke Street
Lancaster, PA 17602

Bucks County Free Library
Pennwood Branch
Pine Street and Flowers Avenue
Langhorne, PA 19047

Monessen Public Library
326 Donner Avenue
Monessen, PA 15062-1182

Oil City Library
2 Central Avenue
Oil City, PA 16301

Free Library of Philadelphia
Logan Square
Philadelphia, PA 19103

Carnegie Library of Pittsburgh
4400 Forbes Avenue
Pittsburgh, PA 15213-4080

Reading Public Library
Fifth and Franklin Streets
Reading, PA 19602

Scranton Public Library
Washington and Vine Streets
Scranton, PA 18503

Citizens Library
55 South College Street
Washington, PA 15301

Bowlby Public Library
311 North West Street
Waynesburg, PA 15370

State Correctional Institution—Waynesburg
R.D. 1, P.O. Box 67
Waynesburg, PA 15370

Midwest

ILLINOIS

Chicago Public Library
Career Information Center
400 North Franklin Street
Chicago, IL 60610

Schaumburg Township District Library
32 West Library Lane
Schaumburg, IL 60194

Skokie Public Library
5215 Oakton
Skokie, IL 60076-3680

IOWA

Bellevue Public Library
106 N. 3rd Street
Bellevue, IA 52031

MICHIGAN

Alpena County Library
Job Launch
221 North First Avenue
Alpena, MI 49707

Willard Public Library
7 West Van Buren Street
Battle Creek, MI 49017

Detroit Public Library
Career & Employment Information Center
5201 Woodward Avenue
Detroit, MI 48202

Flint Public Library
COPE Center
1023 East Kearsley Street
Flint, MI 48502

Peter White Public Library
217 North Front Street
Marquette, MI 49855

Macomb County Library
Education Information Center
16480 Hall Road
Mount Clemens, MI 48044-3198

MISSOURI

St. Louis Public Library
Adult Education Department
1301 Olive Street
St. Louis, MO 63103-2389

NEBRASKA

Broken Bow Public Library
626 South D Street
Broken Bow, NE 68822

Columbus Public Library
2504 14th Street
Columbus, NE 68601

Crete Public Library
305 East 13th Street
P.O. Box 156
Crete, NE 68333

Holdrege Public Library
604 East Avenue
Holdrege, NE 68949

Nebraska Library Commission
1420 P Street
Lincoln, NE 68508

OHIO

Columbus Metropolitan Library
Job/Career Information Center
96 South Grant Avenue
Columbus, OH 43215

Cuyahoga County Public Library
InfoPLACE
5225 Library Lane
Maple Heights, OH 44137

WEST

CALIFORNIA

Los Angeles Public Library
Pio Pico Branch
2631 West Olympic Boulevard
Los Angeles, CA 90006

Santa Ana Public Library
Newhope Branch
122 North Newhope
Santa Ana, CA 92703

WASHINGTON

Everett Public Library
2702 Hoyt Avenue
Everett, WA 98201

Longview Public Library
1600 Louisiana Avenue
Longview, WA 98632

Pend Oreille County Library
116 South Washington Street
Newport, WA 99156-1708

Timberland Regional Library
415 Airdustrial Way, SW
Olympia, WA 98501-5799

Richland Public Library
Education/Job Information Center
955 Northgate Drive
Richland, WA 99352

Spokane Public Library
West 906 Main
Spokane, WA 99201

SOUTH

GEORGIA

Athens Regional Library
Job Center
120 West Dougherty Street
Athens, GA 30601

NORTH CAROLINA

Durham County Public Library
Project LIFT
300 North Roxboro Street
P.O. Box 3809
Durham, NC 27702

TEXAS

Corpus Christi Public Library
Employment/Career Information Center
805 Comanche Street
Corpus Christi, TX 7840

INDEX

Joan C. Durrance is Associate Professor at the University of Michigan School of Information and Library Studies where she teaches courses in public libraries, community information services, access issues, government information, evaluation of Library services. A grant from the W. K. Kellogg Foundation permitted her to visit and study over 40 job and career centers to the literature on communities, reference success, and information needs. She is active in professional associates and served recently on the American Library Association's Intellectual Freedom Committee and the President's Committee on Your Right To Know.